The Captain's Concubine

Love, Honor, and Violence in
Renaissance Tuscany

Donald Weinstein

The Johns Hopkins University Press / Baltimore and London

©2000 The Johns Hopkins University Press
All rights reserved. Published 2000
Printed in the United States of America on acid-free paper

9 8 7 6 5 4 3 2 1

The Johns Hopkins University Press
2715 North Charles Street
Baltimore, Maryland 21218-4363
www.press.jhu.edu

Library of Congress Cataloging-in-Publication Data
will be found at the end of this book.
A catalog record for this book is available
from the British Library.

ISBN 0-8018-6475-5

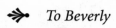 *To Beverly*

CONTENTS

My route to writing a book about a street fight in Pistoia has had as many twistings and turnings as a Renaissance maze. In *Saints and Society*, Rudolph Bell and I noted that holy men and women were much sought after as peacemakers. Clearly, making peace was so important in late medieval and Renaissance society as to be considered a saintly virtue, and I made a mental note to revisit the subject at another time. I did so some years later, although by then my attention had turned to the reasons sixteenth-century people quarreled and came to blows as well as to the ways they made peace. Since fighting was then, as now, almost as common and multifarious as eating or making love, I needed to define my subject more precisely. A conversation with my friend Alison Brown of the University of London helped me get a better grip on it. Why not, Alison suggested, study the duel in sixteenth-century Italy? The idea appealed: I knew the duel to be a highly specific form of violence, culturally defined and socially restricted, designed to be undertaken in the most deliberate, ritually and socially prescribed circumstances, and—the clinching argument—the contemporary documentation and literature were abundant.

I began by reading the treatises that sixteenth-century and seventeenth-century Italian authors fed to an avid market. These "duel doctors" wrote a great deal about honor (who possessed it, how it might be lost, and how it might be defended in a duel) and they laid out the protocol of dueling (the offense, giving the lie, the challenge, the response, the choice of weapons and fields, and so on). But while the doctors set the rules of the game, they had little to say about how the game was played. In the Library of the Vatican and in the Duello archive at the Biblioteca Nazionale of Rome, there were records of a few historic duels, but not very many. I learned a little more by examining government bans and church decrees against dueling and got some information about real duels from some of the countless histories of the subject (among the modern studies, Bryson, Erspamer, and

Billacois are particularly good) but they, too, relied heavily upon the theoretical literature and the more notorious cases. Clearly, even in its heyday, the duel was an abstraction, its elaborate ritual and highminded decorum as much lip service as performance, while historians, instead of surveying actual cases, have treated it as a kind of Weberian ideal type, a conceptual composite. As Robert Dallington, the late-sixteenth-century English diplomat, observed during his travels in Tuscany, dueling there seldom followed the script (see chapter 2). What was wanted was actual cases, but except for a few notorious ones, actual cases were hard to find. Judicial records were an obvious place to look, but unless I could find a jurisdiction in which quarrels of honor, challenges, and personal combat constituted a sizeable part of the record, I would be a long time winnowing them out.

As it happens, there was such a jurisdiction, well known to historians of Tuscany, and it did keep good records. In 1562 Duke Cosimo I, the grandson of Lorenzo de'Medici, Lorenzo the Magnificent, founded the Order of Santo Stefano, a military order. Its members were young nobles (and some aspiring to nobility) who enlisted to fight the Turks on behalf of Christian Europe. Like the clergy, the cavaliers, or knights, of Santo Stefano were largely exempt from the jurisdiction of temporal courts; instead, they were subject to the laws and discipline of their order. Among the many folio volumes of Santo Stefano records preserved in the Archivio di Stato of Pisa, where the order was headquartered, one series contained records of the criminal proceedings against members of the order, another the sentences and penalties imposed. In many cases, the entry ended with a rescript scrawled by the duke himself (the dukes were the grand masters of the order) indicating that he had reviewed the case and giving his disposition of it. Charges against the knights varied, of course; accusations of sexual offenses, rowdiness, unpaid debts, and various forms of cheating and deception were fairly common, but so too were cases in which honor was an issue and swords crossed, either between knights of the order or between knights and outsiders. This was the sort of stuff I was looking for, and I set to work to study such quarrels in the light of the chivalric codes and dueling protocols that were so widely advocated and professed in the sixteenth century.

The reticence of my sources was disappointing. Few of the entries contained more than a statement of the charge, the verdict, the sentence, and ducal rescript—not enough detail for analyzing and making generalizations about feelings and motives. As I continued to work my way through the Santo Stefano records, however, I came upon a separate fascicule of documents with a notation on its cover folio, "No. 43, Processo against Cavalier Mariotto Cellesi," and a notation of costs, "Charges of 117 [scudi] 11 [lire] 10 [soldi]." Unlike the bare summaries of the preceding forty-two entries, number 43 was the complete dossier of a case, the investigation and trials arising from a bloody sword fight between two young nobles of Pistoia. Stretching over many months, it was brimming with the kind of detail I was looking for—declarations of motive, expressions of opinion, and confessions of feelings by the principal actors involved and by the dozens of witnesses and observers who were drawn into the case. This was pure gold for a social historian. I needed to reconsider my project: mining the small mountain of the Cellesi case would be a full-time job; on the other hand, it would be unthinkable to walk away from such a bonanza. So I started digging, first in Pisa, in the trial dossier; then in Pistoia, scene of the quarrel and the early stages of the processo; and finally in Florence, where the grand duke and his secretaries kept a close watch on the unruly Pistoians. The book that has come of it is in the genre of microhistory, a study of a single sixteenth-century fight in a provincial Tuscan town, rather than the general study of dueling in sixteenth-century Italy that I originally set out to write. The field of vision is narrower, of course, but the focus is tighter and renders a sharpness of image and an abundance of detail and local color not possible in a more generalized study. Moreover, the particular circumstances of the case and the people involved in it have taken me well beyond a tale of a simple street fight to observations about social, cultural, and political issues of sixteenth-century Tuscan life and culture.

For directions and assistance along my winding route I am grateful to Sidney Anglo, James Banker, JoAnne Bernstein, Sergio Bertelli, John Brackett, Alison Brown, Jeannie Carlier, David Chambers, Elizabeth Cropper, Gino Corti, Natalie Z. Davis, Trevor Dean, Charles Dempsey, Germana Ernst, Stefano Focacci, Franco Franceschi, John Frymire, Vito Giustiniani, Don Fernando Grazzini, Sarah Mathews Grieco, Gabriele Inglese, Julius Kirshner, Thomas Kuehn, Rita Librandi, Burr Litchfield, Kate Lowe, Ottavio Lurati,

Lissa McCullough, Steve Milner, Heiko A. Oberman, John O'Malley, Letizia Panizza, Adriano Prosperi, Nicolai Rubinstein, Don Sinibaldo Sottili, Joseph Trapp, Armando F. Verde, O. P., Roberto Vivarelli, and Daniel Waley.

The students and faculty of the University of Warwick seminar in Venice were the first public audience to hear my reflections on the Pistoia street fight. Their interest and enthusiasm were a stimulus to begin writing, which I was able to do under the ideal conditions of the Rockefeller Foundation Research and Conference Center in the Villa Serbelloni at Bellagio. My warm thanks to the center's director and staff for their gracious hospitality and to my fellow residents at the center for their interest and suggestions. Further along, I was helped by the advice and criticism of the members of the Johns Hopkins University Seminar in Florence as well as of the members of Nicolai Rubinstein's Renaissance Seminar at the University of London.

The expert guidance of the directors and staffs of the following archives and libraries was indispensable: the Archivio di Stato, Bologna; the Archivio di Stato, Florence; the Archivio di Stato, Pisa; the Archivio di Stato, Pistoia; the Biblioteca Nazionale Centrale, Florence; the Archivio Capitolare of the Cattedrale di San Zeno, Archivio Diocesano, and the Archivio Vescovile, all of Pistoia; the Biblioteca Nazionale Centrale, Rome; the Bancroft Library and the University Library of the University of California, Berkeley; the Biblioteca Berenson, Villa I Tatti; the Biblioteca Forteguerriana, Pistoia; the British Library; the Biblioteca della Sapienza (University of Pisa); the Institute for Historical Research and the Warburg Institute of the University of London; and the Biblioteca Vaticana. A special word of thanks to Monsignor Alfredo Pacini of the Archivio Capitolare, Pistoia, Don Luciano Tempestini of the Archivio Vescovile, Pistoia, and Massimo Buccantini and Franco Savi of the Biblioteca Forteguerriana, Pistoia.

Grants from the University of Arizona Faculty Research Program and the American Philosophical Society helped with the expense of two of my research trips to Italy.

In a characteristic work of supererogation, Lorenzo Polizzotto offered to read the penultimate draft and did so meticulously. His emendations and suggestions were enormously helpful, his enthusiasm invaluable.

I also owe special thanks to Lance Hoopes. Times without number, he interrupted his own work and raced to my side to make peace between me and my computer, greater enemies than the Cellesi and Bracciolini ever were.

Alan E. Bernstein and my wife, Beverly J. Parker, also helped in the task of appeasement, and in many other ways Alan was a ready source of support. Without the repeated interventions of all three, I could not have retained enough of my sanity to complete this book. In preparing the illustrations for publication, I had the help of Maria Segura Hoopes and her computer wizardry.

In addition to her unstinting assistance with a thousand practical details, my wife discussed the writing with me at every stage, offered penetrating insights, and made me rethink and reformulate parts of my argument. This is a better book because of her and I dedicate it to her with admiration, gratitude, and love.

Standards in Sixteenth-Century Pistoia

Time, Weights and Measures, Money, Wages, and Prices
in Sixteenth-Century Pistoia

Time

The Day: In sixteenth-century Italy, the hours were counted from sunset to sunset in a twenty-four-hour sequence. The hour of one was one hour after sunset, two, two hours after sunset, and so on. The sun, of course, sets at different times during the course of the year, and the hour-of-day moved with it. I have converted all times to the modern system, estimating the hour of sunset for the indicated time of the year.

The Year: Pistoia usually dated the new year from March 25, the Feast of the Annunciation, as did Florence. I have converted dates to the modern style.

Weights and Measures

For information on Pistoia weights and measures, I have drawn chiefly from the table in David Herlihy, *Pistoia* n.p., and from Baldassare Licata, "Il problema del grano e carestie," in G. Spini, ed., *Architettura e politica da Cosimo I a Ferdinando I* (Florence, 1976), 335.

There was no standard system of weights and measures in sixteenth-century Italy. The following were commonly used in Pistoia.

Weight: *libbra* = 0.68 pounds avoirdupois, or 323.5 grams; *oncia* = 30 grams.

Length: *braccio* (pl. *braccia*) = 2.1 feet, or 0.613 meters (slightly longer for measuring land).

Dry measure: *staio* = 0.73 bushels, or 25.92 liters.

Distance: The *miglio* had been the common unit of distance since ancient times, when it was equivalent to 1,000 paces—about 1,480 meters. Later it varied from about 1,460 meters at Rome to about 2,466 meters in Piedmont. Shorter distances were often given as so many stone's throws or bow shots.

Surface area: *staioro* = .313 acres (4 *staiori* = 1 *coltra*).

Money

For Florentine money, which included that used in Pistoia, I have drawn mainly upon Carlo M. Cipolla, *Il fiorino e il quattrino* (Bologna, 1982) and *La moneta a Firenze nel Cinquecento* (Bologna, 1987).

In Florentine territory, by the late sixteenth century the *scudo*, or *ducato*, had replaced the *fiorino*, which contained about 32 grams of gold or the equivalent in silver.

7 *lire* = 1 *scudo*; 20 *soldi* = 1 *lira*; 12 *denari* = 1 *soldo*; 4 *denari* = 1 *quattrino*.

Wages

The following are examples of wages (mostly at Pistoia) in the mid sixteenth century.

From S. Pepper, N. Adams, *Firearms and Fortifications* (1986), 30; cited by Sergio Fusco, "Le fortezze secondo Niccolò Machiavelli," *Ricerche storiche* 15 (1990): 40, n. 8):

Tuscan peasant family, approx. income per annum: 5–6 scudi.

Imperial army infantry pikeman, wages per annum: 25 scudi.

From the account book of Giovanni di Bastiano Cellesi, agent of the grand duke, ASF, Monte di Pietà Bigallo 935 fols. 50v, 64v, 46r, respectively (entries dated 1572):

Captain of the guard, wages per month: 30 lire. This was equivalent to the wages for three men (*garzini*).

Chaplain of the Church of Madonna dell'Umiltà, salary per month: 20 lire.

Hostler (*cavallaro*), wages per month: 19 lire.

From Fioravanti, *Ricordi* BNF, MS Rossi Cassigoli 241, fol. 5v):

Domestic servant (female), wages per year: 24 lire plus two pairs of shoes.

From "Relazione del Commissario Gio. Batista Tedaldi sopra la Città e il Capitanato di Pistoia nel anno 1569," ed. Vincenzo Minuti, ASI, ser. 5. 10 (1892), 306:

Commissioner of Pistoia, salary per semester (six months): 3,000 lire.

Prices

In the 1570s the average price of a staio of grain equaled 3 lire, but by 1579 it had almost doubled. The harvest of 1579 was poor and was followed by general famine in Italy (from Giuliano de'Ricci, *Cronaca 1532–1606*, ed. G. Sapori [Milan, 1972], 279, 285). At mid century, a peasant family was expected to subsist on 5 to 6 scudi (38–45 lire) per year (from Fusco, "Le fortezze secondo Niccolò Machiavelli"). The cost of maintaining a rich young man in good style in Pistoia was calculated at between 30 and 50 scudi per year (from ASF, Monte di Pietà nel Bigallo 928, folio not numbered).

THE CAPTAIN'S CONCUBINE

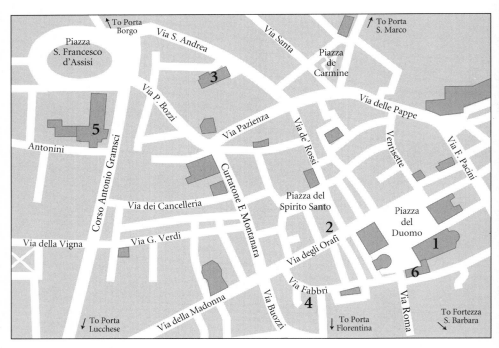

Map of Pistoia. *1.* Cathedral of S. Zeno; *2.* Palazzo Bracciolini; *3.* Church of S. Andrea; *4.* Castel Cellesi; *5.* Church of S. Francesco d'Assisi; *6.* Bishop's Palace. Map by William Nelson.

The Holy Thursday Incident

> Beauty of ladies of compassionate heart
> And cavaliers, in arms, and high in pride,
> And singing birds, and lovers' rhetoric art,
> And painted ships which on the strong seas ride.
> —Guido Cavalcanti

In S. Zeno Cathedral of Pistoia the Washing of the Disciples' Feet was just ending.[1] While elderly Bishop Lattanzio Lattanzi led the celebrants back to their seats in the choir, the Holy Thursday crowd sorted itself out, those who had come only to see the foot washing pushing toward the exits, others pressing forward to hear the sermon. As the massive church doors groaned open, Jacopo, *il trombetto*—the city herald, shoved his way in through the outgoing tide, elbowing through clogged aisles until he found Commissioner Cosimo de'Pazzi and Ser Attriano, his notary, seated well forward toward the high altar. He whispered an urgent message: *a sword fight in the street! . . . Cavalier Mariotto Cellesi and Cavalier Fabrizio Bracciolini—Bracciolini badly wounded.* Messer Cosimo listened to Jacopo's report and gave his orders: to his notary, to issue an immediate *levare l'offesa,* binding the two parties to refrain from further offense and make peace; to his deputy, to proceed to examine and question the wounded man. Then, with the preacher mounting to his pulpit, Commissioner Pazzi despatched the herald and turned his attention to the sermon.

27 March, 1578. By authority of the signor commissioner of Pistoia: Ordered, a cessation of further offenses between Cavalier Mariotto, son of Captain Lanfredino

Cathedral of S. Zeno. Photo by author

Cellesi of Pistoia, of the first part, and Cavalier Fabrizio, son of Messer Francesco Bracciolini of Pistoia, of the second part, and those connected or related to them in the male line to the canonical fourth degree inclusive. To be binding until they have concluded a peace or truce, with penalty of 2,000 scudi to be applied according to the law. Proclaimed on the same day in the usual places by Jacopo, Herald. On the same day notification given at the residence of both parties by Vangelista, Messenger, as reported.[2]

That same afternoon, Daccio Dacci, the commissioner's deputy, and Ser Attriano left their headquarters in the old Palace of the Podestà to interview the reputed victim. They had only to walk next door; the Bracciolini, like the Cellesi and other of Pistoia's patrician families, kept to the city's ancient center.[3] The main entrance of their house on the via degli Orafi opened onto the vast Piazza Grande, slightly behind the Palace of the Podestà, and looked across to the Palace of the Commune, the cathedral, baptistery, and bishop's palace on the far side.[4] Beneath the Bracciolini's shorn-off medieval tower, relict of the family's part in Pistoia's violent history,[5] the two officials entered the arched doorway (lately remodeled in the fashionable *bugnati,* or rusticated, style of Florence). At the end of the bare vaulted corridor (its walls and ceiling would later be frescoed with portraits and battle scenes pointedly linking the service of the Bracciolini to their victorious Medici rulers), they climbed a broad staircase to the family's private quarters on the *piano nobile* above. They found Cavalier Fabrizio in his bedchamber, a doctor treating his wounds. These the deputy and notary examined and duly recorded: "The nose cut almost through, [the cut] starting at the head and reaching almost to the tip of the nose. Another deep cut in the left leg with loss of blood. A third wound in a finger of the left hand, also with loss of blood. A bad bruise from a blow to the fleshy part of the left arm. Numerous other painful bruises in the shoulders."

Sworn and questioned, Fabrizio charged that he had been attacked without warning by Cavalier Mariotto, son of Captain Lanfredino Cellesi, and four other men. Two of the four he could identify: Asdrubale, bastard son of the late Giovanni Cellesi and cousin to Mariotto, and Tonio, son of Lionardo Visconti,[6] known as il Bonzetta; but of the two others he could only affirm that they were armed. Asked why this had happened and where, Fabrizio gave the following story.

I was on my way to confession and the service in S. Francesco. Just past the Canto de'Rossi, Cavalier Cellesi and Asdrubale were in the street in front of me. When they saw me they went toward the doorway of Tonio, an ally of Cavalier Mariotto and his father, and banged on the door.[7] I kept on my way and as I passed them they raised their birettas to me and I to them. After I had passed, Cavalier Mariotto, without saying anything, drew his sword and treacherously, from behind, hit me in the neck and kidneys, as you can see from the cuts in my jacket and cloak, and on the handle of my dagger. Before I could even turn around, Asdrubale also joined in the attack with the cavalier and Tonio threw a stone at me as he was coming out of the doorway with two other armed men, and they attacked me. They all surrounded me, hitting me and throwing stones at me. I pulled away a bit and drew my sword and was trying to turn. Cavalier Mariotto was behind me and hitting me and his last blow wounded me here in the nose, then he ran away with the others. I called to him, but he wouldn't come back, and I heard him say to Asdrubale that Captain Lanfredino Cellesi had put him up to it.

Had there been any enmity between himself and Cavalier Mariotto and the others?

"No, not with any of them. Only two mornings ago we were talking together with some other gentlemen."

Who had witnessed the incident?

"Luca Pazzaglia, some women, and others I didn't pay attention to. I had only my sword and dagger and mail jacket. As I was passing them, Cavalier Cellesi was on one side of the street with a sword and Asdrubale on the other, unarmed, and after I passed, Cavalier Cellesi began striking me, and Asdrubale got a weapon from Tonio's house and came back out."

Ser Attriano confirmed that Fabrizio's jacket had a sizeable rent in the back, another on the right side of the collar, and a large rip in the hood of the cape. There were fresh cuts on the handle of his dagger and on his sword belt. Orders for the arrest of Mariotto Cellesi, Asdrubale Cellesi, and Tonio Visconti were immediately given to the lieutenant—the officer under the bargello, or chief police official—and on the same day magistrates began questioning witnesses.

Witnesses were not hard to find. On Holy Thursday many Pistoians were in the streets making the rounds of churches to hear mass, confess, and garner pardons for their sins, and then, like Commissioner Pazzi, going to the cathedral to see the foot washing.[8] Others (despite the standing orders against working on major holidays)[9] had been at benches and looms, and these rushed to their windows and doors when they heard the commotion in the street. In the next three weeks the Pistoia magistrates questioned fourteen people, seven of them eyewitnesses. What they heard would leave little doubt that Mariotto Cellesi had initiated the armed attack that left Fabrizio Bracciolini wounded. But the other parts of Fabrizio's accusation—that Mariotto and four others had "traitorously" assaulted him, that they had acted without provocation, and that on departing Mariotto had called out the name of his father, Captain Lanfredino Cellesi, as the instigator of the attack—proved much harder to verify.

History and Comedy

> All the world's a stage,
> And all the men and women merely players.
> —*As You Like It*, 2.7

In its general features, the Holy Thursday incident resembles hundreds of other cases recorded in sixteenth-century Italian criminal archives: a young hothead, nursing a grievance or suddenly inflamed by an insult or a slight (aggravated, like as not, by too much wine), either acting alone or with friends, sets upon his enemy with sword and dagger and leaves him bleeding on the pavement. Fights such as these, Robert Dallington, the English traveler in Tuscany, had in mind when, two decades later, he wrote that for all their puffery about honor and the rules of dueling, the Italians' preferred method for righting an injury was to waylay their opponents in the street.[1] If they were caught, they could expect swift justice, with punishment allotted according to the severity of the wound.

In the court record, the summaries of such cases usually occupy a half page or so—not much more than a statement of the charge and the sentence, their brevity a measure of their banality. Not so the Cellesi-Bracciolini affair, which is recorded in abundant—and, by the time the case comes to an end, extravagantly redundant—detail. Unlike the vast majority of cases of armed assault and street fighting that came before magistrates and were quickly disposed of, this one dragged on for more than a year. Before it was over, more than forty people—the protagonists, the other accused, witnesses, and informants—had been questioned; key eyewitnesses were cited to three, in some cases to four, different courts and, as the more spirited among them wearily reminded the magistrates, shunted between Pistoia, Florence, and Pisa to repeat their stories yet another time. Some were confined during the period of their interrogation to the *segrete,* the dungeons of Pistoia and Florence, intimidated by torture threats, and spied on by their cellmates, who reported their conversations to the investigating magistrates. Meanwhile a river of paper ran between the three cities, dumping heaps of orders, interrogatories, depositions, witnesses' responses, personal letters, reports of judges and investigating officials, and instructions from the various authorities, including, from time to time, terse rescripts of Grand Duke Francesco de'Medici himself.

Why was this case unusual? Why should the investigation of a street brawl, at first glance as common as any other, catch up so many people, submit them to such intense and repeated interrogation, and involve the highest authorities? These were some of the questions I asked myself as I began making my way through the abnormally thick dossier of the case against Mariotto Cellesi in the state archives of Pisa. Well before I had finished reading and rereading the more than six hundred pages of browned and rust-spotted folio pages of the transcript and hunting down all my other leads, the Cellesi-Bracciolini affair had me solidly hooked. Page by page, the background of the Holy Thursday incident emerged—first the surface, in blurred outline, then, with ever more vivid detail, the background. For of course the incident *did* have a background, despite Fabrizio's disingenuous assertion that he was the innocent victim of an unprovoked attack. As I came to see it, the same things that made the case so complicated and caused it to drag on for so long were just those that made it so absorbing: the conflicting testimonies about the fight in the street; the intriguing, sometimes contradictory stories about what had led up to it, often recorded in the speaker's own words; the range and variety of individual personalities that came into view; and the legal and jurisdictional intricacies that in part were due to Pistoia's unusual position in the grand ducal Tuscan state, in part to the privileged status of the accuser, the principal accused, and their families.

In the language of theater, the Cellesi-Bracciolini case has a lively and intriguing plot, a rich diversity of characters, and a thickly textured background. Stage language may not be wholly inappropriate to describe it; in the Italy of the High Renaissance, life, art, and theater constantly traversed each other's notional boundaries,[2] most famously in the novella by Luigi da

Porto, *Giulietta e Romeo,* a fictionalized memoir of the author's star-crossed love for sixteen-year-old Lucina Savorgnan and the source for Shakespeare's *Romeo and Juliet.*[3] With varying degrees of self-consciousness, the leading actors of the Holy Thursday drama played parts that might have been written for them by a Niccolò Machiavelli in his comic mode or, closer to home, by Pistoia's popular comedian Francesco Andreini, creator of the swashbuckling il Capitan Spavento—or still closer, by Fabrizio's own cousin, Francesco Bracciolini, a playwright favored and patronized by cardinals and popes.

Still, though Fabrizio's half-severed nose may have been promising material for comedy, among duelists in contemporary Italy, wounds to the nose were more than a joke—a hazard so common and so serious as to bring fame to Gaspare Tagliacozzi, professor in the medical school at Bologna, who specialized in reconstructing them.[4] Nature may in some degree have been imitating art, but the Holy Thursday incident was real, not imagined, its protagonists not fictional characters, but living people. The double wound, to Fabrizio's nose and to his dignity, reminds us that Renaissance comedians and parodists took much of their material from a society they knew at first hand.

No one familiar with Italian Renaissance comedy—or with the satirical pages of Shakespeare or Cervantes—will be startled to learn that the occasion for the quarrel between Mariotto Cellesi and Fabrizio Bracciolini was a woman. And, knowing this much, they will correctly surmise that the issues of the fight in the street were honor, revenge, reputation, and "face" (*figura*, as the Italians would say), sentiments as palpable and vital to the Cellesi and the Bracciolini as the hot blood they spilled over them. Nor will such a reader be surprised to learn that both accuser and accused insisted that their motives and actions were all noble, their rivals' all ignoble, as if rhetorical battles over honor were a zero-sum game.[5] This much Renaissance literature has made familiar to us. On the other hand, about the legal and intellectual aspects of the Renaissance high code of honor, modern readers may not be so well informed, having been put off by the archaic inconsequentiality as well as the turgid prose of sixteenth-century jurists, moralists, chivalry theorists, and duel experts.[6] Besides, who can say that these grave treatises and legalistic "consults" bring us any closer to the way the honor code was formulated and lived? Between the humorous and satirical treatment of questions of honor by sixteenth-century playwrights and novelists on one side, then, and the formal issues gravely debated by sixteenth-century theorists on the other, the Bracciolini-Cellesi case offers a precious third perspective, a real case involving real people.

Virtually all the official orders and instructions issued in the case are included in the surviving dossier; the testimony of the witnesses is complete, much of it verbatim, much in the first person; the interrogatories submitted by the plaintiff and the defendants have been preserved; letters and other writings submitted in evidence were copied into the court record. These sources allow us to follow the case in unusual detail and to hear all parties in their own words. I will quote from them extensively, for even in translation they convey more of their original idiom and sense than my own words possibly could. But while I will encourage the participants to speak, I have no intention of surrendering my historian's mandate to interpret what they say and to draw my own conclusions. I will try to reconstruct the case to make my own sense of it.[7]

My narrative strategy is to let the story unfold as it does in the processo— piecemeal and tentatively; to stay, for a time at least, with the limited perspective of the investigating officials rather than to barge in with preemptive hindsight. This is partly because I want to share with readers the sense of discovery I felt as I first made my way through the documents, but more importantly I want to remind them (as I constantly had to remind myself) that for us the Cellesi-Bracciolini affair has virtually no life apart from the processo it brought into being. Like all stories in court cases, it is a construct—or rather, a cluster of constructs (fashionably referred to nowadays as "texts")—shaped by legal procedures and the strategies of the contending parties, warped by subjective interest, and clouded by imperfect perception and faulty memory.[8] This is brought home to us from the start as we see the magistrates trying to learn from the actors and eyewitnesses the basic facts of the fight—Who was present? What was said? What was done? By whom?—and being met with diverse, sometimes contradictory accounts. We might call this the *Rashomon* aspect of the case, after the classsic Japanese film in which a bandit, the woman he raped, and her husband described the encounter in three different, equally self-serving stories. If anything, the incident in the via S. Andrea was even more complicated, with more people

Hold Pistoia by her factions Florence did, but given the volatility of the parties, especially when abetted by influential Florentines, this was a policy that flirted with disaster. In 1455 four commissioners had to be dispatched to Pistoia "to put an end to the quarrels and fights going on among the various houses, and henceforward parties that broke the peace were required to give bond against new offenses."[5] Judicial restraints, together with strategic favors to key figures and a loosening of control over local offices, helped keep Pistoia quiet for a generation, but in 1499 this arrangement collapsed in the worst explosion of factional violence in Pistoia's history. The trouble began with a Cancellieri-Panciatichi dispute over a patronage plum, the directorship of S. Gregorio, Pistoia's richly endowed foundling hospital. When Florentine supporters of the Cancellieri intervened to ensure the selection of their favorite, Bernardo Nutini, over the three locally nominated Panciatichi finalists, the Panciatichi felt they had been cheated. On February 4, the Feast of S. Agatha,[6] some of their stalwarts attacked Nutini's nephew in front of the cathedral. In the melée that followed, a Cancellieri partisan was killed. Immediately both sides took up fortified positions and sent armed retainers into the streets. With only token intervention from the weak Florentine garrison, they murdered, looted, and burned. Overwhelming the guards, they tore down city gates to admit armed peasants streaming in from Panciatichi and Cancellieri estates. Other bands fanned out into the countryside to enlist additional fighters and to seize key roads, bridges, and fortresses, while volunteers and mercenaries were recruited from Lucca, Bologna, Modena, and even as far away as Siena.

Florence, increasingly in turmoil after the revolt against the Medici in 1494, and divided between Panciatichi and Cancellieri backers, was unable to bring Pistoia's civil war under control until 1502. Four hundred buildings had been destroyed in the city, another sixteen hundred in the contado and mountain areas.[7] Hundreds of people had been killed, lands and crops destroyed, and families forced into exile. Although the fighting in the streets had favored the Cancellieri, the Panciatichi were stronger in the important rural areas, and their relatives and powerful friends in Florence helped them regain dominance, particularly after the return of the Medici to Florence in 1512. Faithful clients of the glittering and triumphant Medici (who, after a short-lived republican interlude from 1527 to 1530, established a hereditary dukedom), the Panciatichi were in the driver's seat. There were further bloody risings in 1529, 1537, and 1539, but the Cancellieri were quelled with exile and fines.[8] Pistoia had become a Panciatichi city.

The violence of "the parties" may have been as much symptom as cause of Pistoia's troubles. From an economic perspective, too many Pistoians were fighting for too few resources. Pistoia was locked in a double bind: lacking the capital, manpower, and industrial capacity to compete effectively with her stronger neighbors for markets, routes, or territory, she was unable to maintain the vigorous rate of growth either in the city or its hinterland that might have eased her domestic rivalries. In this unsettled condition, the Black Death of 1348 was a particularly calamitous blow to Pistoia, and although officials promoted extraordinary measures of sanitation and imposed a quarantine against contamination from outside new waves of plague struck repeatedly in the next two centuries. By 1450 Pistoia's population had fallen from an estimated high between eleven thousand and thirteen thousand to a low of forty-five hundred.[9]

Thus, long before Commissioner Tedaldi wrote his relazione—the time of our story—economic troubles and epidemics as well as internal warfare and Florentine political and commercial domination had hardened the mold of stagnation and provincialism that had begun to encase Pistoia two centuries earlier. Already in 1494 the visiting duke of Urbino commented that although the city was lovely, it "was not kept clean or orderly."[10] Things had no doubt worsened by 1559, when communal officials complained that "our public streets are always full of dirt, stones, and excrement, and everyone is more concerned to clean his house by throwing things out than to keep the streets clean of trash and garbage."[11] Tedaldi reported that Pistoia had fourteen hundred families, compared with a pre–Black Death figure of twenty-three hundred, and a total population of eight thousand (a computation by the fiscale of Pistoia in 1576 gave an exact figure of 6,948, including children and clergy).[12] The condition of the much reduced population varied widely. While wage laborers were very poor, "as they always are everywhere," its artigiani (by which Tedaldi meant to include businessmen and shopkeepers) lived well, getting and spending, taking in money brought into the city by virtue of its privileged status as terra di passo, a required stop for travelers. Especially they profited from the harvesters and sheepherders of the Maremma, who were obliged to stock up there during their seasonal transit with their flocks between the mountains and the coastal plain. Nor did the nobles of Pistoia shun moneymaking, being particularly adept at hoarding grain and selling it when prices rose. Few nobles had less than 3,000 scudi in cash; five had 30,000 or more; most ranged in between.

Tedaldi noted that one-third of the hinterland's yield of grains, chestnuts, beans, and other crops as well as meat and wine fed the whole population and one-third went for seed. The remaining third was converted "entirely into gold, since on market days the surplus was sold in the piazza, furnishing Pistoia, Florence, Prato, and other localities of the state and accumulating money for its citizens, religious foundations, and, in some measure, its peasants." Pistoia also produced silks valued at 10,000 scudi a year. And it exported to France and Flanders the lamb fells of its hinterlands, realizing about 15,000 scudi per year; however, Tedaldi added, this was only one-half of what Pistoian merchants previously netted from sheep fells, before Florentine merchants became aware of Pistoia's monopoly and began to collect and sell sheep fells for themselves, a good example of how the curve of Pistoian prosperity was flattened by the superior resources and enterprise of Tuscany's capital city.

Although Tedaldi recognized that Pistoia's economy suffered from living in Florence's shadow, he had little good to say about the character of its people. Granted, they were "very astute, intelligent, well spoken, ceremonious, likeable, reverent, and obedient," but they were also "miserly, suspicious, flatterers, haughty, vindictive, restless, and ever desirous of seeing new things; as careful, solicitous, and diligent in their own interests as they are lazy, neglectful, and careless in matters pertaining to the public good and general convenience." Not only do the city's nobles "not strive to excel either in letters or in the military field; they do not even take pleasure in horses or building or agriculture or anything else that might make them great and famous or be an adornment of their fatherland with virtuous and magnificent achievements." To be sure, Pistoia had many good Catholics who went to church daily, were devoted to the saints, and faithfully attended sermons and mass. They were also charitable to the poor and completely devoid of any sort of heresy.[13]

The clergy were another matter. Most of them were vain and licentious, gambled, partied, and frequented whores, as if, he said, they were in competition to see which among them could be the worst. Indeed, it seemed that in Pistoia roles were reversed: men had the gravity and moderation of women, women the lasciviousness and sybaritical excesses of men; laymen, for the most part, followed a religious and Roman Catholic way of life, while clerics lived lasciviously and materialistically. Much of this he attributed to the laxity of the bishop (Giovanbattista Ricasoli), who was not old but decrepit and gouty and kept an unsalaried vicar who was worse than any of his priests. This vicar kept a concubine and was avid for money; it was well known that, with enough money, any sin however serious could be made right in Pistoia.[14] Not surprisingly, the commissioner felt that Pistoia's clergy set the city's youth a poor example. The seven hundred young men between fifteen and twenty-five years of age were "very handsome and sturdy to be sure, but wayward *[sfrenato]* and intimidating *[terribile]* and up to any sort of rash undertaking." It was a good thing they had been forbidden to go about armed, Tedaldi continued; the more they became accustomed to this and other restraints, the more peacefully and sociably they will live, "for the Pistoiese are, as they have always been, of a nature much inclined toward idleness *[una vita oziosa]*. This has always been the cause of all kinds of trouble; we have seen many instances of it. What else but idleness caused so many disasters *[ruine]*, conflagrations, murders, and cruel wars in this city in past times? Gaming and drinking in taverns have been the cause of the most serious provocations *[ingiurie],* and this kind of injury gave rise to the perverse and ruinous division of the White and Black Cancellieri [*sic*], which has led to so much ruin and bloodshed from the year 1300 to—we might say—the present day." This would have continued indefinitely, concluded Tedaldi, if not for the "incomparable prudence and excellent justice of His Highness the Grand Duke, our Lord, who has seen to and provided for everything."

Tedaldi's praise of the grand duke's wisdom was the fulsome flattery of a worshipful courtier. But it was also an acknowledgment that Cosimo I had undertaken firm and invasive measures to bring Pistoian factionalism and lawlessness under control and order to the administration of the city.[15] A Florentine-appointed *fiscale* managed the city's financial affairs, as well as other business. In place of the special commissioners who were appointed in times of emergency, Cosimo instituted the office of resident commissioner-general, with responsibility for law and order and justice.[16] Commissioners were prominent Florentines, senators who served a six-month term. The *famiglia* of the commissioner-general included an officer of the household *(cavaliere)*, heralds *(trombettori; araldi)*, messengers *(messi)*, and notaries *(notai)*. Also under the commissioner's orders was the *bargello*, chief police officer, who had his own *famiglia*, consisting of a lieutenant and his men— the lowly *sbirri* (or *birri*, as they were called in Pistoia). Even this sizeable array did not satisfy Cosimo: in 1545 or shortly thereafter, he established the special secretariat known as the Pratica Segreta to oversee Pistoian matters directly from Florence.[17]

From its chamber in the Palazzo Pitti, literally at the right hand of the grand duke himself, the *signori* of the Pratica Segreta kept close watch on the affairs of Prato and Pistoia and intervened via the commissioner in any matter they considered important. Even verbal altercations that smacked of Cancellieri and Panciatichi factionalism brought a speedy and effective response from wary authorities. In 1551, when Cammillo Bracali, "of the Panciatichi persuasion," and Fabio Gatteschi, a supporter of the Cancellieri, exchanged words "that might easily lead to disorder," the commissioner reported to Florence that he had summoned both men and imposed a *levata d'offesa* binding to the fourth degree of kinship. Moreover, since Fabio was unable to come up with the obligatory monetary bond he was taken into custody.[18]

Such minute supervision from the capital had its drawbacks, however. Routinely, the Pratica acted on the basis of the commissioner's reports, but it might also take action upon receipt of information from some other local source, or upon the request of a private person. It also acted in obedience to ducal rescripts—the personal orders his highness routinely scribbled in the bottom margin of the documents that came across his desk. The grand dukes regularly reviewed decisions of officials and judges and also might intervene in a particular case in response to a *supplica* (petition) from a subject. This was one way the capital kept in close touch with its dependencies, the grand duke in personal touch with his subjects. There were other ways, such as employing informers and, as Cosimo I liked to do, going about incognito in the streets. The trouble was that this short-circuiting of institutional channels, whereby petitions could move directly to the center and orders return to the periphery without the intervention of local magistrates (sometimes even without their knowledge), could undermine the ability of officials to maintain control of cases for which, structurally, they were responsible. In the Holy Thursday case, Pistoia's Commissioner Pazzi often seems, in the technico-bureaucratic jargon of a later age, to have been left out of the loop.

FOUR

The Cellesi

Eleventh-century records show that the Cellesi were landowners and castellans, people of some means and authority, in and about the village of Celle, in the mountain valley of the river Vincio, northwest of Pistoia. Nearby were the ruins of the old road that may have brought their forebears over the mountains from Lombardy[1] in the great *incastellamento,* the settling of the area, a century or so earlier.[2] Around 1200, members of the family moved down to Pistoia, where they tended to congregate in the parish of S. Anastasio, located in the quarter of the Lucca Gate. Their origins were preserved in their surname (de Cellis, da Celle, de Cellensibus, and others) and, as with so many other urban "new men," in their continuing economic and social ties to the land. Their farm estates, increasingly worked by *mezzadristi,* sharecroppers, provided surplus wool and chestnut flour that they could sell in local markets, and they prospered in commerce and moneylending. In the years that followed, some Cellesi accumulated additional farmlands, woods, mills, and flocks, not only in their mountain homelands but also in the more fertile alluvial plains south and east of the city, and with the yields of these extensive holdings as well as other goods, they traded in Florentine and European markets.

With growing wealth came standing in the commune; soon there were Cellesi priors and gonfaloniers—the highest officials of civic government. The family also vaunted kinship with a saintly bishop, the Blessed Atto, who presided over the Pistoia diocese until his death around 1295.[3] The claim may have been connected to the Cellesi's reputation as defenders of the church against heresy and to their domination of Pistoia's elaborately symbolic ceremony of the Entry of the New Bishop. Time-honored, sharply contested, and jealously guarded, the Cellesi privilege of leading the welcoming party when a new bishop arrived at the city gates attested to their powerful position in the civic arena, where religious and political prominence reinforced each other. Their role is colorfully and forcefully represented in the following description of the Bishop's Entry in 1562.

On 23 February, 1562, Messer Giovanni Battista Ricasoli, bishop of Pistoia, made his solemn entry in procession. He had been informed of the Cellesi privilege by which, according to ancient custom and right, he would be introduced into the city. So, when he arrived at the drawbridge of the Lucchese Gate, he asked if [members of] the house of Cellesi were present. At these words, everyone seated behind a triumphal arch near the gate rose to his feet. In the frieze of the arch was a Latin inscription reading: "We are able to enter here safely because your ancestor conquered the heretics."[4] Seventy-five-year-old Bastiano di Filippo Cellesi, as the senior member of the whole family, replied that [the family] was at the service of his serene most reverend holiness, begging him to maintain its privileges. [The bishop] replied that he wished not only to maintain but to augment them. Messer Fabrizio di Atto Cellesi delivered an oration on these matters, to which monsignor made a brief reply.

Then, ranged two by two around the canopy, they conducted [the bishop] into the city, accompanying him to [the Convent of] S. Piero Maggiore. Fabio di Benedetto Cellesi dismounted and, approaching the [bishop's] stirrup, removed [the bishop's] spurs, took his gloves, and mounted his palfrey. The others followed monsignore into S. Piero to celebrate the marriage to the abbess.[5] Then they went to the cathedral, where the Cellesi family were allowed to sit on special benches near the high altar. After monsignor performed the customary rites at the altar, the clergy and all the magistrates departed, while the Cellesi were called by his curate [name illegible] to kiss his hand, and following them all the people so that they might acquire indulgences.

When [the bishop] left the cathedral, everyone again followed him as far as the entrance to the bishop's palace, where Bastiano [Cellesi] gave the reins of the palfrey and the spurs and gloves to his serene holiness, while asking him to observe the Cellesi privileges. [The bishop] replied [a second time] that he would do everything in his power to augment rather than to diminish them. As a sign of this, he gave Bastiano, the eldest, the palfrey with its accoutrements and his spurs and gloves, and after they were dismissed by him everyone went to Bastiano's house. In accord with a decision by Monsignor Antonio Pucci, formerly bishop of Pistoia, the saddle was removed and covered in white ermine, and Fabio di Benedetto, Andrea di Luca, and Ridolfo di Francesco Cellesi, in the name of the whole family, presented the palfrey to the abbess of San Piero, together with a tabernacle of Christ. To Bastiano, the eldest, was given the saddle, bridle, gloves, and spurs, according to a perpetually binding decision recorded by the notary Ser Giovanni Cioci on 22 January 1520.

Nevertheless, on 25 February the whole family deliberated and decided to present the saddle to the most reverend monsignor. They had heard that the abbess had decided to return the palfrey to him, bareback as it was. They returned the saddle with the bridle, so that there remained to Bastiano only the gloves and spurs, which he kept in eternal memory of the privilege.

This account is one of a sheaf of aggressively defensive family documents supporting the Cellesi's right to precedence in the entry ceremony against a succession of rival claimants.[6] In an independent account of the entry of 1400 by the chronicler Luca Dominici, a member of the Buonvassalli family gives the official address of welcome. Still, the chronicler assigned a "customary and proprietary" role to the Cellesi and described a member of the family delivering "a pretty speech" at the Lucca Gate before taking the bridle of the bishop's horse.[7] It was about this time, however, that the Cellesi's privilege began to be contested by the Opera di S. Jacopo, Pistoia's largest charitable foundation.[8] The wealth of S. Jacopo and the prominence of its *Operai*, or lay officials, together with its quasi-public, quasi-ecclesiastical status, made it a formidable rival for processional honors. But the Cellesi held their own against S. Jacopo, even though the foundation officials twice appealed to the grand duke for support, first in the 1570s and again in 1599. Apparently the grand duke did not favor their suit; the officials continued to dispute the Cellesi claim until 1650, when they resigned themselves to the more modest role of welcoming the bishop in their own chapel.[9]

Pistoia's ceremonial calendar offered plenty of occasions for the intermingling of the sacral and the secular aspects of communal life (the city had, for example, at least three *palios*, or horseraces—the palio of S. Domenico, the palio of the Opera di S. Jacopo, and the palio of S. Bastiano)[10] and, as in other towns, quarrels over ceremonial precedence were common. In Florence "the hypertense competition of even the most stable of feasts" not infrequently exploded in violence.[11] In Pistoia, the Cellesi's long drawn-out battle over precedence in the entry ceremony is a measure not only of tenacious family ambition but also of the significance of the Bishop's Entry in Pistoia's ritual life. Every joining of the new bishop to his diocese renewed the union of the spiritual and temporal spheres and enhanced the auspices for the city's well-being. Although they played supporting roles to the bishop and abbess, the Cellesi and other lay participants performed ritual offices,

too—preparing the liturgical setting, accompanying the new prelate, inton-
ing the prescribed speeches, and handling charismatic objects—all necessary to the effective conduct of the holy rite. In return they received the
bishop's gifts of saddle, spurs, and gloves, radiant talismans of the ceremony's mystical power. As Richard Trexler puts it of the very similar Florentine entry ceremony, "lesser men, realizing the power of precedence, tried
to establish a right to share the bishop's charisma."[12] We might think the
Cellesi exceedingly pushy for insisting that their privilege be confirmed and
notarized on the spot, but this was common practice; in the Florentine
entry ceremony, even the abbess made such a request.[13]

Whatever blessings the city derived from the marriage of the bishop and the
abbess, peace and harmony were not prominent among them. Nor were the
Cellesi noted for their pacific virtues. "The family Cellesi is numerous, with
more men than any other in the city," reports Francesco Franchini, the fiscale, or financial magistrate, to the Pratica Segreta in Florence in 1588—
Franchini's way of saying that the Cellesi *casata* was well represented and
prominent in Pistoian affairs.[14] One of the family's own partisans agrees,
noting that after 1500 the Cellesi were "more numerous than any other" and
became factional chiefs.[15]

As with so many violent conflicts, the Cancellieri-Panciatichi war of
1499–1502 was almost as cruel to its winners as to its losers. Victory went to
the Panciatichi party, but the once-mighty family that led that faction was
so weakened that it was forced to cede precedence to others. Chief among
the families that succeeded to leadership was the Cellesi. They had been
in the forefront of the fighting from the earliest days. When Bartolomeo
Cellesi was killed at the bloody battle of S. Angiolo in 1500, so elated were
the Cancellieri that they cut off his head, carried it back to Pistoia on a sad-
dlebow, and publicly displayed it for three days. Most of the other members
of the Cellesi family were forced into exile and their houses in central Pistoia were sacked and burned to the ground.[16] When the war ended, the
Cellesi returned and rebuilt on a grander scale. To the "cramped and small"
houses burned in the Piazzetta Romana, they made major "additions and
improvements,"[17] while the fortunes and misfortunes of war provided them
with opportunities for further aggrandizement at the expense of friends

and enemies alike. La Magia, the Panciatichi stronghold in nearby Quarrata, passed first into Medici, much later into Cellesi, hands. Years later Captain Lanfredino purchased the Panciatichi family palace, one of Pistoia's great houses. When the Cancellieri were expropriated from their rural holdings north of Pistoia in the wake of the rising of 1529, the Cellesi succeeded them as landlords in Lanciuole, Crespole, and Calamecca, villages north of Celle.

As leaders of the pro-Florentine, pro-Medici faction, the Cellesi had special claims on the goodwill of the Medici regime. Mariotto di Atto Cellesi, grandfather of the Mariotto of our processo, won glory for fighting courageously at the battle of Gavinana in 1530, when the Medici crushed the Florentine republicans who had driven them from the city three years earlier. Mariotto's son Lanfredino, born in 1518,[18] succeeded to extensive holdings in town as well as the agricultural and pastoral properties acquired by his ancestors, and he made considerable additions on his own. Besides managing his lands, Lanfredino dealt in cloth, grain, and sheep fells in both regional and foreign markets. He also derived income from functioning as a *mallevadore,* or guarantor of private loans. He kept a *banco* in Pistoia, in rented premises on the ground floor of the bishop's palace,[19] but he was often in Florence, where he did much business with the Ricci and other leading commercial and banking firms.

Around 1545, Lanfredino, now calling himself Captain Lanfredino (he had acquired the rank in service with the emperor's forces in Hungary in 1543, and he continued to insist on it despite allegations that his military career had been something short of distinguished) made a brilliant marriage to Giulia Malaspina, daughter of the late Marchese Teodoro, of the ancient feudal family from the Lunigiana, and his second wife Angela de'Medici. Giulia was also the protégé of the Duchess (later Grandduchess) Eleonora of Toledo, consort of Cosimo I.[20] Lanfredino and Giulia kept a Florentine residence on the via Martelli, a stone's throw from the baptistery and cathedral and just down the street from the palace of the Medici on the via Larga.

By the time of the Holy Thursday incident, however, the captain had been a widower for many years. Crippled by what was diagnosed as gout, he spent less time in Florence than he did when Giulia was alive, preferring, when he felt well enough, to be carried by his servants into the country, to

Castel Cellesi, exterior view *(above)*, interior view *(facing page)*. Photos by the author

one of his several properties in the Apennines, north of Pistoia. Mostly, however, he kept to his main residence in Pistoia, in the family compound in the Piazzetta Romana.

The piazzetta, also known as Castel Cellesi since it consisted entirely of houses owned by the family, retained (and still retains) the ovoid shape of the ancient stronghold that had once stood there, near the center of the old Roman city. Separated from the via Fabbri by massive curving walls, the piazzetta (as would be importantly noted in our processo) could be entered only from the street through two huge gateways. When the gates were shut and barred, it was completely closed off, although neither walls nor gates had saved the Cellesi houses from being burned down in the civil war. But that was seventy-five years earlier, before the Medici regime imposed its peace upon the factions. Now the gates remained open, and the Piazzetta Romana—or Castel Cellesi—was, officially at least, public space.[21] In 1580, Captain Lanfredino affixed to the outer walls, at intervals between the shops, reliefs of shields inscribed with the Cellesi coat of arms, a lion rampant surmounting a field of diagonal stripes, and an inscription informing

passersby that this was the entailed property *(fidecommisso)* of Captain Lanfredino Cellesi. Although heavily weathered, the shields and inscriptions are still visible.

For two years before the incident in the via S. Andrea, Captain Lanfredino's gout had kept him virtually bedridden, although he remained active in business. The captain was a feisty character—quick to take offense and, in his younger years, quick to violence.[22] Even in his crippled sixties he remained unflaggingly contentious. As his kinsman Tommaso Cellesi reported in 1574: "Continuously for the last ten or twelve years Captain Lanfredino has had many, diverse, and very lengthy quarrels with many diverse sorts of people." Since Tommaso was in the midst of a lawsuit with the captain, he is perhaps not our most objective informant on this, but Giovanni Fabroni, Lanfredino's own procurator in the case, had to allow that what Tommaso said was true.[23] Everyone involved in the Holy Thursday case four years later could expect that the captain would use every means, including his fortune and his influence at the Medici court, to defend the interests of his family in this latest quarrel. Besides, Captain Lanfredino's involvement was more than that of a parent protecting his son; named in Fabrizio's deposition as the instigator of the attack, he was added to the list of the accused.

Mariotto, born in November 1558, was the elder of the two surviving sons of Captain Lanfredino Cellesi and the late Giulia Malaspina. Only twenty at the time of the Holy Thursday affair, he was married to Ippolita Cancellieri (what better example of the waning of the old party feud!) and the father of a one-year-old son, Cosimo. From the age of eighteen, Mariotto had been a *cavaliere*, or knight, of the military-religious Order of Santo Stefano and was away for some months each year, either in barracks in Pisa or serving in the order's galleys.[24] By 1578 he had completed three voyages and accumulated enough seniority to be eligible for a *commenda*, or benefice, from the order, but since his family had not provided him with a family-endowed benefice and one had not become available from the order, he was forced to continue routine service.[25]

Before the Holy Thursday street fight, Mariotto had experienced the Order of Santo Stefano's discipline only twice. Four years earlier he had been confined to barracks in Pisa for six months for an unspecified violation. Just a year before the Holy Thursday incident, while hunting in the mountains north of Pistoia at Vacca Morta, above Belriguardo (site of one of the fortresses of Castruccio Castracani, the fourteenth-century Lucchese despot), he had been involved in a dispute over possession of a hare with one Giovanni di Piero of Coreglio. Mariotto was accused of beating Giovanni over his whole body with the handle of a lance. Mariotto admitted taking the hare, claiming that he had recovered it from Giovanni, who had seized it from Mariotto's dogs, but he denied the beating. The Council of Santo Stefano heard the case, noted that the two had made peace, and dismissed the charge for lack of evidence.[26]

But it was one thing to administer a beating to a peasant—possibly one of his father's tenants—another to set upon a fellow cavalier of Santo Stefano and shed his blood. Mariotto, Captain Lanfredino, and the family procurator knew the difference, and they carefully prepared their strategy to defend father and son against the Holy Thursday charges.

FIVE

The Bracciolini

The Bracciolini had migrated to Pistoia from Buggiano, near Pescia, in 1269. Like the Cellesi, they soon became involved in Pistoia's communal politics, with the first of their family elected *Gonfaloniere,* or standard bearer, of the commune in 1339. Many more Bracciolini would follow in high civic office in the years to come. In his application for admission to the Order of Santo Stefano, Fabrizio would have no difficulty establishing his patrician lineage: his mother was a member of the important Pucci family of Florence, and his family quarterings included the aristocratic Lapi of Florence and Fabroni of Pistoia. Extensive property owners in the city and contado, the Bracciolini, like the Cellesi, had claims on the favor of the Medici. Traditionally they had belonged to the anti-Florentine Cancellieri party, but shortly before the Pistoian civil war of 1499 they had hitched their wagon to the rising star of the pro-Florentine and pro-Medici Panciatichi. Niccolò Bracciolini openly murdered Baccio Tonti, a Cancellieri chief, in 1527, fought on the Medici side at Gavinana in 1530, and again, after flirting with Filippo Strozzi and the republican exiles, fought for Duke Cosimo I at Montemurlo in 1537.[1]

At the time of the Holy Thursday incident, the Bracciolini had no patriarch as rich or as powerful as Captain Lanfredino Cellesi. The family's males seemed to be inclining toward the professions and the liberal rather than the martial arts,[2] so Fabrizio was something of an exception, the first (although by no means the last) of the Bracciolini to enter the Order of Santo Stefano. Fabrizio's father, Francesco di Vincenzo, a doctor of laws, was a career administrator, serving as a castellan and commissioner in the papal states under Pope Clement VII (Giulio de'Medici).[3]

A young cousin, also named Francesco, son of Giuliano Bracciolini and

Marietta Cellesi, followed his father into the law but achieved fame in Italy as a poet and playwright. Born and reared in the Bracciolini palace, this Francesco was twelve at the time of the Holy Thursday incident and may well have been watching as Fabrizio limped home from the via S. Andrea to lick his wounds. Some time later, Francesco went off to Florence, where he began his literary career. In 1594 he moved to Milan as secretary to the great Cardinal Federigo Borromeo, then in 1600 to Rome, where he became secretary to Cardinal Maffeo Barberini, later Pope Urban VIII, and helped found the Accademia degli Umoristi. As a reward for his *The Election of Pope Urban VIII,* he was granted the honor of adding the Barbarini bee symbol *(api)* both to the family name and to its coat of arms, a distinction the Pistoia Bracciolini continued to exhibit with pride. Did Francesco regale his Umoristi companions with the story of the fight between his Bracciolini and Cellesi cousins? Might he have found inspiration in it for any of his comedy plots? If so, he covered his tracks well. Besides, he and the other Bracciolini had reason to keep silent about an affair that could only have been a family embarrassment. In 1605, now a distinguished poet, Francesco returned to Pistoia, remaining for some years. He would have found Fabrizio still living in the family palace on the via degli Orafi, at the edge of the Piazza Grande.

Thirty-three years old at the time of the Holy Thursday incident, Fabrizio Bracciolini, in contrast to Mariotto Cellesi, was no stranger to street fights, broken heads, and prison cells. At seventeen he had been a student at the University of Pisa, where he was part of a group of avid *calcio* (soccer) players whose gambling and unruly behavior caused some concern to local magistrates.[4] In 1566, when he was twenty-one, he applied for admission to the Order of Santo Stefano, but he was not accepted until three years later. The reason for the delay can only be guessed at: the order required good moral character of its members; perhaps Fabrizio's student carousing in Pisa, where the order had its seat, had hurt his chances.[5] In any case, his admission came after his family endowed a *commenda,* or benefice, for him.

As a knight of Santo Stefano, Fabrizio's chief duty was to fight in the order's maritime campaigns against the Turks and to defend his prince, but as a *commendatario di padronato,* holder of a family-endowed benefice, he was

Palazzo Bracciolini. From an early drawing, ASPist, Sapienza 440

exempt from routine barracks service—the lengthy stays *in convento* in Pisa and the peacetime voyages aboard the order's galleys required of unbeneficed knights. This left Fabrizio—Cessio, as he was known to his friends[6]—largely free to live the life of a gentleman of leisure in Pistoia.[7]

In 1578 Fabrizio had been married for more than ten years and was the father of two sons and a daughter.[8] Neither marriage, fatherhood, nor the oath he had sworn to live a chaste and Christian life as a knight of Santo Stefano—to "become a new man," as the statutes put it—kept him from pursuing his pleasures in the streets and wineshops of the town and in the company of women other than his wife. Or the wives of other men: in March 1577, the Pratica Segreta ordered Fabrizio and Livia, wife of Vicenzo Biagiuoli, arrested and confined in the dungeons, *segrete,* of the bargello, in Florence, and instructed officials in Pistoia to find out why Mona Livia had left her husband, whether she and the cavalier had exchanged letters, and whether they were *innamorati.*[9] The archives are silent over how long Fabrizio and Livia remained in detention and how the case was disposed of. Presumably Fabrizio was not charged; if he had been, he would have had to answer to his superiors in Santo Stefano, but in the detailed records of the order there is no mention of the incident.

If Fabrizio seldom raised his sword against the Infidel Turk, he drew it frequently in quarrels with his fellow Pistoians (although in one instance he played peacemaker in a brawl at the house of the prostitute Locchina). In 1569, the very year of Commissioner Tedaldi's report and the year Fabrizio entered the order, Tommaso Isolavi, fiscale of Pistoia, complained that Bracciolini was one of six local knights who were *in disservitio* to their prince— arming and providing mounts for their servants and retainers and riding about with them at night, beating people with the flat of their sword blades. Although the grand duke banned servants from carrying weapons and jailed some of the offenders, the practice continued. Another of Fabrizio's servants was punished for a similar offense in 1571, and two years later Isolavi reported that Fabrizio was still helping his retainers get horses and weapons. Fabrizio's street brawling must have been the reason for the suspension of his cavalier's privilege of carrying arms in the city. After he petitioned the grand duke in June 1573, his weapons were restored to him, but in October he was again cited for a similar transgression.[10]

In April 1576 Fabrizio was summoned before Santo Stefano's Council of Twelve after a row in the *bottega* of Battista Ferretti. Accused of administering a sword-beating to Alessandro Bichi, then to Alessandro's brother, Fabrizio produced witnesses who testified that he had entered Ferretti's shop on business for the Company of S. Jacopo (a religious confraternity, not to be confused with the Opera of S. Jacopo),[11] in which he served as *festaiuolo*, the officer in charge of the confraternity's feasts. In the shop he encountered Bichi, who reportedly sneered at Fabrizio's pretensions to having the competence to do the company's business. The two men traded insults. Fabrizio drew his sword partway out of its sheath. Alessandro, who was unarmed, threw a brass candelabra at him, missed, and ran out of the shop. Fabrizio gave chase. At this instant (still according to witnesses) Alessandro's brother Cosimo appeared, sword in hand, and exchanged blows with Fabrizio. After Alessandro threw a rock and missed, the Bichi brothers ran for home with Fabrizio in hot pursuit, raining blows on them with the flat of his sword. The council decided that Fabrizio had been provoked and, considering that he and the Bichi subsequently made peace, recommended to the grand duke (who reviewed criminal sentences) that he be exonerated and set free. But his highness, Francesco I, thought otherwise: perhaps wearying of Fabrizio's persistent misbehavior as well as determined to punish unauthorized violence, Francesco sentenced him to two months exile from Pistoia and two months loss of seniority in Santo Stefano, making him less eligible for further preferment.

Soon afterward, Fabrizio was embroiled in an even more serious incident. On a November evening, he and Lionetto Bracciolini accompanied a certain Madonna Agnoletta to her door and were talking with her when Fabrizio was called aside by Giovanni Fioravanti, a fellow knight of Santo Stefano. "When Cavalier Bracciolini approached him they began to argue; whereupon the said Fioravanti gave the lie [dette una mentita] to Bracciolini and each drew his sword and began to strike the other." Fabrizio suffered three wounds, two on the head and a cut on his left arm that "drew blood and endangered his life." Fioravanti had three slight face wounds.

The indictment further noted that before Fabrizio struck a blow he fell to the ground, and that Fioravanti wounded him before he could get up. Santo Stefano's Council of Twelve decided that Fioravanti was the aggressor, noting that he had summoned Bracciolini to fight him, had given him the lie, and was the first to draw his sword. As giving the lie was the first formal step toward fighting a duel, it, like dueling itself, was expressly forbidden by both the ecclesiastical and the temporal authorities.[12] The Twelve recommended that Fioravanti be imprisoned for eight months, a sentence the grand duke stiffened to two years. This time Fabrizio was acquitted, but he was required to pay court costs of twenty-nine lire, nine soldi, and six denari.

In late October 1577, the council was still trying to collect this money, as well as the few lire Fabrizio owed for administrative costs connected with his brief exile,[13] fairly trifling sums, but apparently Fabrizio was hard put to pay them. The life of a man-about-town was expensive, particularly if he kept armed retainers, and Fabrizio, with little income apart from his commendatario's stipend, a modest 23 scudi per annum,[14] was constantly short of funds and frequently in debt.[15] He might hope for relief when he came into his inheritance, but in 1578 Messer Francesco was still very much alive (he died in 1580); besides, Fabrizio would have to share the estate with his brother Mario, named as coheir in the will, and with his four sisters, Olympia, Virginia, Dorotea, and Lavinia, who were promised dowries of 700 scudi each. All this from an estate that, while substantial, was far from being among Pistoia's richest.[16] By contrast, Camilla had brought a dowry of 4,000 scudi to her marriage to Fabrizio—and seen her husband squander one-third of it. The Holy Thursday imbroglio would produce even greater strains in Fabrizio's fraying relations with family, wife, and order.

SIX

The Order of Santo Stefano

In the Cellesi-Bracciolini affair, jurisdictional responsibility was even more overlapping and the commissioner's authority even more compromised than usual because both Mariotto Cellesi and Fabrizio Bracciolini were *cavalieri,* or knights, of the Order of Santo Stefano. The Order (or "Religion") of Santo Stefano had been founded in 1562 by Cosimo I on the model of the old crusading order of the Knights of S. John, or Knights of Malta as they had come to be known since taking up residence on that island. Santo Stefano's principal mission was to defend Christendom against the Infidel, mainly by engaging the ships of the sultan on the high seas.[1] More than half the order's recruits came from Tuscany, although a sizeable contingent of other Italians and even non-Italians gave it a broader identity.[2] Although designated cavaliers, they bore little resemblance to the knights-on-horse-back of medieval lore. Gentlemen marines, they rode into battle on the decks of Santo Stefano's galleys, armed with pikes, harquebuses, and swords. Alongside the galleys and galleasses of the Knights of Malta and of Venice, they fought in some of the major naval actions of the Mediterranean wars, including the relief of Malta in 1565 and the great victory at Lepanto in 1571.[3]

Santo Stefano helped the Tuscan rulers polish their image as champions of embattled Christendom and enhanced their prestige and influence among the European powers. It also served Medici domestic policy by offering a variety of material and social rewards to young, well-born Tuscans in exchange for service to their prince. To be accepted as a cavalier of Santo Stefano a young man had to offer, as well as evidence of good character, proof that he was nobly born. For Tuscans this could be tricky, since most of the Tuscan communes had long since exiled or suppressed their patrician families or induced them to formally divest themselves of their status as *ottimati,* or nobles.

Now, however, the current was reversed. In founding the Order of Santo Stefano, Cosimo I had thrown up a bridge over which important families of the republican era could cross to noble status in the new age of the principate. Beside the usual guarantees that no parent or grandparent had stained the family honor by engaging in manual labor, a craft, or petty trade, a candidate for admission to the order was required to furnish proof that his father and grandfathers had held high elective office in the republic. Exceptions could be obtained for a consideration: a young man whose pedigree was tainted might still hope to be admitted if his family were wealthy enough to endow a benefice for him. This not only relieved the order of providing for his maintenance, but also enriched it, since the real property on which benefices were based ultimately reverted to Santo Stefano. In this way, since acceptance into the order was an automatic guarantee of noble status, the order also served as an avenue of social mobility and, by giving the cavalier opportunities to display his personal qualities under the eye of the grand duke and his ministers, a ladder for advancement. Drawing both on the established nobility and nouveaux riches, Santo Stefano was an inspired device for creating a service gentry, a critical element in Medici state building.[4]

Whether acquired through noble ancestry or family wealth, the red cross of Santo Stefano on the front of a young man's doublet certified his high social status and his profession of a chivalric ethos equally compounded of Christian and warrior values. The order subscribed to a modified form of the Rule of S. Benedict, with cavaliers sworn to charity, obedience, and chastity (this last, since celibacy was not required, was interpreted as fidelity in marriage). Although they were laymen, free to marry and, when not on duty, to live at home, cavaliers were periodically subject to a discipline that was both monastic and military. In times of peace, they were required to spend two months of the year living in the order's "convent" in the Piazza dei Cavalieri in Pisa, magnificently restored for the purpose by Giorgio Vasari (himself a cavalier of the order from 1571). There they recited their daily office, trained in horsemanship, weaponry, and marine combat, and stood on call for service on the galleys patrolling Mediterranean waters.

The prerogatives of the order, spelled out in papal and ducal privileges,[5] were jealously protected by its officers and generally observed by the civil authorities, whose master, the grand duke, was also the grand master of Santo Stefano. Chief among these prerogatives was the exercise of jurisdiction in civil and criminal cases involving the order's cavaliers, with its executive Council of Twelve acting as a high court.[6] The statutes set out rules for the conduct of its members and a schedule of penalties and punishments for transgressions. Local authorities were expected to notify the council when a matter arose involving a cavalier, either remitting the case to Pisa or, at the council's choosing, conducting the investigation on its behalf. In either case, officials were expected to send copies of all pertinent documents to the Council of Twelve, the ruling body of the order, at its headquarters in Pisa. In the Cellesi-Bracciolini affair, Commissioner Pazzi in Pistoia regularly complied with this requirement, although the council frequently complained that he was slow to act. For their part, the Twelve appointed a special commission to adjudicate the case of Mariotto in Pisa. The commission held some hearings of its own, but its distance from the scene and the linkages between Mariotto's case and that of the other accused who were not under the order's jurisdiction inclined the Twelve to delegate to local officials much of the work of investigation and interrogation.

SEVEN

The Processo

He lies like an eye witness.
—*Russian saying*

Most street brawls, even between contentious Pistoian nobles, were resolved speedily. The clumsy duel of the previous year between Fabrizio Bracciolini and his fellow Santo Stefano cavalier Giovanni Fioravanti had brought quick action, swift judgment, and a stiff verdict against Giovanni.[1] But this case, pitting Fabrizio against the rich and irascible Cellesi patriarch with a direct line to the grand duke, and with its tangle of temporal and ecclesiastical jurisdictions, made for a complicated judicial equation. Besides, in most street brawls the facts were not so elusive; in the Holy Thursday affair, agreement on the facts was hard to come by.

The difficulty began in trying to verify Fabrizio Bracciolini's deposition, both in what he asserted and what he denied. In questioning Fabrizio and recording his statement, the commissioner's magistrate had taken the first steps of the judicial proceeding known as *processo*, which was central to the prevailing inquisitorial system of Tuscan criminal justice. The processo was both more and less than the modern Anglo-American trial, combining the investigative functions of the grand jury with the deliberative functions of the trial proper. In a processo, all these responsibilities centered in a single official, the magistrate, or judge (or judges), who, assisted by his notary, acted as investigator, prosecutor, judge, and jury.[2] Thus the next step for the officials in the Holy Thursday case was to examine Fabrizio's charge that Mariotto and Asdrubale Cellesi, armed with swords, had attacked him from behind, "traitorously" and with no warning, after an exchange of greetings performed by the mutual lifting of birettas, and that Tonio Visconti and two other armed men had burst out of the Visconti house to join the attack.

This examination of Fabrizio's account the officials opened on the very day of the fight, but if they hoped to begin by questioning Mariotto and his alleged accomplices, they were already too late. Felice di Giovantonio, guard at the S. Marco Gate, informed them that he had seen Mariotto, "pale as a freshly dug-up corpse, and Asdrubale, who they say is always with Cavalier Cellesi" (and who, he observed, was carrying a weapon) pass by his post on their way out of the city, and he had lost sight of them as they took the road to Prato. Two armed soldiers from the fortress had accompanied them as far as the bridge to Campo del Colle before turning back to Pistoia. Felice would recognize the two "because they were beardless."[3] He did not see them return.

The next day (28 March) the magistrate ordered the arrest of Tonio Visconti and began calling eye witnesses to the fight. What he heard confirmed part, not all, of Fabrizio's story. Luca, the thirty-year-old son of Captain Giovanni Pazzaglia, testified that he had left his house (it stood at the northwest corner of the via S. Andrea, toward the Church of S. Francesco) and was on his way to mass in the duomo when he saw Cavalier Mariotto standing on one side of the street and Asdrubale on the other. He lifted his biretta to them and continued on his way. Next he passed Cavalier Fabrizio, who was headed toward Piazza S. Francesco, in the opposite direction. Luca was about to stop off at the Company of S. Giuseppe, adjacent to the Church of S. Andrea, when he heard a noise.

I turned around and saw Cavalier Mariotto, who had his sword in hand and was striking Cavalier Fabrizio with it. Cavalier Fabrizio had turned back, avoiding the blows of Cavalier Mariotto, and when he was opposite the stairway of S. Andrea he drew his sword and just as he did and was turning a little he was hit in the face by Cavalier Mariotto, who almost cut his nose off with a blow. At the same instant, Asdrubale came at Cavalier Fabrizio with a sword and swung at his legs, but his sword hit Cavalier Fabrizio's sword, which he had lowered while he was holding his wounded nose with the other hand. And when Cavalier Mariotto saw that Cavalier Fabrizio was wounded, he said to Asdrubale, "Let's go!" and they turned back toward Prato S. Francesco. I saw that Cavalier Fabrizio was in the condition I've described. I went up to where his cape had fallen and picked it up. He took it and wiped the blood with it and I accompanied him to his doorway.[4]

Church of S. Andrea. Photo by Roberto degli Innocenti, with permission of the Ufficio Beni Culturali, Diocese of Pistoia

No, said Luca, he had not seen Tonio, son of il Bonzetta, or two armed soldiers or anyone throwing stones, "and that's the truth; if it were otherwise I would say so because I'm going to take communion after tomorrow morning." Before the fight began, he saw Mariotto armed, Asdrubale not; but no one knocking at the door of the Visconti house and no one coming out. He saw only some little girls "whom I didn't know" on their way to the sacrament "and a poor old man, a veteran of Candia,[5] who retrieved Cavalier Fabrizio's biretta. I don't know where he is; I think he's one of those people who go around begging, because he was so badly dressed, with no cape and a tattered hat."

Polita di Giovanni Battista, who described herself as the wife of Vittorio, unemployed, testified that she and her mother had been on their way to the Pardons (a form of indulgence),

and when we had left the Company [Confraternity] of S. Andrea, looking down the street I saw Cavalier Fabrizio wrapped in his cloak coming up the street. Turning to go to the Crucifix of Ripalta,[6] I saw Cavalier Mariotto standing at the wall almost directly across the street from the doorway of Nardino Bonzetta and Asdrubale at the door, which was closed, with his hand on Nardino Bonzetta's bell. We continued on our way when we heard noises and yelling and we turned back and began to run, and we were frightened because Asdrubale and Cavalier Mariotto were striking at Cavalier Fabrizio. I saw the sword out just as it hit Cavalier Fabrizio and they left him and ran away, Cavalier Mariotto with a sword and Asdrubale with a storta,[7] which he couldn't get back into its sheath, and they were afraid they weren't going to be able to get away.

Like Luca Pazzaglia, Polita had first seen Asdrubale unarmed, then with a weapon, joining the attack, yet she too testified that the Bonzetta doorway remained closed. Her mother, Maria di Giovanni Lombardo, told the same story. Pressed to tell who had thrown stones at Fabrizio, Maria replied, "I've told you what I saw; I don't want to damn my soul for anyone else."

The weaver Stefano Ruffino said he had been home at his loom when "I heard some women say that it seemed a fight had started down below, so I went to my door and saw Cavalier Mariotto and Asdrubale pass by, going up the main street. I went to see what had happened and I saw Cavalier Fabrizio holding a hand to his face. I went to him and asked him if he wanted me to go for a doctor, and he said yes, so I went to fetch Maestro Giovannino. Then I left, and that's all I know."

The testimony of ten-year-old Rinaldo di Alidonio reinforced the impression that the attack was by stealth, and it salvaged something for Fabrizio's pride.

I was leaving Magrino's, going home, and I saw Cavalier Mariotto at the well opposite the house of Nardino del Bonzetta, and Asdrubale was at Nardino's door, and I saw Cavalier Fabrizio pass and they tipped their birettas to each other. When Cavalier Fabrizio had passed, Cavalier Mariotto ran after him and without saying anything began to strike at him with his sword. And Asdrubale also began to strike at Cavalier Fabrizio with a storta and Cavalier Fabrizio was wounded in the face; I saw that when Cavalier Fabrizio was wounded he drew his sword and they ran away and Cavalier Fabrizio then turned to Luca Pazzaglia and said, "I want you to be a witness to how I was set upon!"[8] and Luca replied, "I'll do it."

So far, no witness had placed Tonio Visconti at the scene of the fight or espied an open door at the Bonzetta house; but the widow Camilla, daughter of the packsaddle maker Piero Celli, told a different story. Camilla had gone to S. Andrea for the pardoning and was just leaving when she saw Cavalier Mariotto at Nardino Bonzetta's doorway and Cavalier Fabrizio passing by. After they tipped birettas to each other and Fabrizio had gone on about thirty feet *(sei braccia)*, Mariotto drew his sword and ran after him, and without saying anything—so far as Camilla could tell—struck Fabrizio a blow in the kidneys. Fabrizio turned, crying, "Oh, me! Ah, traitor!" and in that same instant, Asdrubale and the son of Nardino il Bonzetta came out of the house, Asdrubale holding a weapon—she didn't know what kind it was. Cavalier Fabrizio said, "Three against one!" "And I was so terrified," said Camilla, "that my eyes began to cloud over and my stomach began to heave so that it seemed it was taking me a thousand years to run away from there and get back into the church, and I didn't see anything else."

After languishing *in segrete* (in the dungeons) for three weeks, Tonio was called in for questioning on 16 April. On Holy Thursday he had dined at the family home; he saw no one come to the house.

Afterward I went out to our Company of S. Giuseppe nearby; I stayed less than a quarter of an hour and then I went straight to the house of Agnolo Campanaio[9]— that is, to his serving woman, who was sick; the priest Bartolomeo del Siena also came, and we stayed about two and a half hours. [Bartolomeo] wanted to see the *festa* of our company so we went there and stayed until we received the pardon. From there we went to the duomo, arriving just as monsignor was washing feet, performing the ceremony of washing the feet of the disciples. I stood right in front of the sacristy near Atto Bracciolini, and when the bishop had finished the ceremony of washing the disciples' feet, Atto and I went to sit near monsignor's chair and we stayed there until a woman told Atto that Cavalier Fabrizio had been wounded. Atto said, "I want to go to Cavalier Fabrizio's house," so I went out with him and went as far as the shop of Agniolo Campanaio, where I stopped, and Atto went on his way.

Of the details of the encounter in front of his house on the same day, Tonio professed to know little, and denied seeing either Asdrubale or Mariotto at his door. He and the priest had stayed at the house of the sick woman about three hours. "Then we heard the bell for mass, and the priest Bartolomeo said, 'I have to go to the duomo to mass, but I'm waiting until the bishop finishes the foot washing.'" Tonio had left with the priest and returned home only at dusk. Two women who had been with the sick woman, Pellegrina, widow of Jacopo da Parma, Angolo's serving woman, and Fiore, a "foreigner" from S. Quirico, a district of Lucca, testified that Tonio and the priest had arrived "about the time of the midday Ave Maria as well as one could judge by the sun, because the [city] bells weren't being rung." They stayed about two to three hours, joking and laughing to amuse the shut-in Mona Sandra, while she drank sarsaparilla.[10] When the bell rang for mass, the priest said he had to go to the cathedral. Tonio said he had never seen the foot-washing ceremony and would like to go with him, and they left together.

Tonio's arrival at the duomo in time for the foot washing was confirmed by Atto di Vincenzio Bracciolini, a cousin of the wounded man. Questioned on 21 April, Atto stated,

When I arrived in the choir they were just performing the Washing of the Feet. . . . I was alone, but just then Antonio, the son of Nardo Bonzetta, showed up. We stood together until the bishop got up from his place, then went into the choir to hear the sermon. I asked Antonio if he wanted to come sit in the choir and he said yes. So he came and we sat on a bench in the choir, on the side where the bishop sits. Messer Camillo Alberti, of the bishop's household, and my nephew Camillo Bennozzo were also there. When we'd been there about the length of a credo I heard from Mona Portia, the widow of Andrea Zozzifante, that Cavalier Fabrizio had been wounded. So I said to Antonio and Messer Camillo that I wanted to go to see him. Antonio said, "I want to go, too," so we left and went to the house of Cavalier Fabrizio. Both of us went into his bedchamber, where we found the cavalier being treated. After he was treated, I went home. I didn't see whether Antonio left.

Asked how long it was after Tonio arrived in the cathedral that the news came about Cavalier Fabrizio, Atto replied that it had been only "a short time." Could the fight have already happened when Antonio arrived in the duomo? Atto did not know. Nor did he know how long the wounded Fabrizio had been home before he and Tonio arrived in his bedchamber, "although when we saw him he had already been stitched up and they were applying the egg white."[11]

Tonio's alibi was not airtight. Of the eye witnesses to the fight, one, Camilla, partly corroborated Fabrizio's charge, placing Tonio at the scene; the others denied seeing him there. Since estimates of how long Tonio stayed with the sick woman varied from two to three hours and the exact time of the confrontation in S. Andrea had not been determined, it was difficult either to confirm or disprove his story on the basis of Atto's testimony. Would Tonio have had time to take part in the attack on Fabrizio before slipping into a seat next to Atto at the foot washing? If so, why had he been invisible to most of the witnesses to the fight? The most puzzling discrepancy lay between Tonio's account of his movements after leaving the duomo and Atto's recollection that they had gone together to visit Fabrizio. Evidently, the Pistoia magistrates were not convinced by Tonio's alibi: on 22 April, the day after questioning Atto, they announced an official action against Tonio, Asdrubale Cellesi, and Captain Lanfredino Cellesi.[12] Tonio and Asdrubale were charged with taking part with Mariotto Cellesi in assaulting Fabrizio Bracciolini, while the captain was named as the instigator of the attack ("All this was done at the instance of the said Captain Lanfredino father of the said Cavalier and took place on his behalf"). The fugitive Mariotto Cellesi was not named as a defendant in this action; his case would be considered by the superiors of the Order of Santo Stefano.[13]

On 24 April, Captain Lanfredino wrote to the grand duke:

Lanfredino Cellesi of Pistoia, most humble vassal of Your Most Serene Highness, states that an inquest has been officially mounted against him by the signor commissioner of Pistoia on the grounds that on his orders his son had engaged in a fight with Cavalier Fabrizio Bracciolini. He did not want to inform Your Most Serene Highness of this until the real reasons for his son's action had been explained. Hopeful that Your Most Serene Highness has now been so informed, as well as of the culpability of the said Bracciolini, he petitions and begs that you deign to grant him the favor of having the Magnifica Pratica Segreta take up the case; this for the true reasons expressed in person to Your Most Serene Highness, and out of respect for whom they have been kept confidential. May it become clear that the complaint is unreasonable—as if his son, who is incapable of anything improper, did not know good from evil. For this, along with other kindnesses received from [Your Highness], I will be forever obligated. May Our Lord preserve and exalt you.

Whether Captain Lanfredino had personally spoken into the ear of Grand Duke Francesco I or someone had done so on his behalf, clearly the old soldier and Panciatichi chieftain enjoyed some degree of confidential access to his prince. A ducal rescript on the same day instructed the Magnifica Pratica to "take up this case and do justice." On 26 April the Pratica lords sent a letter to Commissioner Pazzi: "That he proceed no further in [the matter of] the above mentioned quarrel, but that he leave it to the cognizance of the Magnifica Pratica, and that he send a copy of the entire processo to date." Commissioner Pazzi complied on 29 April. So it was that the case of Lanfredino and Asdrubale Cellesi and Antonio Visconti came to be tried in Florence rather than in Pistoia.

By 7 May, the Pratica had had the opportunity to review the processo. The bargello of Pistoia was ordered to bring Antonio Visconti to Florence under guard and to summon Asdrubale to appear within five days. Captain Lanfredino Cellesi was not summoned, even though he had been included in the Pistoia commissioner's action. Two days later, Tonio was taken to Florence and placed *in segrete,* and on 15 May the Pratica's magistrates began their inquiry into his part in the Holy Thursday affair.

Their first witness, Bartolomeo d'Alberto, chaplain of S. Jacopo of Pistoia, appearing with the express permission of the episcopal vicar, confirmed that on Holy Thursday he and Tonio had remained at the bedside of the ailing Sandra about three hours. They left together at the hour of the office, going first to see the holy-day display (of the Eucharist) at the Company of the Humility,[14] and after participating in the Forty-Hour Prayer (the vigil of silent prayer in front of the displayed Eucharist),[15] they left for the duomo, arriving just in time for the Washing of the Feet. Bartolomeo found Tonio a seat inside the railing of the high altar, near the priest who was in attendance on the bishop, and next to Atto Bracciolini. Just as the sermon was beginning, Jacopo the herald came to tell the commissioner about the fight in the street. If Tonio had remained in his seat in church, how could he have taken part in the fight? Dramatically placing his hand on his heart, Bartolomeo swore "as a truthful priest" that during this whole time Antonio did not leave: the fight, he said, took place while they were in the duomo.

Don Bartolomeo's testimony strengthened Tonio's alibi, but the Pratica magistrates were still not ready to acquit him; they sent him back to prison while they reexamined the eye witnesses of the Holy Thursday fight. This would be no mere rehash; the Florentine officials had acquired enough additional information to easily deconstruct some of the stories told in the Pistoia court.[16] Camilla, the only witness who placed Tonio Visconti at the scene of the fight and identified him as one of Fabrizio's assailants, now reconsidered: she was sure she had seen one of the sons at the fight, "but I don't want to tell any lies; I don't know the sons of Nardino by name, but one of them was there." Would she recognize him if she saw him again? She couldn't say: "I was so confused; anyway I wouldn't know him again."

Tonio was brought in. Was this the man she had seen? "I can't say because I don't know one from the other."

Camilla was removed while Tonio was questioned about this new lead. His brother's name was Giovanni. Midway in Lent Giovanni had quarreled with their father and left home. Tonio had not seen him since and did not know where he was. Could Giovanni have been present at the scene of the fight? "He can't have been; he's a beardless kid and he doesn't have anything to do with anyone."

A few days later, the missing Giovanni was found and brought in to confront Camilla. She was unable to say whether he was the third assailant, repeating that she did not know Nardino il Bonzetta's sons. Then how did she know the man she had seen at the fight was one of the Visconti brothers? "I don't know him, but I was told this." By whom? "I don't know."

Young Rinaldo di Alidonio also revised his earlier testimony on two key points. No longer was he willing to say with certainty that Mariotto and Fabrizio had tipped their birettas to each other as the latter passed; instead, he agreed with the magistrates' suggestion that it was equally possible both men had been exchanging greetings with a third party, Luca Pazzaglia, who was also passing at that moment. Moreover, although he was still certain he had seen Mariotto and Asdrubale attack Fabrizio, Rinaldo now declared that he had heard Mariotto call upon Fabrizio to draw his sword before lunging at him.

Removed from their familiar surroundings—in Camilla's case to be imprisoned in the bargello's dungeon and threatened with torture—the simple woman who scratched out a living by doing a little weaving and selling old clothes and the ten-year-old schoolboy were out of their element and beyond their depth at the hearings in Florence. Under the sharper probing of these lofty officials, neither Camilla nor Rinaldo was likely to stick to their original stories once it began to be apparent that they had withheld important information.

The magistrates first disclosed their suspicions in their questioning of

Menica Celli, Camilla's mother. Had Camilla told her that the priest Bracciolini or anyone else had tried to influence her testimony?[17] Menica said no, but Camilla herself was now more forthcoming: when she went to her mother's house two or three days after the fight, her mother told her that Cavalier Fabrizio had sent for her; he wanted to know what she had seen of the fight in the via S. Andrea. "Then I told him that I didn't want to say I'd seen him get hit. I told him everything I'd seen, just as I just told it here [that she had seen Mariotto, Asdrubale, and "one of the sons of Nardino Visconti" strike at Fabrizio]. Then he told me not to say anything to the court about his having sent for me, but I'm scared, so I have." After this admission, magistrates had little trouble getting Camilla to confess that she did not know one son of Nardino from the other. Nor had she seen whether this son of Nardino had thrown stones because she had become faint and quickly retreated inside the church. It was while she was inside that she had heard Cavalier Fabrizio cry out, "Three against one!"

Camilla's second arrest took place in the house of the priest. Had he tried to tell her what to say and what not to say? Camilla maintained that he had only told her not to be afraid, advised her to stick to her story as she had given it the first time, and to tell the truth. This ambiguous answer was all the magistrates could get out of her for the present, but they had another card to play. Returned to the *segrete,* she was brought back for further questioning on 2 June. While in prison, had she spoken with any other woman? Camilla said she had not—if she had she would say so. But confronted with an anonymous report that she had spoken with another prisoner, Mona Santa di Andrea, of Pistoia, Camilla admitted, "I only told her I didn't want to confess, but that they called me to the court and I had to tell." Santa was summoned: she confirmed that Camilla had told her she had been forced to testify and to say what she had said, but Santa was not clear whether Camilla had meant she had been forced by the court or by someone else. Again Camilla was summoned and "warned and terrified with threats of the rope,"[18] but she continued to insist that she had told the truth. The magistrates ordered her returned *in segrete* "to see if they could pull anything more out of her." By 7 June, however, the Pratica had reviewed Camilla's testimony and concluded that they would get nothing more from her; she was released. Camilla's testimony, they decided, was "a tissue of lies, not to be given credence, as demonstrated by the investigation."

By that time, the lords of the Pratica had (on 22 May) declared Tonio innocent, acknowledging his alibi for the time of the fight. Dismissed too, for lack of evidence, was the charge against Captain Lanfredino.

We may sympathize with Mona Camilla at the scene of the fight: frightened, dizzy, and nauseated by the shouts and the clanging of swords, she thought of nothing but getting away. The sudden explosion of violence and sickening gush of blood seem to have confused the senses of more than one witness, leaving them with clouded and contradictory memories. As to who was present, what they said and did, whose swords were drawn, what blows struck, what cries uttered—these ought to have been matters of fact, presumably observed by the townspeople who were there to see and hear them. Yet, although the magistrates tried to wring every detail out of the witnesses, they were stalled by contradictory assertions and wavering perceptions. None of this helped Fabrizio press his charges. Parts were flying off his story like shingles from a wind-battered roof. Of the original list of attackers, said by Fabrizio to number five, the dismissal of charges against Tonio Visconti left only two, Mariotto and Asdrubale Cellesi; the "two armed men" seemed to have been phantoms, visible only to Fabrizio (or were they the two armed men who accompanied Mariotto and Asdrubale through the S. Marco Gate?). Fabrizio's story of a "traitorous" attack—a story he apparently tried to buttress by suborning witnesses—was undermined by these same witnesses now claiming they had heard Mariotto call to him to draw his sword. Moreover, what he described as falling back to make a stand was regarded by some as headlong flight. Instead of valiantly calling out to his tormentors to come back and fight, he seems to have downed his sword and leaned on it while holding his other hand to his bloody nose.

If Fabrizio magnified the odds and exaggerated his defiance, it is hardly surprising. More even than his desire for revenge, his need to repair his wounded dignity and protect his cavalier's reputation shaped his memory of the event and persuaded him that he had been unfairly attacked and had responded bravely. But subjective perception was one thing, concealment another: when Fabrizio denied that he knew any reason why Mariotto Cellesi might wish to fight him, he was not only telling a lie, knowing very well what those reasons were, he was telling a foolish lie, since, as we shall see, the reasons were bound to come out—if, indeed, they had not already done so.

Peacemaking I

> Pursue him, and entreat him to a peace;
> He hath not told us of the Captain yet.
> — *Twelfth Night* 5.1

When the report of the fight in the via S. Andrea interrupted his Holy Thursday devotions, Commissioner Pazzi's first act was to dispatch his herald with instructions to impose a *levare l'offesa*, on the two principals and their families. Here again is its gist:

Ordered, a cessation of further offenses between Cavalier Mariotto, son of Captain Lanfredino Cellesi of Pistoia . . . and Cavalier Fabrizio, son of Messer Francesco Bracciolini . . . and those connected or related to them in the male line to the canonical fourth degree inclusive. To be binding until they have concluded a peace or truce, with penalty of two thousand scudi to be applied according to the law.

Commissioner Pazzi's order resonates with confident authority: fighting between the grand duke's subjects was a disruption of the public peace, its suppression and control the business of public officials. Theirs was no new-minted prerogative; rulers and governments had been asserting what Max Weber called the state's monopoly of violence—with varying degrees of consistency and success, to be sure—since the early Middle Ages.[1] If there was one kind of private violence that still challenged sovereignty's claim to puissance, it was the feud. The persistent fear of feuding explains the formulaic wording of Pazzi's *levare l'offesa,* addressed not only to Mariotto and Fabrizio but also to their close kinsmen and associates. In the code of the feud, an offense done to one member of a house is an offense done to all, and a man who violates that principle is a man dishonored.[2] By ordering both families to keep the peace, the state was trying to interrupt the cycle of violence set in motion by Mariotto's act.

Peace, however, was not something to be preserved but something to be made, not a natural condition protected by the state but a social arrangement, a precarious equilibrium between disputing families who must balance their need for security against their fear of losing honor and respect. As is evident in Commissioner Pazzi's *levare l'offesa*, the government of the grand duke regarded these as legitimate concerns and recognized the crucial public role of notable families. The instructions from the council of Santo Stefano and the Pratica Segreta are even more emphatic on this point.

The Council of Santo Stefano to Commissioner Cosimo Pazzi, 19 April 1578:[3]

We have received your notification of the *levare l'offesa*. . . . Now we would like you to proceed as soon as possible to constrain the said cavaliers to make a peace or truce with a bond in the amount you deem appropriate. Require them to draw up a contract and send a copy to this council at the order's expense. The bond is to be paid into the treasury of the religion [order]. Also send a copy of the investigative processo concerning the fight between them.

The Magnificent Pratica Segreta to Commissioner Pazzi, 13 May 1578:[4]

We understand that the council of the knights of the Religion of Santo Stefano has commissioned you to arrange a truce between Cavalier Mariotto Cellesi and Cavalier Fabrizio Bracciolini. Therefore to avoid scandal it is our wish and order that you summon those closest to Cavalier Fabrizio, that is, in the Bracciolini family,[5] and Giovanni Fabroni, procurator of Captain Lanfredino Cellesi, and constrain them to make a truce between the said Bracciolini family and the said Captain Lanfredino in the masculine line to the fourth degree. They are to be required to post bond of at least 1,000 gold scudi. You should take a suitable security to ensure their observance and report to us all that takes place.

It was one thing for the state to command its subjects to make peace; it was another thing for them to comply. The disputing parties had to negotiate terms. First they must agree to a truce for a specified period while discussing the conditions of a permanent peace. But even here difficulties might arise: one or both of the parties, or some of their members, might balk at the amount of the bond, or one might complain that the amount set was too low to effectively restrain the other from further aggression. Captain Lanfredino was adamant that there should be no peace until the reasons justifying the fight were acknowledged. As we shall see, Commissioner Pazzi's order was met by all these difficulties simultaneously. Ironically, while intending to expedite a truce, the intervention of the council of Santo Stefano and the Pratica Segreta made matters even more complicated. Pistoia had repeatedly to seek and receive instructions, Florence and Pisa constantly to be informed. All this slowed the proceedings, and when the authorities in Florence and Pisa decided to dictate terms, the confusion mounted still further.

Fabrizio Bracciolini to the Council of Santo Stefano, 15 May 1578:[6]

By order of Your Illustrious Lordships, I have been cited by the magnificent commissioner of this city to make a truce with Cavalier Mariotto Cellesi. I appeared and told the signor commissioner that Your Lordships had been commissioned by the magnificent signori of the council [of Santo Stefano] and the Pratica Segreta of His Serene Highness to constrain four of my closest blood relatives to the fourth degree to make a truce with Captain Lanfredino, father of Cavalier Mariotto, under bond of 1,000 scudi, and that four of my relatives were called for this purpose and that I was included. Although I was disposed to obey, it did not seem reasonable to constrain me to make another truce or to have a double burden [i.e. of the Pistoia commissioner and the order]. But when the procurator of Cavalier [Mariotto] said he would make a truce for 1,500 scudi, I replied that the ordinances of this city require that it be according to one's ability [to pay] as determined by the signor commissioner. Since I have no property but my commenda and my wife's dowry, I was not able to afford more than 200 scudi.

The signor commissioner declared that it was to be made for 500 scudi, so, to obey, I said I was ready to do it even though it would be a heavy burden and I would have trouble finding security and [I pointed out] that of 100 truces made up to now, 86 of them were for less than 500 scudi and those involved a death and were among the leading [richest?] families.[7] Since the procurator of the said [Cavalier Mariotto] refused to do it [for less], nothing else was done. I beg Your Illustrious Lordships not to cause me the burden of a double truce or force me to bear a heavier burden than I am able, since it is known that the said signori of the Pratica have required my four relatives to post bond of 1,000 scudi, that is, 250 per person. I am poor and have nothing but my commenda. The other side is not going along with this because they want me to die in prison.

I trust in your compassion and good justice and that you will take pity on innocent and poor people. My commenda could be my security for the truce. I doubt you want me in prison, but I have nothing else to pledge.

Fabrizio's plea of poverty and his offer to pledge his commenda were obviously manipulative. So was his complaint that the Cellesi were holding out for a higher bond in order to make it harder for him to pay—a patent effort to gain sympathy—although it was probably true. In fact, both sides used the peacemaking process itself as a means of continuing their quarrel even as they negotiated the terms of a truce.

Commissioner Cosimo Pazzi to the Council of Santo Stefano, 16 May 1578:[8]

I cited both men to appear. Cavalier Fabrizio appeared and Giovanni Fabroni appeared as procurator for Cavalier Mariotto. They were not able to agree on the amount of bond. I have taken into consideration the possibility that Cavalier Fabrizio has little or nothing besides his commenda and his wife's dowry. According to this court's records of peace and truce, the truce bond has for years normally been not more than 500 scudi, a few 600, and one 800 scudi. Pursuant to the commission of the lords of the council and Pratica Segreta . . . I called four of the closest relatives of the said Cavalier Fabrizio to be guarantors by making a truce with Captain Lanfredino Cellesi, father of Cavalier Mariotto, under bond of 1,000 scudi. I set the bond for the truce between the two cavaliers at 500 scudi, as is customary in important truces of this tribunal, so that together with the guarantors this comes to 1,500 scudi. Cavalier Mariotto's procurator said he did not wish to make a truce for less than 1,000 scudi.[9] Unable to constrain him without summoning his client, I asked Your Illustrious Lordships for another commission to order the said Cavalier Mariotto to appear today at 4 o'clock to make a peace or truce with the said Cavalier Fabrizio. He did not appear this time either, but again his procurator Giovanni [Politi] came to say that he did not wish to make a truce for less than 1,000 scudi. Giovanni returned with a letter from Cavalier Mariotto that commissioned him to make a truce for 25 scudi. I replied that this was great foolishness and that the truce was to be made for 500 scudi. I want to notify Your Illustrious Lordships of all this and to ask you how to proceed since this is a matter between two cavaliers. I will not fail to carry out your orders.

Commending myself to you.

The officials of Santo Stefano also heard, and immediately rejected, the 25 scudi offer.

The Council of Santo Stefano to Commissioner Pazzi 21 May 1578:

[T]he sum of 25 scudi offered by Cellesi is not worthy of acceptance. Although the Council usually takes security of no less than 500 scudi, since the Magnifica Pratica has ordered each to pay 1,000 scudi . . . it seems to us you should constrain both cavaliers as principals in the matter to obey what the council in its wisdom has resolved and post the sum of 1,000 scudi, all payable to the common treasury of the Religion.

[Copy of the Pratica Segreta's order of 13 May enclosed]

Mariotto's offer to call a truce for 25 scudi had arrived in a letter from his place of refuge: just when he had arrived in Pontito, a mountain town in the Val di Ariana, north of Pescia, or where else his flight had taken him in the two months since he and Asdrubale disappeared on the Prato road, is not clear. But some time after leaving Pistoia on Holy Thursday, Mariotto had gone up to these mountains, his old hunting grounds. With extensive family lands in the area he could hide out among Cellesi tenants and retainers.

Mariotto Cellesi to Giovanni Fabroni:[10]

Most Magnificent and Honored Giovanni. I understand everything. If I had been there I would have come to an agreement with Bracciolini. I would have made the truce with him for 25 scudi just to wipe out the offense. Since he says he can't afford it [i.e., the higher amount], and since I could not return, I should have told you to tell the signor commissioner to let Bracciolini know that you have my authorization to make the truce for 25 scudi. If you have not already been constrained to make peace for 1,000 scudi, make my opinion known to everyone and see that everyone is put on notice. That's all for now. I commend myself to you. May our Lord God preserve you.

Pontito, 16 May 1578
Obediently Yours, Mariotto Cellesi

Mariotto's proposal to seal the truce with a token payment of 25 scudi seems disingenuous. As a fugitive from the law, no one could have known better than he that both the state and the Order of Santo Stefano were too deeply involved in these peace arrangements and regarded the achievement of a binding truce as too serious to allow the matter to be sloughed off so cheaply. If Mariotto and Fabrizio had been alone in their quarrel, free to settle the matter between them, there would have been no need for the *levare l'offesa,* no reason for the state to level charges or initiate a processo, no investigation by the Order of Santo Stefano—and no reason for him to go into hiding. The time when a private quarrel—especially one in which noble blood had been spilled—was allowed to play itself out without the intervention of Authority had long since passed, if such a time there had been. Perhaps Mariotto made the offer to promote his image as a peaceloving gentleman, confident that the authorities would reject his proposal, so at variance even with the offer of his own negotiator, Fabroni. Perhaps, less deliberately, it was an impetuous gesture of knightly generosity, a self-conscious display of proud disdain for the grubby calculation that would stamp a money value on his noble action. Realists might label the mentality from which such gestures flowed as archaic and, with Commissioner Pazzi, brand the offer (and the street fight itself) as "great foolishness," but such thinking was common among young Italian nobles and budding *gentiluomini*. The code that inspired it was too important to their way of being in the world to be relegated to the lumber room of an earlier, feudal age.

While Mariotto proposed to "wipe out the offense" with an offer of a token truce, Captain Lanfredino tried to reach a private accommodation by working the kinship network connecting his family to the Bracciolini.

Jacopo Cellesi to Lanfredino Cellesi, 17 May 1578:

Most Magnificent Signor Captain.

Signore, I have received your letter of the thirteenth concerning what has been done for you and your sons. In reply, in my view you wrong me and much offend me. You know that where an unfortunate disagreement arises, every relation or friend, indeed, every man of honor, is obliged to try to stop it, and that he not only wins merit from God but also from the world. So, if I have not done more for you or for your children, it is because I didn't know [what to do] or wasn't able [to do it]. In the future I will always do what I can, aware that this is my obligation, not failing to do my best for you, signore, as for any other man if I have the opportunity, knowing that you are the kind of man that would do the same for me. Everything I can do I will not fail to do with all my life and my small amount of goods. As to commending your sons to me, I assure you I will do whatever I know how and am able to do, because I have always loved them and you as I love myself. Pardon me if I've taken so long to reply to you; I had to go to my brother-in-law, Cavalier Fabrizio, to see if I could get him to make peace with you and your sons. He promised me he would [make peace] just as soon as you want to give him the satisfactions that he thinks he should have. If you wish, please let me know at once so that the truce does not fail to be made. I will then send you my opinion, as in such a matter would any other man of good faith and intelligence.

Signore, be so kind as to reply at once by the bearer so that we may advance this matter as it may please God. I conclude, commending myself to you with all my heart.

Pistoia, 17 May 1578
Affectionately and like a brother, Jacopo Cellesi

Jacopo di Battista Cellesi was a good choice to serve as personal mediator between the two disputing houses. Not only was he brother-in-law to Fabrizio and part of the extended Cellesi clan, as a fellow knight of Santo Stefano he was also a comrade-at-arms of both Fabrizio and Mariotto.[11] Besides, Jacopo had firsthand experience of quarrels and imposed truces. In one incident he was briefly imprisoned, then exiled from Pistoia for two years and banned from carrying arms.[12] In another, after a quarrel with Francesco di Piero di Giorgio Cellesi over a male Turkish slave presented by him to Francesco years earlier, the truce bond was set at 1,000 scudi—the usual amount (as Commissioner Pazzi was to insist in the Holy Thursday incident) for fights involving the spilling of blood.[13]

Lanfredino Cellesi to Jacopo Cellesi, 18 May 1578:

Magnificent Signore.

In reply to yours of the seventeenth I want to say that I know for sure that before leaving for a galley voyage you tried on numerous occasions to persuade your brother-in-law [Fabrizio Bracciolini] that he did not do well in causing trouble for me and my people, especially given the close friendship and familiarity he had with my son, known to you and all the world. Further, I feel obliged to thank you again, as I did in my letter of the thirteenth.[14] I have no doubt, signore, that you will continue as before (although, of course, in a different way). From your letter and in other ways I know that you have exhorted and begged your brother-in-law as well as myself and my sons to make peace and union. I am infinitely grateful to you for this. In reply let me say that I and my sons neither disturb peace nor flee from it, nor will we do so. Others who were close to us have created and carried on the disturbances. Just as soon as the truth is made clear or admitted I will not only accept peace and see that the others accept it if it is offered, but I will demand that they do so, and in such a way that you, signore, and all the world will be satisfied.

For now it remains only to kiss your hands and pray that our Lord God grant you every felicity, commending myself to you.

Florence, 18 May 1578
Lanfredino Cellesi

So, at the same time Commissioner Pazzi was struggling to bring the two parties into agreement on the amount of a truce bond, Cellesi and Bracciolini were negotiating privately over the issues at the heart of their quarrel—provocation, satisfaction, and honor. Fabrizio wanted "the satisfactions that he thinks he should have" before agreeing to a peace. For his part, Captain Lanfredino promised to make peace as soon as "the truth is made clear."

In short, each side wanted the other to concede that it was in the wrong, each wanted an acknowledgment from the other that its behavior had been honorable.[15] To the captain, public opinion, the regard of "all the world," was a trophy he had always coveted and pursued along with the treasure of commercial profits, lands, and estates.[16] For Fabrizio, reputation was all-important, since he had so little else. (This being so, we might wonder Fabrizio was so reckless with it, but rightly or wrongly he must have believed that "the world" loved its swashbuckling brawlers and devastating lovers.)

Jacopo Cellesi to Lanfredino Cellesi, 19 May 1578:

Most Magnificent Signor Captain.

I understand what you say in your latest letter regarding the peace between your son Cavalier Mariotto and my brother-in-law Cavalier Fabrizio. I only want to remind you that there is no concealing that Cavalier Fabrizio has taken a hit, so if you want to make peace with him, it seems to me, signore, that you have to take a hit, too, and not claim all the right or insist on the complete satisfaction you feel is coming to you before making peace.

Let me know so we can send someone there to talk to you personally; I'm sure, signore, that if you were here we could say things to each other privately that we can't put on paper. I beg you to be satisfied with a peace that is just and honorable. I will do anything for it that is good. Please reply as soon as possible. I commend myself to you.

Appropriately enough, in mediating the quarrel between his kinsmen, Cavalier Jacopo Cellesi borrows from the language of dueling: Fabrizio has taken a hit; fairness demands that the captain's side take a hit, too. He appeals to the captain to admit that since the Cellesi have already exacted a payment from Fabrizio in bodily pain and public humiliation, they must now be prepared to pay a price in return.

But Captain Lanfredino holds out for a formula of resolution more to his liking:

Lanfredino Cellesi to Jacopo Cellesi, 20 May 1578:

Most Magnificent Signor Cavalier.

In answer to yours of the nineteenth I want to say that I demanded an admission or recognition that my family has been unjustly abused and its trust violated. I would hope that once that is done, it will only remain for the official inquest and examination of witnesses to show we are in the right. Again, I reply to you that when the truth of what my son did is recognized or is admitted, I will not only accept, I will insist on a peace and I will give such satisfaction to you, signore, and to your brother-in-law that he, you, and all the world will be amazed and be satisfied. Do not think, signore, that this demand is a pretext for a refusal to make peace; rather it is in the interest of the truth, from which we ought never to run no matter what other great obligation there may be whether due to an insult or an injury. In whatever cause, I am resolved to speak on behalf of any matter that concerns my son.

Florence, 20 May 1578, Lanfredino Cellesi

Magnificent Pratica Segreta to Commissioner Pazzi, 23 May 1578:[17]

Do not continue to constrain the Bracciolini whom you have detained for the truce with Captain Lanfredino Cellesi until you receive new orders, but release them. If anything else comes up appropriate to your magistracy, we will notify you.

This is our first indication that some of Fabrizio's relatives had been detained for refusing to underwrite a truce. Why the lords of the Pratica now decided to instruct Commissioner Pazzi to release them they do not say. Perhaps they felt that since the principals themselves were unable to agree on terms, it was unjust to penalize other members of the family. At any rate, it comes at a time when both the public and private negotiations seem to be faltering.

For his part, Jacopo Cellesi acknowledged the failure of his efforts to bring the two parties together.

Jacopo Cellesi to Lanfredino Cellesi, 24 May 1578:

I regret extremely that I have not succeeded in bringing about a peace between your son Cavalier Mariotto and Cavalier Fabrizio Bracciolini. It seems bad luck on my part. As to your offer of peace, signore, I thank you. I hope for a better opportunity in the future to break another lance.[18] For whatever good purpose I offer myself to you and your son.

And there, for the time being, peacemaking efforts rested.

NINE

Chiara

Being a woman is a terribly difficult task,
since it consists principally in dealing with men.
— Joseph Conrad

Even before Camilla and Rinaldo and the other witnesses were brought to
the bargello's palace in Florence—indeed, even before the incident in the via
S. Andrea—Secretary Conti had been busy questioning someone else who,
while not an eye witness, was central to the Holy Thursday drama. She had
made herself known to their lordships of the Pratica Segreta some weeks
before the Holy Thursday incident in the following undated letter.

Signori of the Pratica of Florence of the Grand Duke,

I, Chiara, living in the Prato S. Francesco in Pistoia, am presently in the house of
Captain Lanfredino Cellesi. I am locked in, not allowed to go out or to go to my own
house. They are keeping me here by force, watching me and telling me that they will
mark me, cut my nose and ears, before letting me go. This is due to jealousy. I beg
you to have me set free so that I may go to my own house and safely go out without
their doing anything to me. After I was locked in a little room for several days by the
captain, I ran away to the house of Mena Maria di Biondo. Cavalier Mariotto arrived
and promised that I would be allowed to go to my own house that evening, so they
brought me back to his father's house and now I am locked in, unable to go out. So
I beg you, for the love of God, have me set free so that I may leave and be secure. Do
it right away, because I am afraid they will send me away after doing something bad
to me. The *birro* (policeman) Francesco, il Maestro, the servant Giovannino, and the
serving women of the house could tell the truth if they wanted to; they know I have
been locked in again and cannot go out to my own house—that I have been locked
up again by the captain—but they won't say so. For the love of God, have me set free
so that I don't die here without anyone knowing.

Chiara in Pistoia, locked in the house of Captain Lanfredino.

Piazza (Prato) S. Francesco. Unknown artist. Museo Civico di Pistoia

A postscript follows:

> If you can have me freed to go to my own house please do it in such a way that I can be sure nothing bad will be done to me, and please do not say that I have written to you or it will be bad for me. He'd have me killed. Have me set free soon, I pray God for you and also for the safety of my children because they won't give them to me.

On 7 March, the lords of the Pratica sent a letter to Commissioner Cosimo de'Pazzi in Pistoia ordering him to investigate Chiara's appeal for help and to keep her available for further questioning. The commissioner seemed in no hurry to comply: two weeks later, he reported that on the previous day he had sent his lieutenant and notary to Captain Lanfredino's house.[1] Finding her in bed with the captain, the officials roused her and took her out of earshot to question her. She confirmed that she was being held against her will, although she had not otherwise been mistreated and was, in her phrase, "not allowed to want for anything." She was conducted to the commissioner's office, where she handed him a letter containing an appeal much like the one she had sent to the Pratica in Florence. "I ask for God's sake because I have no one who is for me, only reason and God, and I beg that you keep this secret and see that he is unable to do anything to me."

Under oath before the commissioner, Chiara told more of her story. She was the wife of Piero, called il Morino, the little Moor, of Bologna, but she lived in Pistoia with Captain Lanfredino Cellesi, dividing her time between his house and one he provided for her use in the Piazza S. Francesco. Her current troubles began one evening during Carnival.

I went out masked with two of Captain Lanfredino's servants. He was informed of this, and also that I had done a lot of other things. He kept repeating that he wanted to know what I had done and he locked me into an antechamber without my clothes, which he kept in a chest. His bedroom has two doors, one leading to the terrace, which he had nailed up. He said he wanted to clear up certain things. After eight days, he made me sleep with him and all night he kept telling me to confess what I had done and saying that if I confessed to him he would forgive me. I told him I couldn't confess and he began to threaten me, saying that if I confessed he would forgive me and if I didn't he would throw me out and lock me in a room and let anyone do whatever they wanted to me. In the morning, covered only by a heavy coat and the captain's cloak, having no other clothes, since mine had been locked up, I ran away to the house of Mena Maria nearby. And when he learned of my flight, he ordered a search, and Cavalier Mariotto, the captain's son, found me and came to Mena Maria's house and she begged me to return. I didn't want to go back but Mariotto said, "Come back and talk to the captain; as soon as you do you'll be able to go back to your house."

So I was won over by promises and went with him and with the woman servant and I dined in his house and after dinner I went to the captain's house. As soon as I arrived, he began screaming and threatening me and saying, "What crazy things are you up to? Confess what you've done; you're going to stay here and not go out without permission." I was afraid he would mark me and then send me back to my house so I decided to escape and ran to the court. The errand boy and Teodoro, the captain's [other] son, ran after me and reached me in the court and begged me to return, saying I didn't have anything to fear and that he wouldn't let anything bad be done to me. The captain had his servants carry him there, and when he arrived he said, "Come back! Come back!" Seeing that I couldn't run away, I returned against my will, and when I got back the captain sent for a locksmith and had him make a key and a shutter for the door at the head of the stairs so it couldn't be opened without the key. Since then I have been locked in there, only permitted to go around the inside rooms, but when I did go out of my chamber, I was watched by a guard.

Pressed for more details of her relationship with the captain, Chiara said:

For some years now the captain has been doing a lot of weird things to me.[2] Once I pawned a pair of bracelets and he wanted to know who had pawned them for me, and when I wouldn't tell him he wanted to cut my nose with a dagger to force me to tell him. Sometimes he beat me, sometimes the whole night long, chasing me, with nothing on but my shirt, around the bedroom, and hitting me with the flat of his sword, hurting me badly. Now the latest thing, the night of Carnival, because I had gone out masquerading, he punched me. I was afraid he would really do what he had threatened to do other times, so I ran away. This is why I have made up my mind that I won't stay with him or with anyone else anymore. I'll stay by myself, and live like a Christian, go to confession and live free.

Shortly after her flight—she thought it was the second day of her return but she had been too agitated to note the day—she got someone to write to the Pratica Segreta in her name and found a messenger to deliver the first of her two letters, "but I beg you not to press me to tell you who wrote them or who carried the message because I don't want to cause any scandal, as there will certainly be when it is known."

After these revelations, Commissioner Pazzi had Chiara escorted to her own house; but this period of freedom was almost as brief as the first. On 1 April, the Pratica ordered her brought to Florence and consigned to the bargello's prison. She was escorted by the Pistoia bargello's lieutenant. Although the Pratica said she might bring a woman with her, she was alone.

In this latest letter to the commissioner, the Pratica lords also took up another matter: they had heard that Cavalier Mariotto Cellesi had wounded Cavalier Fabrizio Bracciolini and they were surprised and annoyed that Commissioner Pazzi had not already reported it to them. "As soon as you are well informed of the circumstances, let us know so that we may give you instructions as we see fit. In the future, when other cases of this sort happen, you are not to fail to tell us about them as soon as possible. This is the duty of your office." Although they did not say so, the juxtaposition of Chiara's troubles with the news of the fight on Holy Thursday, four days earlier, suggests that the Pratica lords had information connecting the two matters. By 23 April, when they resumed their investigation of Chiara's complaint, they knew a great deal more, for by this time the "true reasons" for the imbroglio had been whispered into the ducal ear by the captain or his man at court, and undoubtedly passed on to the Pratica for investigation. They had also found witnesses who could supply information that Chiara herself was unwilling to give up.

In the month that followed, Chiara struggled to turn aside Secretary Conti's probing into her secret life, but the testimony pouring out in his hearing room overwhelmed almost all her defenses. She was forced to reveal what the reader will already have guessed—that her scribe and messenger was her own ardent knight, none other than Fabrizio Bracciolini. The bargello's night guard provided damaging information connecting her with this eager suitor (and demonstrating the evasiveness of Fabrizio's deposition of 27 March). But the main agents of Chiara's undoing were her own servants, women who were privy to her secrets and witnessed most of what went on behind the closed doors of the little house in the Piazza S. Francesco.

With Secretary Conti confronting her with these intimate, vivid revelations, she was forced, step by unwilling step, to admit that the story she had given earlier was marred by half-truths and omissions. Still, it was easier for the secretary to unravel Chiara's version of her story than it is for us to knit up a better one. None of the witnesses, not even Chiara, possessed all the facts or a complete perspective, and the details they provided were disconnected, piecemeal, and seldom disinterested. With informants hazy about dates and times and the court notaries careless about dating letters, the chronology of the affair is vague. By the time the Pratica Segreta first hears from Chiara, on 7 March, she has been suffering Captain Lanfredino's nighttime antic jealousy for some years. Whether the old man had real grounds to be suspicious she does not say. Just when Fabrizio entered the picture is unclear, although from the combined testimony of Caterina *la Genovese,* part-time servant, part-time prostitute, and the widow Ceccha, Chiara's live-in servant for some three months, it appears that Fabrizio had begun courting Chiara some time in the fall, possibly late summer, of 1577. Secret exchanges of messages and gifts followed, with the two serving women acting as go-betweens. Fabrizio sent Chiara a ring; she sent him one in return "as a token of her love," although, since it had been a gift from the captain, she had Caterina take it to be altered by having it covered with enamel and its "ugly little stone" replaced by a beautiful turquoise. Fabrizio sent Chiara his portrait in a little box. Four days later, she returned the portrait and had Caterina explain that she was afraid the captain would find it. Another little box arrived, containing a golden heart and ten silver piasters. Chiara sent back the coins but told Caterina she would keep the heart "as a token of his love." She instructed Caterina to bury the heart in the garden, but instead she hid it in the coal pile until Chiara took it for safekeeping to her confessor, fra Bartolomeo of the Church of S. Francesco. Other gifts were a *corona* (headband) of red wool, some little vials of scented water, and a basket containing lemons and *butagra* (a fish-roe delicacy).

Cautious and secretive at first, Fabrizio grew more reckless in his wooing. Many witnesses reported seeing him in the Prato S. Francesco keeping vigil in front of Chiara's house. Caterina, too, saw him there, day and night imploring Chiara "in that restless and insistent way he has." Chiara's neighbors saw him climbing her garden wall. Caterina said she warned the cavalier many times that if he did not leave Chiara alone he would offend the captain. But Fabrizio retorted, "I don't want to leave her alone, I'm not afraid of the captain or anyone else; if they come one at a time, I'll give it to them. She's the captain's woman, not his wife. If she were his wife I wouldn't bother her." Ceccha, too, tried her hand at putting a damper on the affair. She carried Chiara's messages to the cavalier, but when Caterina gave her a letter from him, Ceccha threw it in the fire in Chiara's presence.

Chiara's country friend Sforzo di Chiarito from nearby S. Moné hectored her repeatedly about her need to "live a better life." The Cellesi and Bracciolini should always be friends, he told her, but if she persisted (in what he did not say), she would create a scandal between them and they would become mortal enemies. Sforzo di Chiarito took it upon himself to enlist the help of Lionetto Bracciolini, Fabrizio's cousin. One day traveling in the Maremma, he passed Lionetto at the barrier where he served as a customs guard. He urged Lionetto to persuade Fabrizio to give up his pursuit of Chiara, because he could see that there was going to be big trouble between the cavalier and the captain. Lionetto replied with little grace: he did not need to be taught by Sforzo, he huffed, but he would talk to his cousin when he returned to Pistoia in three or four days' time.

But Fabrizio persisted. He was seen talking to Chiara at her doorway. On 2 November, All Souls' Day, he gained admission to her house. Caterina was present, as were Francesco Bizzo and his wife, when Fabrizio entered. He and Chiara talked and she heard Chiara tell him, "I'm fine; please don't give me any trouble; the captain doesn't let me want for anything." But the cavalier, insistent as always, as Caterina put it, did not cease pressing her. Some time before Christmas, bloodstains appeared on the lintel of Chiara's doorway. It was the cavalier's blood, said Caterina, but Ceccha insisted that it

Site of Holy Thursday attack, S. Andrea.
Photo by Lorenzo Polizzotto

was the blood of a chicken killed for the holiday. The source of the blood remained a mystery, at least to the court, but the line of questioning implied that Fabrizio's efforts to get into the house were not always peaceful.

Though Caterina could not, or would not, say whether Chiara's suitor had gained entry to her mistress's bed, Ceccha was more forthcoming. She had come to stay with Chiara in December, except for three weeks when she went home to Bagni di Lucca. During that time, she had not only seen Fabrizio in the house on several occasions, two or three nights she had seen him enter Chiara's bedroom. Each time he stayed for two or three hours. She could not say what they had talked about (she was a woman who minded her own business, she declared) but on those nights she had found the two in bed together when she came in to warm it, and very cozy they appeared.

If Ceccha's testimony is trustworthy, then, some time after 2 November Chiara's "No" changed to "Yes," and she and Fabrizio became lovers. How often and under what circumstances they saw each other afterward, other than the times Ceccha reported, we have no way of knowing. Judging from the exchanges of letters, messages, gifts, and declarations of love, the affair grew in intensity until the crucial night of Carnival when they went masquerading together. This was during the week preceding Ash Wednesday, 12 February. Chiara made no mention of Fabrizio in her account to Secretary Conti, but Caterina told a more plausible story: Fabrizio had sent her to Chiara with "two pairs of velvet knee breeches *(braconi)*, one red the other black, a mantle *(tabaretto)* of turquoise satin, two hats, one of turquoise satin, the same color as the mantle, the other of yellow satin, a pair of little boots of yellow satin, a pair of black knitted stockings, and a pair of silver leather shoes." Chiara put on the red velvet breeches and the turquoise hat of satin, and over a white cloth coat of her own she put on an old woolen coat and went out with il Maestro and Giovannino, the captain's servant, who also put on costume. Caterina herself put on "a grey and white damask skirt belonging to cavalier Fabrizio's wife, and the cavalier [Fabrizio] put on a green taffeta vest *(traversa),* and Giannino, the son of the bargello's lieutenant [did she mean Giannozzo, the commissioner's son?] put on the cavalier's short cloak *(panni).*" She and Fabrizio and Aurelio, his secretary, nicknamed Iandone, then went to the party at Francescone's house, leaving the lieutenant (this seems to be an error) at Fabrizio's house to wait for some other maskers. The cavalier danced with a young girl and also with Caterina and Chiara (who by then had arrived with il Maestro and the servant Giovannino).[3] Afterward, Caterina, Fabrizio, Chiara, il Maestro, Giovannino, and Giovanna, the wife of Lanzi, went to several other parties.

If Fabrizio and Chiara hoped their Carnival masks would protect them against scandal, their ardor deluded them; gossip about their affair had already spread beyond their domestic circles. Whether or not rumors had reached Captain Lanfredino prior to their outing, what he heard afterward so enraged him that he locked Chiara in his room. And there, through February and most of March, she remained, except for her brief flight, when Commissioner Pazzi sent his men to investigate her cry for help.

With Chiara a prisoner in the captain's house, Fabrizio took a reckless— a disastrous—step. Between 9:00 and 10:00 on the Friday evening before Palm Sunday, Luca del Capitano Domenico, lieutenant of the bargello's night guard, came upon Fabrizio, his friend Giannozzo de'Pazzi, and a professional singer named Thomio di Domenico, called the Frenchman, loitering in the Piazzetta Romana, the Cellesi compound. The better to observe what they were doing there, Luca and his *sbirri* concealed themselves in the nearby Canto di S. Giovanni delle Legne. From the compound, they heard whistling and Cavalier Fabrizio calling "Baby *(Bimba)* come back, run, and other things of that kind," while Thomio sang "When the New Season is Upon the Fields," "If You Were a Lover Like Me," "Fortune's Wheel Goes Up and Down," and other Neapolitan songs, with Giannozzo accompanying him on the lute.[4] The half-hour serenade was heard by neighbors, members of the Cellesi family, the Genovese woman, and by Chiara herself, in bed with the captain and trembling with fear of "the scandal." The attack on Fabrizio in the via S. Angelo came the following Thursday.

During the month that Secretary Conti was probing into her secrets, Chiara, in her cell in the bargello's dungeon in Florence, must have wondered whether she was any better off than when she had been locked in the captain's bedroom. Her liberators had become her jailers and inquisitors and, with the help of her once-trusted maidservants, they had wrung out of her one damaging admission after another—first the name of her suitor, then Fabrizio's entry into her house—even, finally, into her bedroom. But not into her bed: when asked point-blank if the cavalier had had sex with her, she replied, "Signore, no, and it would never happen." Then, confronted with Ceccha's report of having seen them in bed together, she conceded that Fabrizio had entered her room, even that he had stood at the foot of her bed, but still she continued to deny that he had crossed that ultimate threshold. By this point in her interrogation, Chiara's "No" was not credible. Nor would it have mattered much had she really said no to Fabrizio in her bedroom, so grievously had she compromised herself, first by admitting him, then by finally confessing she had done so. Whether she had slept with Fabrizio or not, she was undone. She had admitted enough to be branded as faithless— to her patron because she had accepted Fabrizio's attentions; to her suitor/ lover because she had revealed his identity. No matter that she had resisted; both times she had surrendered more than she could afford. She could expect no sympathy or indulgence from either patron or lover.

Chiara longed for independence, to be neither the concubine of the captain nor the mistress of the cavalier, but the setting of her dream was the little house in the Prato S. Francesco, and, though she liked to think of it as her own, the house, like everything else she possessed, was the captain's. Now that Lanfredino's suspicions had been confirmed, she could hardly expect he would let her go on living there, certainly not on her own terms. She could not turn to her lover, a married man with children, noble and a cavalier of Santo Stefano. Fabrizio's taste was for furtive conquests, not open liaisons. For all his swaggering and defiance of public opinion, he had repeatedly warned her about the need for secrecy, and, though she could hardly have done otherwise, he was not likely to forgive her for revealing him as her lover. He had wooed and, probably, won her by swearing to protect her against the world; whether she was aware of the irony, we can only guess.

Once the questioning of Chiara and her friends and servants had ended, the Pratica Segreta's investigation into her situation was over. Their lordships made no further inquiries into her claims of mistreatment, nor did they concern themselves with her future. Having determined that Chiara's troubles stemmed from her dalliance with Fabrizio, they shifted their attention to the Holy Thursday processo. When, soon afterward, she was released, the Pratica's notary did not take the trouble to note it in the record. She will be mentioned occasionally in the continuing investigation, usually as Captain Lanfredino's concubine or as his whore.

I found no trace of any further communication between Fabrizio and Chiara. Captain Lanfredino's prompt reaction to the disclosures in Florence is evident in the two documents that follow, the first a letter from Teodoro Cellesi and Giovanni Politi to a certain Guaspare of Castelvecchio (this is probably Castelvecchio di Piancaldoli in the valley of Santerno, near the village in the mountain district of Bologna where Chiara had lived with her husband), the second a contract between the captain and Pierantonio Manzini, Chiara's lawful husband.

Teodoro Cellesi and Giovanni Politi to Guaspare of Castelvecchio, 23 May 1578:

Most dear, like a brother, Guaspare:

We have received your letter directed to Captain Lanfredino, our father and uncle, together with one from his son, Cavalier Mariotto. We have not wanted to show it to him because he is seriously ill, but having been informed of everything by both of them, knowing the captain's views, and out of goodwill on our own part, we are able to reply to you. Since September [that is, of the year before the Holy Thursday incident], il Morino, through Don Bino and Bastiano of Lizzano Matto,[5] has been very insistent about his wife and has not changed his mind. This he demonstrated by having these same men promise they would ask the captain on his behalf to return Chiara to him and forgive him everything and make a holy peace.[6] You may ascertain that this is so and that we are trustworthy by asking Giorno and Menico di Sforzino and others of Castelvecchio about us. We wrote to you about them a few days ago in connection with other matters. So, dearest Guaspare, if you are persuaded that il Morino is being sensible and does intend to do this, you may urge him to do it through them and let us know. If so, you'll see what we will do and how we'll do it. We see no better course than this. Since it could go one way or the other, we can assure and promise you that Captain Lanfredino will not do or have done anything against il Morino through the whole of next June; indeed he will treat him as if he had never known him until now and he will do what he can for him. We promise to speak to him about it and read him your letter and the letter of the cavalier his son when he seems better.

Contract between Captain Lanfredino Cellesi and Pierantonio Manzini of Rocha Corneto:

16 September 1578[7]

The Magnificent Captain Lanfredino di Mariotto Cellesi of Pistoia . . . gives quittance to, absolves, and frees Madonna Chiara, daughter of Domenico de Fioresi of Lizzano Matto, district of Bologna, and wife of Pierantonio di Martino de Manzini of Rocha a Corneto, County of Bologna, although absent. He frees her husband, the said Pierantonio, and his notary . . . from liability for any thing, occasion, and in whatever way or whatever sum for which she may be in debt to Captain Lanfredino . . . and similarly of all the goods which in any way she may have taken for herself or which were sent to her. . . . To Chiara he gives these goods . . . on condition that she return, reside with, stay, and remain with the said Pierantonio her husband and that she live with him with every due matrimonial observance.

In the event that she does not return to live, stay, and remain with her husband in matrimonial observance . . . he [Captain Lanfredino] wants every . . . enfranchisement and guarantee he has given to be null and of no value or effect . . . as though he had never made [such an agreement].

And the said Pierantonio her husband gives his word to Captain Lanfredino and his sons and . . . to the reverend don Bino di Anibale de Fronzamoli [the name is obscure in the text] and to his brothers in the presence of Captain Lanfredino and myself the notary . . . that he, Pierantonio, will not harm the said Chiara his wife either with weapons or without, or with words or deeds, or have her harmed in any way for anything that may have happened up to the present, but to live [with her] as true and good Christians and to treat her well and support her as a husband should a wife: . . . under penalty of 200 scudi . . . applied according to the form and statutes and promises, and he swears with his hand on the sacred scriptures. Public contract is made of these matters in Pistoia in the Cappella of S. Michele[8] in the house of the said captain by the hand of Ser Giuliano Cattani, notary of Pistoia.

So, after seventeen years, Pierantonio ("the little Moor") got his wife back.[9] If the husband's efforts to recover Chiara had been a problem for the captain in September, by May they had become a solution. With a penstroke, Captain Lanfredino banished a wayward mistress and shifted the burden of her support to her legal husband. By the same stroke, he freed Mariotto and Teodoro of a rival for his affection and property. Chiara herself seems to have had no say in the matter. Her estranged husband's campaign to get her back was directed to the captain, and now the two men, through intermediaries, negotiated the contract by which she was returned. Chiara's signature was not required on the agreement, nor was her presence required at the signing. Obey she must, unless she chose to surrender the goods she had from the captain and join Polita, Maria, and her own former servant Caterina on the streets. Her former homes, Lizzano Matto or Rocha Corneto, could hardly have been her idea of the safe haven she so urgently wanted and needed. To her reasons for leaving those places years earlier, she must now add the fear of a jilted husband's jealous (and, most of her contemporaries would have said, righteous) anger. To be sure, the contract foresees this danger and binds il Morino to treat her well or pay a fine of 200 scudi; but a contract drawn up in Pistoia in the grandduchy of Tuscany would give Chiara little protection in a remote mountain village in the district of Bologna. There is no mention of her children.

Asdrubale

> Therefore let this be ordained as the first law of
> friendship: Ask of friends only what is hon-
> ourable; do for friends only what is honourable
> and without waiting even to be asked.
>
> —Cicero

To the blast of a herald's trumpet, notices were posted on 14 May summoning Asdrubale Cellesi to answer the charge of assaulting Fabrizio Bracciolini.
Last seen striding through the S. Marco Gate on Holy Thursday, Asdrubale
had ignored every summons of the Pistoia commissioner. But this latest
order was *perentorio* and in the name of the Pratica Segreta in Florence—as
compelling as a command from the grand duke himself. And this time
Asdrubale responded, though not in five days as ordered, and not in person.
On 28 May, Giovanni Politi, Captain Lanfredino's nephew (he was the son
of Lanfredino's sister Francesca) and procurator, appeared before the Pratica lords on Asdrubale's behalf. Ser Giovanni presented two documents, a
notarized copy of Asdrubale's ordination as a subdeacon by the archbishop
of Savona on 18 April 1566, and a recent letter of Alberto Bolognetto, apostolic nunzio in Florence, which confirmed Asdrubale's ordination and absolved him of any irregularity in his clerical status. As a member of the clergy,
Asdrubale had the privilege of being tried in an ecclesiastical court, and this
privilege Politi now claimed for him. The Pratica lords deliberated and three
weeks later remanded him to the ecclesiastical forum. Pistoia's Bishop Lattanzi instructed his vicar, Alessandro Cespi, to proceed.

Arraigned before the vicar on 10 July, Asdrubale affected to be indifferent.

Did he know why he had been summoned? "I couldn't say—because of a citation sent to me by Your Reverend Lordship."

Did he know the reason for the citation? "What would you have me know, signore?"

Had he not had other summonses in the previous three months? "Not that I know of, not me personally, not at my house, as far as I know."

Asked about his actions on Holy Thursday, Asdrubale explained that he had been knocking on Nardino del Bonzetta's door to ask for a glass of wine when he heard Cavalier Mariotto Cellesi say "Draw your sword." He saw Cavalier Mariotto running after Cavalier Bracciolini and Bracciolini falling back. Each man struck at the other and Fabrizio was wounded.

When the court notary read the charge against him, Asdrubale burst out, "That isn't true, and I deny this whole complaint, and I don't have to respond to it here." As to having been armed: "Signor, no, I never carry arms in Pistoia."

Questioned about his clerical status, Asdrubale replied, "I'm a subdeacon, Your Lordship, and I have been for a number of years, just how many I don't recall. I think it was in the time of Pius IV [1560–65]; I was ordained in Rome, examined by a Jesuit father."

But then why did he not wear clerical dress or have a tonsure? Asdrubale explained that when Pope Pius V issued a breve allowing priests to join the fight against the Infidel, he had volunteered. Since then he dressed as a soldier and recited the office only irregularly.[1] "His Most Reverend Monsignore knows the whole story; I talked with him before Lent and I promised him I'd start wearing the habit in Lent, but I don't have the wherewithal."

At this point the vicar ended the hearing. Asdrubale was led away to a prison cell and Fabrizio was summoned to declare whether he intended to proceed against him.

Ordered to appear within five days, Fabrizio came in two, but only to denounce the proceedings. It was not up to him, he declared, to prove the case against Asdrubale; the court could do that itself by studying the testimony of the witnesses examined by the Pistoia commissioner and reexamined by the Pratica Segreta. Besides, the case should not have been remanded to the ecclesiastical court at all; as far as he, Fabrizio, knew, Asdrubale was no priest; he had always worn secular dress and lived a secular life; he had even gone to war. He knew Asdrubale had once had a church, but here was a document of this very court depriving him of his church because of his irregular life. Asdrubale ought to be constrained to demonstrate how and where he had been ordained, so it could be seen whether he was a priest or not. As for himself, Fabrizio concluded, the ecclesiastical court had no business telling him he must prove his case by a certain date. Once again, he had no obligation to prove anything. The court should uncover the truth and so inform His Most Serene Highness.

Fabrizio's documents showed that in 1569, Jacopo Ansaldi, then episcopal vicar of Pistoia, had deprived Asdrubale of his living in the parish church of S. Pietro in Campiglio, a mountain village in the Pistoia diocese, on the grounds that he had "transgressed and damnably incurred the penalties prescribed by the sacred canons and synodal constitutions imposed on negligent clerics." On appeal, the Florentine archdiocese confirmed Asdrubale's removal from S. Pietro, together with the loss of all its fruits. What the nature of these transgressions was is not specified, but together with Asdrubale's more recent irregularities the decision indicates a pattern of misbehavior stretching back to the early years of Asdrubale's ordination. Still, they did not disprove Asdrubale's claim to clerical status; quite the opposite, in fact, as he was quick to point out when he followed Fabrizio back into court.

Gone now were all signs of nonchalance and defiance of authority. Reminding the court that he was still suffering "the evil of prison," he asked that Fabrizio be held to his deadline so that his judges might proceed expeditiously, find him innocent, and make his accuser pay court costs.

Ten days later, Vicar Cespi announced that he was granting Asdrubale's request: the ecclesiastical trial would proceed. Fabrizio was given three days to produce his witnesses and present his charges.

On 22 July, Asdrubale was unshackled and brought to hear the charges again. Once more he acknowledged that he had been present but had not been involved in the fight with Fabrizio: "I was at Nardino's doorway, as I said in my first statement; I didn't see Cavalier Fabrizio when he passed, but it's true, I was in the company of Cavalier Mariotto. We had gone out walking together. None of the rest [of the charge] is true. I stand by what I said in my first examination."

How had he been dressed? "The way I am now is the way I usually go. [The notary recorded that Asdrubale was wearing black sailor pants, a jacket of white canvas, and a short cloak down to mid thigh, a laced shirt, and a felt cap.] But I had a black jacket; [not] this one they gave me in prison."

Asdrubale was given ten days to designate a procurator and prepare his defense. He would be permitted to examine the testimony of the witnesses who had already been questioned in the civil courts and decide whether he wished to present interrogatories for cross-examination. Asdrubale designated Giovanni Politi as his counsel and was taken back to prison.

Appearing on 24 July, Giovanni Politi argued that everything that had been deposed against "Presbyter Asdrubale" in the secular court was null—in the first place because the secular court had no competence in the matter, and in the second because Asdrubale had not been properly notified or cited. He won his point: the vicar agreed to disregard the earlier testimony and sent Fabrizio a notice to this effect. Politi's strategy was developing nicely. Having first secured the change of venue to a church court, he then managed to have the vicar disregard the earlier proceedings. As a result, Fabrizio was in the position of either making his case against Asdrubale de novo in a forum whose jurisdiction he refused to recognize or of forfeiting his role as accuser. He chose the second. Politi, on the other hand, was now free to cross-examine, without rebuttal from Fabrizio, the witnesses whose testimony seemed to confirm the charge against Asdrubale. To exploit this advantage, he quickly produced his interrogatories.

Politi opened by asking each witness whether they knew Asdrubale and could describe his appearance. The schoolboy Rinaldo said he had known the defendant for about a year; he was a guard of the Sanità at the Borgo Gate.[2] He was a well-built man with a beard that was rather red than dark. Mena Maria di Giovanni Lombardo, the mother of Polita, had been in service with Captain Lanfredino over a period of five years and had often seen Asdrubale there; "He's red-haired, with a reddish complexion, a good-looking man." Luca Pazzaglia had known Asdrubale as long as he could remember; he was of medium height and had chestnut-colored hair. Mena Camilla had known Asdrubale since he was a little boy, but she could not recall his height or hair color.

If the four witnesses were less than unanimous about Asdrubale's appearance, the next four witnesses agreed that he was destitute. Simone Panciatichi knew the defendant was a pauper who never had anything of his own. Simone himself had kept Asdrubale in his house at his own expense two or three times, a month or two at a time. As far back as he could remember, Giovanni Fabroni had been keeping him at his place in Pistoia. All of them—he, Giovanni Fabroni, and others—did it out of charity. All this was common knowledge in town. Giuseppe Fabroni agreed: Asdrubale was very poor; he had nothing of his own and he had lived in the house of Giovanni Fabroni, Giuseppe's uncle, four or five months at a time, at his host's expense. As long as Giuseppe could remember, he had been receiving alms in Pistoia. Asdrubale's poverty was also known to Alessandro Bicci and Battista Partini.

The relevance of Asdrubale's poverty is unclear, although Politi was obviously trying to downplay his part in the assault on Fabrizio. Most of his questions were aimed at Fabrizio's original deposition of 27 March. Detailed questions about the witnesses' perceptions of the fight broke the flow of each of their narratives into separate frames, isolating each moment of the action.[3] Did Cavalier Mariotto raise his biretta at the very moment the fight began—or an instant earlier? Did Cavalier Bracciolini immediately raise his biretta in turn? Was he going toward S. Francesco and was Mariotto standing still at the well while looking in the direction of S. Andrea? Did the two cavaliers turn to look at each other at that moment? Did Luca Pazzaglia hear Mariotto say to Bracciolini, "Draw your sword," or other such specific words, or were there other things said that the witness could not make out? Did Luca, when he heard the noise of the fight, turn toward S. Francesco and see Cavalier Bracciolini returning in the same direction from which he had come and did he see Cavalier Mariotto pursuing him and striking at his back with his naked sword? And did Fabrizio then turn around toward Mariotto, opposite the middle of the stairs of S. Andrea, and did Mariotto just then strike and wound Bracciolini in the face?

Thus on reexamination Rinaldo said he had seen Cavalier Bracciolini pass but he could not say whether he had raised his biretta to Cavalier Mariotto or to Luca Pazzaglia, who was also approaching; nor could he tell to whom Mariotto raised his. He had seen Mariotto draw his sword and go after Fabrizio and he heard him say something; he thought it was "Draw!" but he wasn't sure. Polita now said that she had not actually seen Asdrubale and Mariotto striking Fabrizio, she had only seen Fabrizio holding his head. Luca Pazzaglia recalled tipping his hat to Mariotto as he passed and Mariotto tipping his in return. Then he encountered Fabrizio and they, too, exchanged the greeting.

By focusing on what may have been the false perception that Mariotto had saluted Fabrizio in order to disguise his intentions, Politi deprived the charge of treachery of a good deal of its force. By showing that exact observations of each gesture—something no witness could claim—was critical to the perception of the whole, Politi aimed to demonstrate that there could be more than one reading of the incident.

Politi's questions also insinuated an alternative reading of the evidence— to wit, that Mariotto gave Fabrizio fair warning and attacked him honorably, while Fabrizio responded with something less than his usual bravado: "and did Cavalier Bracciolini, as soon as he was wounded in the face, drop his sword toward the ground, supporting himself on it, and with the other hand hold his nose? As soon as he was wounded, and directly afterward, were Cavalier Fabrizio's eyes covered with blood, and was he in such straits that if Cavalier Mariotto had wished to kill him he could have done it easily?"

Besides stressing the imponderables in the witnesses' accounts of the fight, Politi exploited the mounting suspicions that Fabrizio had suborned witnesses. Rinaldo now revealed that before the official hearings, Cavalier Bracciolini had him called out of school by Sano, his teacher, to ask him "how I'd seen the fight, and I told him I'd seen him tip his biretta but didn't see to whom, and that I'd seen Cavalier Mariotto standing on one side of the street with one foot on the well and Asdrubale on the other, at Nardino's doorway, and that I heard Cavalier Mariotto say 'Draw!' when he went after Cavalier Bracciolini, and saw Asdrubale also draw and go to help Cavalier Mariotto."

Then Cavalier Bracciolini asked if he had seen Nardino's door open and Rinaldo said it had been closed. He also wanted to know if Rinaldo had seen Tonio, Nardino's son, throw stones at him. Rinaldo replied that he had not, that Tonio was not there. Whereupon the cavalier replied that if Rinaldo did not say he had seen Tonio there he would have him beaten and whipped. But Rinaldo replied that he did not want to say what wasn't true. Had Rinaldo's testimony been read back to him after the notary had taken it down? "No," replied Rinaldo, nor even summarized for him.

The testimony was now read verbatim. Rinaldo declared that it was accurate except that—startling correction—he had omitted to say that Cavalier Mariotto had said "Draw!"—or words to that effect—to Cavalier Fabrizio.

There was more to come: After Fabrizio promised Rinaldo money in exchange for testifying that Tonio di Nardino had been at the scene, he dismissed the boy, saying, "Go! You've got an order," and again admonished him to say that Tonio had been present. But Rinaldo was not to mention that Cavalier Mariotto had called upon Fabrizio to draw. And the cavalier had added, "Don't worry, the judge belongs entirely to me." The servant Iandone (Aurelio) accompanied Rinaldo to court and gave the judge a message from Cavalier Bracciolini to the commissioner. Rinaldo did not know what it contained. Afterward, although he didn't want to go, Iandone took him to Cavalier Fabrizio's house. The cavalier asked Rinaldo what he had told the court and he replied that he had told the truth. (But, evidently, not the whole truth.)

Polita now admitted that she had been questioned in the Palazzo Bracciolini prior to the commissioner's hearing; she did not recall by whom, but she thought it had been by the cavalier himself. But neither he nor anyone had asked her to falsify her testimony or promised her anything if she did so.

Camilla, daughter of Piero the saddle maker, weaver, and vendor of old clothes, was even more muddled than in her earlier appearances. Camilla knew nothing about bribery attempts. She had been present at the beginning of the fight but not at the end because she felt faint and went back into the church. That was all she could remember. Nevertheless, she remembered enough to repudiate part of her earlier testimony. Asked about her observations of Tonio, Camilla insisted she had not told the Pratica that Tonio was not there, only that a son of Nardino was there whom she didn't know. No, she had no business of any sort with Cavalier Bracciolini, either for herself or any of her relatives. As to what the priest Jacopo Bracciolini had said to her before her first examination, it was only to encourage her to tell what she knew.

Once he had pried these reconsiderations out of the main eye witnesses, Giovanni Politi proceeded to discredit some of them personally. A string of witnesses belied Polita and Maria's descriptions of themselves as honest workers of loom and needle. Simone di Filippo Battifolle testified that Polita was a public prostitute; he himself had had sexual relations with her. As to Maria, her mother, he knew that once, while the late Andrea Manni was with Polita, Maria came to ask her for money for household expenses. During the eighteen months or so that he and Andrea were carrying on with Polita, Maria had acquiesced in her daughter's "evil life." That must have been four or five years ago, since Andrea Manni had been dead that long. Simone knew that the two women loitered about the public places frequented by other prostitutes and were friendly with them, and as far as he could see, mother and daughter were no different than the others.

Giuseppe di Pier Jacopo Fabroni knew from some of his friends that Maria went about hawking her daughter. Some of these friends, Michelangelo Gai, for one, had had relations with Polita. Giuseppe had been present when Maria came to them and when they talked to Polita. He knew she was a prostitute; she had had a baby baptized at a time when she had no husband, some time after she had begun her evil ways, maybe six or seven years ago. Giuseppe saw her at the places frequented by public prostitutes and saw her talking with them, and others told him they had seen her, too. Alessandro, son of the late Captain Gianbattista Bicci, had known Maria for a long time; for years she had been the servant and procuress of Calochina, a public whore in Pistoia. For the past eighteen months, she had been back with her daughter Polita, acting as her procuress. Alessandro had been present while Maria solicited men for Polita. Polita had been a prostitute and still was; it was common knowledge in Pistoia. Besides, he had seen Maria at all hours of the day and night taking men to Polita's house as to a public house of prostitution.

Francesco di Giovanni Bacciotto had known Polita and her mother Maria for about ten years; they had been women of ill repute and low life and were still, and he knew that Maria had approved her daughter working the prostitute's trade and still did so. He had spoken many times with men who had had Polita. At times he had seen Maria fetch Polita home, telling her that some man-friend or other was there. All this, he declared, was known to most of the men of Pistoia. Battista, son of the late Bartolomeo Partini, called Maria a procuress and Polita a prostitute. He himself had been with Polita. Although he had not had sex with her, he had felt her up and he knew she would have agreed to do it. And Maria had come to his house many times to get him to have sex with Polita. Since 1572 many men in Pistoia had told him she had done the same with them—in particular, Girolamo di Bartolomeo Forteguerri, the late Michelangelo Gai, and others.

By inducing Rinaldo and Camilla to admit that they had been coached by the Bracciolini, demonstrating Camilla's unreliability as a witness, branding Polita and her mother as disreputable and even showing some slight disagreement among the eye witnesses as to what Asdrubale looked like, Ser

Giovanni had probed the weak spots in Fabrizio's deposition and undermined much of it. At the same time, Politi had made no attempt to discredit Luca Pazzaglia, the one eye witness of some social standing. Luca's insistence that he had seen Asdrubale striking Fabrizio with a storta went unchallenged. That ought to have weighed heavily against Asdrubale, but whether it was enough to outweigh the other side of the balance containing Politi's skillfully heaped mass of contradictory and suborned testimony remained to be seen.

Fabrizio, representing himself, played his cards less skillfully.[4] By refusing to return to Vicar Cespi's court, he renounced the opportunity to present his own interrogatories and shore up his faltering deposition. Did he think the case against Asdrubale so strong that it needed no further help from him, or, on the contrary, was he convinced that in the vicar's court a verdict favorable to Asdrubale was a foregone conclusion that it was hopeless to prevent? More likely it was nothing so deliberate: Fabrizio was simply being Fabrizio—impulsive, defiant, and reckless. Since he had failed to get his way in arguing that the vicar had no jurisdiction in the case, he simply boycotted the ecclesiastical trial, whatever the consequences.

Two months later, on 11 October, Asdrubale was brought into court to hear Cespi's verdict. The vicar noted Asdrubale's admission that he had worn lay dress and lived as a layman, even as a soldier, for many years, and that he had often neglected to recite the daily office. For these violations of sacred canons and Tridentine and synodal decrees (and notwithstanding the letter of absolution from the papal nunzio in Bologna), Cespi suspended Asdrubale for one year and fined him fifty staie of grain, Pistoia measure, to be distributed at the discretion of the bishop.

On the charge of the assault on Fabrizio Bracciolini, because it has not been fully and canonically proven that subdeacon Asdrubale entered into and assisted the said cavalier Mariotto with arms, Asdrubale was absolved and excused court costs. He was ordered to reassume clerical dress on pain of excommunication and he was to remain in prison until he paid his fine.

Having lived as a layman for years, Asdrubale's violation of his clerical vows would probably have been a dead issue if he had not claimed benefit of clergy in the Holy Thursday case. This was a calculated risk: instead of allowing the civil processo to go forward, he had gambled—no doubt, on the advice of Procurator Giovanni Politi—that the hand of the church would be lighter than that of the prince. The gamble began to pay off almost immediately, starting with the early rulings by the vicar favoring his defense. When Fabrizio played into this strategy by failing to appear or submit interrogatories, he left a clear field for Giovanni Politi, whose unchallenged interrogatories dominated the rest of the hearings and undermined much of the eye witnesses' testimony. Besides, whether Politi had foreseen this or not, Vicar Cespi proved to be more concerned with Asdrubale's violations of clerical discipline than with his alleged violation of the public peace. Cespi's ruling provided that after a year of good behavior, Asdrubale would recover his clerical status—and with it, presumably, his eligibility for a church living. That much a civil processo could not have done for him, even if it had exonerated him from the charge of assault.

In moving for an ecclesiastical trial for Asdrubale, Politi surely calculated how this would affect his principal client, Mariotto. His interrogatories suggest as much. Sooner or later, unless he chose to go into permanent exile, Mariotto would have to appear before officials of the Order of Santo Stefano to answer the charge against him. If he could show that Fabrizio's deposition had already been impugned in an ecclesiastical court, this would be an important talking point for Mariotto's defense. Furthermore, if Mariotto could present himself as the lone, chivalric avenger of his family's honor rather than as the ringleader of a gang of assailants, he would surely have a greater claim on the sympathy of his judges. Now, with Tonio freed, the assault charge against Asdrubale dropped, and the two armed men literally out of the picture, Mariotto would be able to make that claim.

Although the documents do not say so, we can only suppose that the cost of the impoverished Asdrubale's defense, as well as his fine, were—like the bread that he ate—paid for by Captain Lanfredino and his friends, so that he did not have to remain in the bishop's prison much longer. Charity and family loyalty apart, the Cellesi father and son had had a crucial stake in the outcome of this trial, and the cost to them of Politi's expert counsel on Asdrubale's behalf was more than justified by the outcome.

Mariotto

Whether 'tis nobler in the mind to suffer
The slings and arrows of outrageous fortune,
Or to take arms against a sea of troubles.
                                    —*Hamlet* 3.1

At the end of May, the Council of Twelve of Santo Stefano received these short communications:

25 May 1578
I, Bernardo Santucci of the vicariate of Coreglia,[1] district of Lucca, resident of Borgo, have visited Signor Cavalier Mariotto Cellesi, who is in bed; I am told he has been this way for three days. I have prescribed a diet and bleeding. I shall do my best for him, relying on a judgment better than mine.

From Decimo, on the day given above.

I, Maestro Tommaso, surgeon of Decimo, district of Lucca, attest that today I drew blood from Signor Cavalier Mariotto Cellesi of Pistoia, who has been in bed in Decimo for three days. I drew this blood at the prescription of the excellent physician Messer Bernardo Santucci and in good faith have written the above in my own hand.

On the above day I, Francesco Lunardi, pharmacist at Decimo, attest that the above Signor Cellesi received the materials for his purge by written prescription of the above Messer Bernardino, and in good faith I declare this on the above date in Decimo.

I, Giuseppe di Antonio Lippi of Decimo attest that on 22 May 1578, [Mariotto Cellesi] arrived in my house ill. Here, by orders of the excellent physician Messer Bernardino Santucci on the 25th, he has been bled according to the written prescription. In good faith I have written this in my own hand this 25th day of May, 1578, in Decimo.

Decimo, or Diécimo, where Mariotto had come to ground, is a village in the Val di Serchio, so named because it is ten Roman miles, or about eighteen kilometers, north of Lucca. Apparently Mariotto had gone there from Pontito, where, on 16 May, he had written his first letter in the peacemaking negotiations. Then, ill with fever, he had left this refuge and made his way down to Decimo for treatment. Since there was no road across the mountains from Pontito to the Serchio valley, it would have been a difficult trip even for a healthy man. We can guess why Mariotto took this route instead of traveling down the easier and shorter road from Pontito to the city of Pescia, where he would have had a larger choice of physicians: Pescia was part of the grand duchy of Tuscany, whereas Decimo was in the autonomous republic of Lucca. In Decimo, Mariotto could prudently remain outside the jurisdiction of the grand duke while he recuperated.

But Mariotto's days of freedom were numbered. Either in Pontito, Decimo, or somewhere in between, he was overtaken by a summons to appear before Santo Stefano's Council of Twelve on 26 May. After ignoring repeated citations by the Pistoia commissioner and the Pratica Segreta, Mariotto now had to decide whether to ignore the superiors of his order as well. If he did so, he would not only be declared contumacious and an outlaw, but he would probably be expelled from Santo Stefano as well. This would end his military career and strip him of the order's protective jurisdiction. Mariotto decided to respond to the summons. First, however, he wrote to Grand Duke Francesco I, his prince and grand commander of his order.

Most Serene Grand Duke,
   Mariotto Cellesi of Pistoia, cavalier of Santo Stefano, humble vassal of Your Most Serene Highness, asks for a benign judgment of Your Most Serene Highness in the matter of the investigation of the complaint and the causes that moved him to fight with Cavalier Fabrizio Bracciolini. The inquest is pending before the Magnifica Pratica Segreta. In order to find out the truth of the incident and the suborning of witnesses appearing for official questioning, [the Pratica Segreta] continues to detain in prison the persons under investigation as well as the witnesses. This evidence is indispensable for arriving at the truth of the matter, for the case has infinite particularities, about which the present petitioner has written to Your Most Serene Highness. The petitioner has been cited by the most illustrious Twelve Lords of the Coun-

cil [of Santo Stefano] to respond by 26 May to the complaint formed against him on the basis of the testimony of witnesses examined in Pistoia and presently held by the Magnifica Pratica under suspicion of subornation. He begs Your Most Serene Highness to be so kind as to extend his term for responding to the investigation until the most illustrious Twelve Lords of the Council have received the processo and information from the Magnifica Pratica. The time allotted for his defense is so short as not to allow the petitioner to present his evidence, which is still in the hands of the Magnifica Pratica. Otherwise he might be considered contumacious and justice might not be done.

For such favor he humbly supplicates you, praying that Our Supreme Lord God grant you happiness and contentment.

Mariotto makes no reference here either to his flight from Pistoia on Holy Thursday or his failure to respond to earlier citations. Perhaps he had already made his excuses—those "infinite particularities"—in the earlier letter, which has not come down to us. The grand duke seems to have been satisfied: on 26 May, Secretary Antonio Serguidi issued a rescript granting the extension, and on 28 May the Twelve gave Mariotto an additional twenty days to appear. By that time, late June, the hearings in Florence on the charges against Tonio Visconti and Captain Lanfredino were over, and Asdrubale's trial, in which many of the same witnesses were involved, was about to begin, so Mariotto's appearance was again postponed.

While out of sight, Mariotto had not been out of touch. The letter of 16 May to Giovanni Fabroni in Pistoia (see chapter 8) shows him well informed about the progress of the judicial proceedings and peace negotiations. The timing of his reappearance and the coordination of his defense with Asdrubale's suggests that the two fugitives had remained together for part of the time, or had at least kept in touch with each other and with their mutual procurator, Giovanni Politi, as he shuttled between Pistoia and Florence on their behalf.

Since the vicar was not to make his decision in Asdrubale's case until October, Mariotto had grounds for delaying his appearance before the commissioners of Santo Stefano until the decision was announced. Meanwhile he was obliged to remain in Pisa at the headquarters of his order.

Captain Lanfredino Cellesi, guarantor for his son Cavalier Mariotto Cellesi, 9 July 1578:

In the Name of the Lord Amen . . . 9 July 1578 . . . Pistoia.

The valorous Captain Lanfredino Cellesi, son of the late Mariotto Cellesi of Pistoia . . . makes this agreement, although absent, through his procurator Messer Giovanni Politi, son of the late Ippolito Politi of Pistoia . . . on behalf of his son, Signor Cavalier Mariotto, that he will observe a truce made between [Mariotto] and Signor Cavalier Fabrizio Bracciolini and promises under bond in whatever amount is set that the said Signor Cavalier Mariotto will not leave the city of Pisa or the palace of the lord cavaliers of Santo Stefano in the city of Pisa or whatever place is chosen. . . .

Done in Pistoia in the Chapel of S. Michele tra Fabbrum.
[Names of witnesses follow.]

Mariotto's situation was not quite as bad as Captain Lanfredino represented it in a letter of 17 July to Bernabò Trevi in Florence: "My son has had to go to prison in Pisa on account of the fight and it troubles me a lot. So I'm going there to stay until his case is settled."[2]

On 8 November, Mariotto appeared before his judges, where he was sworn and ordered to tell how the incident in the via S. Andrea had come about.

When I returned from galley service last year, I went to Pistoia. I got along fine with Cavalier Fabrizio Bracciolini; we had always been friends. When I noticed that he was constantly around S. Francesco, I said to him, "Cavalier Fabrizio, I want a few words with you. My father is crippled and bedridden; I want you to leave his girl alone. I wish you wouldn't carry on that way around her. It seems to me that for the sake of our friendship you would respect her as well as everyone of our house. So I'm telling you as a friend, cut it out; if not, we're not going to get along." And he told me that it wasn't true, that he wasn't hanging around her, and that he had respect for all of us and for her and our whole house because we had always been friends, and that I shouldn't think this of him—that he had always considered Captain Lanfredino as a father and me as a brother, and if this weren't true, Christ might break his neck and bury him. He swore it in so many ways I can't remember now to repeat them all. I replied that if what he told me was true, I would feel very kindly toward him, that even though I don't speak to my father I still want some consideration for him. And he said to me, "And so you should."

Then my father sent for the girl and he kept her in his house, sometimes for a month or two, sometimes for a couple of weeks at a time, to take care of him because he's sick. Then, in our enclosure, in front of the door of my father's house, I began to hear singing, whistling, stamping of feet, and someone saying "Baby, come back, run away, run away poor little thing," and stones thrown on the walk in the compound, and singing of songs making fun of my father. This went on several nights, until one morning, after an evening when Cavalier Fabrizio was there singing and whistling and doing all the same things as the other nights, she ran away from my father's house in her shirt to Biondo's house, nearby. My brother called me right away saying, "Cavalier, come here quickly!" I said, "What's the matter?" He told me Chiara had run away in her shirt, and when I asked why, he said, "Haven't you heard the singing, whistling, and all those goings-on on all those nights?" I said, "Yes, who's doing all that shameful stuff in disrespect of my father?" And he said, "I don't know." I went to [the house] where Chiara was and led her back to my father's house. Meanwhile, Cavalier Fabrizio Bracciolini got the commissioner of Pistoia to issue an order to my father and his sons not to remove anything from Chiara's house. We asked her if she had made him her procurator to do such a thing or if she had asked anyone to do this, because we had asked Ser Giuliano Gattani [the official from whom they tried to find out who had represented Chiara in obtaining an injunction against them]. She replied that she did not get anyone to do this and she had not talked to anyone.

The night of Passion Friday at around eleven or twelve o'clock, I began to hear singing and playing and calling "Baby, come here, come back; poor little girl, your nose and ears are going to be cut off." Stones were being thrown in the street and there was foot stamping and yelling and whistling, and disrespectful songs were being sung about my father. When I heard it, I went to the window and saw a lantern uncovered and I heard, "Halt for the guard!" and Cavalier Fabrizio Bracciolini answer, "I'm Cavalier Fabrizio Bracciolini." Then the guard said to him, "Cavalier Fabrizio you shouldn't cause such trouble to Captain Lanfredino; you know you've always been very close." And Cavalier Fabrizio replied, "Go on about your business and do your duty." Hearing this I didn't want to go out because he was in a company of five or six, all covered from head to foot in white woolen mantles, so I went back to bed and in the morning I went to Chiara's house. No one was there because she was at my father's house, and I began to empty the closets; I found some letters and an inventory of things being held by a friar of S. Francesco called fra Bardo [i.e. Bartolomeo]. When I saw these letters and the inventory, I went to fra Bardo and made him give me the stuff which was from Cavalier Fabrizio, who was always sending pimps and procuresses to my father's house. One time he sent her ten piasters, which she didn't want and sent back to him, keeping only the picture he had sent her of himself. So, on Palm Sunday Cavalier Fabrizio wrote in Chiara's name to the Pratica that my father was holding her bound hand and foot, on bread and water, so she could not go home. When I had the letters Cavalier Fabrizio wrote to Chiara in his own hand, and entirely clear that they had done these villainous things to my father and to the rest of us, I went to find him on Holy Thursday around two o'clock and I found him on the via S. Andrea, near the entrance to the house of Nardino del Bonzetta. We met as he was coming from the direction of his house and I from the direction of S. Francesco, and as soon as I saw him I went up to confront him and I said, "Cavalier Fabrizio, draw that sword because you haven't behaved toward me as a cavalier or a gentleman!" We both drew at the same time and began to strike at each other until he started to run away. I said to him "Turn toward me!" but he kept running away and I kept striking at him, thinking he was wounded, while he kept running back in the direction of his house, where he had come from. I ran after him for about two bow shots, but when I saw he was wounded, I left off.

This is how it came about. My father cared more for her than for us. You can see that in what he did for their daughter, when he made her a nun with a dowry of 400 scudi—more than I ever had—and for their son, whom he wants to make a cavalier with a commenda. That didn't make me feel very good. If my father had been well and not crippled in his hands and feet, I would have let him get out of this himself, just as he has done other times. But when I saw that his hands and feet were crippled, I decided that it was up to me to pay back whoever wronged my father, even though he has shown little regard for me and cares more for that whore and their two bastards than for the two of us who are legitimate.

Was Mariotto alone when he went to fight Cavalier Fabrizio, or accompanied, and if so, by whom? "I went alone, but at the corner of the Porta Vecchia I met Asdrubale Cellesi and he came with me."

What weapons did he have when he went to fight with Cavalier Fabrizio? Was Asdrubale armed? How was he outfitted?

Asdrubale was unarmed. "I had a sword, dagger, mail jacket, and vambraces *(maniche)*, an under helmet *(segreto)*, and a gauntlet on my bad hand."[3]

Questioned about Asdrubale's part in the fight, Mariotto insisted that his cousin had known nothing about it and did not intervene. He further maintained that both he and Fabrizio had drawn their weapons simultaneously.

How many wounds were there and in what parts of his body? "One in the face—in the nose."

Did Mariotto hit him from the front or the rear? "I hit him from the front, as you can see from the wound."

Did he wound Cavalier Fabrizio before he drew his sword? "No, because he had drawn and each of us had struck several times before he was wounded."

Who came running to the fight? "I didn't see anyone."

Did he speak to, confer, or make any agreement with anyone about starting this fight, and with whom? "With no one."

Who came out of a nearby door, running to join the fight to help him? Was this Asdrubale? "I didn't see anyone; there didn't seem to be anyone but

Asdrubale and he had come [with me] and didn't do anything, as I already told you."

Warned to tell the truth: "I told you the truth; I have nothing else to say."

Asked to be more candid, for the truth is that Antonio Bonzetta ran to the fight to help and Asdrubale had a storta and all of them set upon Cavalier Fabrizio: "I tell you the truth is as I have already said, and not otherwise."

Did he and Cavalier Fabrizio raise their hats to each other when they met, and after letting Cavalier Fabrizio go on for about four or five paces did he (Mariotto) strike at Fabrizio several times without saying anything until he wounded him? "That's not true, I say, the truth is what I've already told you."

Again warned to tell the truth, Mariotto stuck to his story, after which he was dismissed.

Having completed the investigatory part of Mariotto's *processo*, the vice-chancellor decided to pursue the charge.

Official proceeding against Cavalier Mariotto,
son of Captain Lanfredino Cellesi, of Pistoia.

Whereas on 27 March, 1578, with the intention and purpose of confronting and fighting Cavalier Fabrizio Bracciolini of Pistoia, and having conferred in all this with Asdrubale Cellesi and Antonio di Nardino del Bonzetta,[4] the said cavalier armed himself with a sword, dagger, mail jacket, mail vambraces, mail gauntlet, and under helmet, and the said Asdrubale, armed with a scimitar taken from the house of the said Antonio, met the said Cavalier Fabrizio Cellesi [*sic*] on the via S. Andrea, in front of the house of the said Antonio, on the said day of 27 March, Holy Thursday, who [Cavalier Fabrizio] was going toward S. Francesco to mass. After the cavaliers greeted each other with their birettas, after the said Cavalier Fabrizio had passed, the said Cavalier Mariotto drew his sword and began striking at the said Cavalier Fabrizio. The said Asdrubale did likewise with his scimitar and made several cuts in his [Cavalier Fabrizio's] clothes. The said Antonio, coming out of his house, took their side, throwing stones and hitting the said Cavalier Fabrizio in the fleshy part of his left arm while he [Cavalier Fabrizio] was wounded by the said Cavalier Mariotto with a cut almost through his entire nose. After they had done this, they departed, leaving Cavalier Fabrizio wounded in this way.

These aforesaid actions are charged against him.

On the twelfth day of November, 1578:

Appeared personally before the illustrious lords of the council assembled, etc. The aforesaid Cavalier Mariotto Cellesi of Pistoia, under investigation [*inquisito*] to respond to the charge, to which after it has been read to him, he replies under oath, "I deny it." He denies the contents of the charge in its present manner and form, confessing that it is true that he fought and wounded Cavalier Fabrizio Bracciolini for the reasons and in the manner that he described in his statement taken by the chancellery. For the truth that statement is to be referred to in every particular. He fought as a knight, on equal terms and honorably.

The council appointed Grand Prior Eneo Vaini and Grand Chancellor Benedetto Vivaldi as special commissioners to hear the case, and Cavalier Mariotto Cellesi was ordered not to leave Pisa without permission of the council on penalty of expulsion. That permission was soon sought and obtained.

In council, Order of Santo Stefano, 21 November, 1578.
    Cavalier Mariotto Cellesi is given permission to leave Pisa for ten days on account of his father's life-threatening illness. Giovanni Politi posts 200 scudi security for his return.[5]

After Mariotto's arraignment and initial statement, the Santo Stefano council ordered his accuser to make a counterstatement to be taken by the commissioner of Pistoia.

Fabrizio appeared on 24 November. He was much more respectful than he had been at the court of the Pistoia vicar, perhaps because he knew that his words would be reviewed by the superiors of his order. He insisted that his original deposition was accurate and asked the new commissioner, Bartolomeo Panciatichi, to order a repeat of the testimony already taken by his predecessor, Commissioner Cosimo de'Pazzi. "From this," he argued,

it will appear whether the said Cavalier Mariotto has fought as a Cavalier or not. . . . This is not to aggravate Cavalier Mariotto's punishment in consideration of which, in order to free him from all punishment, he has offered before Your Lordship and Your Lieutenant to grant him peace[6]—but for further verification of the fact, and to demonstrate that Cavalier Mariotto had no reason whatsoever to act conspiratorially against him as he did.

First . . . the truth was and is that on Holy Wednesday 26 March past, the said Cavalier Mariotto Cellesi, Messer Giannozzo di Messer Cosimo Pazzi of Florence and the said Cavalier Fabrizio Bracciolini after dinner were in company together in the shop of Maestro Lodovico, the barber in Pistoia, familiarly and talking amicably, joking and laughing together as friends, as were other friends and companions . . . which Cavalier Mariotto would not have done if he had had any resentment against Cavalier Fabrizio.

Finally, all this is public knowledge, and to prove these articles . . . he calls Jacopo di Lorenzo Chiti of Pistoia and asks that he be examined by Your Lordship and, most importantly, Messer Giannozzo de'Pazzi, who, since he is presently on Elba, I request that the said magnificent and illustrious lord commissioners [of Santo Stefano] order the rector of that place to examine Messer Giannozzo on the above articles.

The newly designated Santo Stefano commissioners now moved to the deliberative processo, that stage of the proceedings in which the accused was examined on the charges and found guilty or innocent. In some respects the deliberative processo resembled the Anglo-American trial. New witnesses could be introduced and questioned and witnesses who had already been questioned in the investigative phase might be subjected to cross-examination. But unlike Anglo-American trial procedure, all questions took the form of written interrogatories presented to the court by the parties or their procurators. Interrogatories might be general, addressed to all witnesses, or directed to specific witnesses, but neither the parties nor their counsel interrogated witnesses directly; all questions were put to the witnesses by the presiding magistrates. In contrast to the adversarial system of the English and American criminal-law traditions, the deliberative processo was not intended to be a contest between antagonistic lawyers battling for the minds and hearts of a citizen jury with a judge acting as referee. There was, as I pointed out earlier, no jury. In a system that derived from imperial Roman law, the court, not the people, represented the sovereign authority, and the court investigated, deliberated, rendered a verdict, and pronounced sentence. Truth was decided, and justice handed down, from above.

Detachment, impartiality, and rational inquiry were the hallmarks of the system. It was the task of magistrates to discover truth in accordance with the evidence and say what it was *(veredictum)*. It would be naive of course to think that opinions from laymen had no influence in judicial decisions, that magistrates were unbiased, incorruptible, and deaf to the murmurings of special interests, or that procurators were helpless to shape the court's perception of the facts. The case we are following shows the opposite. Indeed, for procurators who hoped to undermine seemingly solid facts and influence outcomes by giving a different spin, not only to the evidence but even to the charge, the trial of Mariotto could have been a textbook case. Without the opportunity of direct cross-examination, the chief, almost the only, way a procurator could influence the direction of a case in this system, in addition to choosing effective witnesses on his client's behalf, was through his interrogatories. These might seem a limited instrument for maneuver, but, as we saw in the trial of Asdrubale, in the hands of a shrewd advocate like Giovanni Politi, interrogatories could be a flexible and effective instrument, masking arguments and value judgments, cross-examining witnesses, and shaping the judges' perception of the issues. Often they were designed to induce the witness to make a point that would favor the questioner's client— to lead the witness, a tactic frowned upon by modern judges in an adversarial trial. The term *interrogatori* does not fully convey the multiple uses to which these "questions" could be put: many of them were not questions at all, but assertions, a set of arguing points constituting a kind of lawyer's brief for the court's consideration. The interrogatories that Messer Giovanni Politi submitted to the commissioners on 24 November, the same day Fabrizio had made his rebuttal to Mariotto, are of this kind.[7] Moreover, together with Mariotto's earlier statement, they provide us with our fullest version of the story of the captain and his concubine from the Cellesi perspective.

For the past seventeen years, up to the time of the outbreak of the said fight, Captain Lanfredino Cellesi . . . has continuously kept as his concubine, supported and clothed, sometimes in his own house and sometimes in another house he set up for her and put at her disposal, Chiara, wife of Pier Antonio, called il Morino, of Lizzano Matto . . . the captain fathered two children with Chiara—a male named Raffaello, now about twelve, and a female named Dianora, of about fifteen, whom he has always treated, reared, and educated as his own natural children, keeping them with him, setting the boy on the path of good morals under the care of a private tutor in his own home, and putting the girl in the custody of a convent of the city of Pistoia. . . . Captain Lanfredino monachized Dianora in the monastery of S. Caterina of Pistoia with a gift of 400 scudi and . . . before the said fight he had petitioned His Highness to make the said Raffaello commendatario in the Order of Santo Stefano, with a commenda of 5000 scudi. . . . All this was common and public knowledge in the city of Pistoia to all the men and people of the city, or at least to the more important and nobler part.

There is more of this, then the interrogatory turns to Fabrizio:

Cavalier Fabrizio Bracciolini, contrary to every obligation of reason and civility, contrary to the respectable and decent behavior that one citizen ought to observe to another, especially by those who are friends and familiars, as he has been for four years with Cavalier Mariotto, for eight months, right up to the day of the fight, continuously harassed Chiara, sending her embassies daily, writing her love letters and sonnets, sending her money, a ring, a perfumed heart, tiaras, his picture and other presents. He sent these through low women [ruffiane] to the house provided for her by Captain Lanfredino, as witnesses will testify in greater detail. . . .

Cavalier Fabrizio Bracciolini, from November 1577 until the herein described fight, adding error to error, with little respect and against praiseworthy and good manners, especially those of cavaliers and gentlemen, many times at night when he knew Chiara was in the house of the captain, with his companions entered the compound of the Cellesi, where normally people go only if they are visiting one of the Cellesi houses. Playing, singing, whistling, yelling, calling, and throwing stones without restraint, he dishonorably signaled to Chiara that he was there. As a result, one morning before daybreak Chiara left the captain's house in her shirt. . . .[8]

On the night of Passion Friday, Cavalier Fabrizio entered into the Cellesi compound and playing, singing, yelling, whistling, and stone throwing with his companions right in front of the door of Cavalier Mariotto, he shamefully called out these, or similar words in a loud voice, "Come, baby, come, baby, come back, come back home, run, baby!" And one song particularly that kept repeating "run away, run away poor little thing," over and over. . . . For eight months prior to the outbreak of the fight, when Chiara was staying in the house in S. Francesco loaned to her by Captain Lanfredino, Cavalier Fabrizio continually stood in front of the house during the day importuning her by means of low women with embassies, letters, and presents, and at night many times entered into the garden of Chiara's house, climbing the walls of the gardens of neighbors against their will. . . .

Finally, after many months of following and importuning Chiara, Cavalier Fabrizio by night entered the house set up for her by Captain Lanfredino and went to bed with her and knew her carnally many times. . . . When relatives of the family and house of Bracciolini learned that Cavalier Fabrizio was behaving toward Chiara in this sinister and evil and disrespectful way, realizing that something unpleasant would result, they warned him repeatedly, urging and praying him to stop. Cavalier Bracciolini told them to mind their own business, that he had no need of a teacher, that they should go read their breviary—that was their duty; he would do what suited him. . . .

Shortly after his return from sea, when Cavalier Mariotto Cellesi learned of these sinister ways and evil behavior and of these warnings, and of the little respect displayed by Cavalier Bracciolini, thinking him a close friend and an intimate of the family as they had been with each other the past four years, he asked him not to harass or trouble Chiara, out of consideration and respect for his father, even though he [Mariotto] was at that time estranged from his father. . . .

Instead of desisting, Cavalier Bracciolini increased his untoward and shameful behavior, and to show that he had no respect for anyone, whenever he passed or stopped in a public place where there were a lot of people, he would say, "If anyone asks for me I'll be at the Prato S. Francesco until nighttime." When he was there opposite the house of Chiara, if anyone he knew passed he would say, "If anyone asks for me tell him that you've seen me here and that I'll be here until night, and I'm not afraid of being chased out of this public place; let them come one at a time; I'll give them what's coming to them." . . .

Cavalier Fabrizio got the notary of the commissioner of Pistoia, without the knowledge or the orders of the commissioner, and without the orders of Chiara, to command Captain Lanfredino and his sons not to remove anything from Chiara's house under penalty of a 25 scudi fine and a judgment. . . .

When Chiara learned of this, she sent a representative to the signor commissioner to find out at whose instance that command had been given, and the commissioner and his judge replied that they did not know anything about it. They called the notary and asked him who had requested this, and he replied that one time it was a man and at another a woman; he didn't know them. For this reason the commissioner and his judge had the command revoked. . . .

After that . . . in Passion Week, Cavalier Bracciolini wrote a letter to the Magnifica Pratica saying that Captain Lanfredino was privately holding Chiara prisoner in order to maintain his power over her. . . .

Since all or most of these things were matters of public notoriety, and since Cavalier Fabrizio Bracciolini's behavior has been so scandalous as to warrant a coming to blows, it was daily and hourly expected that a fight or some other strong reaction would take place between Cavalier Mariotto and Cavalier Bracciolini, especially since it was known that feelings between them had intensified.

The interrogatory now raises the matter of Mariotto's situation, as a man of honor:

Captain Lanfredino Cellesi, father of Cavalier Mariotto, has had gout for about two years and his hands and feet are so crippled that he can't stand and can't use his hands; most of the time he stays in bed. . . . Any gentleman soldier and honorable knight whose father is powerless to revenge himself for an injury done to him is obligated by his honor and the code of chivalry to defend and repay the injury to his father. Otherwise he will be held an unworthy knight. So every right-thinking man and worthy cavalier has always and will always maintain. . . . Finding himself forced by his honor and the code of chivalry, seeing that his father was in the condition just described, on Holy Thursday after breakfast, as soon as Cavalier Bracciolini's improper behavior had been made clear to him by letters [written] in Cavalier Bracciolini's hand, Cavalier Mariotto went to the via S. Andrea in Pistoia and, meeting [Cavalier Fabrizio] as he went toward Chiara's house, he called upon him to draw his sword and fight. In the exchange of blows, he wounded him in the face. . . .

Cavalier Mariotto Cellesi is a peaceful and quiet knight and minds his own business. He is known and reputed to be a man who always strives to make peace and settle differences wherever they arise. . . . All these things are open and public knowledge in Pistoia and all other places where there is information about them, and to prove the [contents of] the above clauses, the following witnesses are summoned.

The names of fifty-nine men and six women follow.

Politi's interrogatories have swept away the shredded remnants of Fabrizio's cover, but Fabrizio, desperate to protect his stance as the victim in this affair, can think of nothing better than to persist in his original statement, ignoring mounting evidence that he had wooed Chiara and suborned witnesses to shore up his story. Then, in an ill-considered moral appeal, he attacks Mariotto for taking action to protect an illicit relationship:

Interrogatories to be put to witnesses of the procurator of Cavalier Mariotto Cellesi by Cavalier Fabrizio Bracciolini who says that the things alleged by Cavalier [Mariotto] as to [what occurred in] the place of the concubinage of the captain his father were not and are not true and offer no grounds for the insult he committed against Cavalier Fabrizio. Moreover, Cavalier Mariotto's action is unworthy of an honorable knight, especially since his allegations concerning the behavior of Cavalier Fabrizio with that concubine are not true. Nor is it true that Cavalier Mariotto ever tried to get him to stop harassing the said Chiara, nor could he have done so, because Cavalier Bracciolini has never harassed Chiara, and if it had been true Cavalier Mariotto would not then, on Holy Wednesday, have spent time in Cavalier Bracciolini's company nor conversed familiarly with him, as he did that day and other days previously.

He asks that witnesses be sworn again and warned of the severe penalty for giving false testimony under oath.

He asks that witnesses first be read the following preliminary interrogatories:

Do they know Cavalier Fabrizio Bracciolini? For how long?

Do they consider Cavalier Fabrizio an honorable knight and one who would not behave in ways inappropriate to an honorable knight?

Should an honorable knight seek to insult or fight another knight over a whore?

Do not witnesses believe that there is no good or honorable reason for a cavalier of honor to fight over a whore?

Are they servants or employees of Captain Lanfredino? Do they have any connections with him or with Cavalier Mariotto, his son?

Who asked them to come forward for questioning in this case?

Were they told what to say?

Are they enemies of Cavalier Fabrizio Bracciolini, or have they ever quarreled with him?

Do they know that whoever wishes may pass back and forth in either direction in front of the house of Captain Lanfredino and in the Piazzetta Cellesi publicly as in other streets?

Do they work as servants for Chiara, said to be the concubine of Captain Lanfredino Cellesi, or did they work for her during the previous Lent? . . .

Is it not true that often one is deceived in identifying someone by voice and confuses one person for another, particularly at night? . . .

In what day and month did Cavalier Mariotto seek out Cavalier Fabrizio for the purpose described in this article? In what place, who was present, what words did Cavalier Mariotto use and what did Cavalier Fabrizio reply? . . .

Were the letters written to the Magnifica Pratica registered by the coadjutator of the chancellor of their lordships? Were [the witnesses] present and did they see the said letter being written? Where was it written? . . .

Should not an honorable knight and good Christian sooner try to get his father to leave his concubine than to fight or insult [someone] for something that might have been said or done to that concubine? Have there not been many others, who, when something unpleasant happened to their concubine, did not take offense, but instead reproved and punished the concubine so as to avoid coming to blows with anyone on her word? . . .

By what letters did Cavalier Mariotto became convinced, as described in this article, and who brought them to him?

Were they (the witnesses) present at the said fight?

Have they heard it said publicly in Pistoia that Cavalier Mariotto in meeting Cavalier Fabrizio raised his biretta to him in order to determine whether [Cavalier Fabrizio] was wearing an under helmet?

Have they heard it said publicly that Cavalier Mariotto was accompanied by Asdrubale [who was] armed?

Did they hear it said that Asdrubale and Cavalier Mariotto together and at the same time drew their weapons and advanced on Cavalier Fabrizio from behind, and that both, without saying anything, began striking him, and that Cavalier Fabrizio finding himself assaulted in this way by someone who had just declared himself to be a friend by tipping his biretta, had no chance to draw his sword?

Have they heard it said that Tonio di Nardino Bisconti came out of his house armed to help Cavalier Mariotto, who was assaulting Cavalier Fabrizio Bracciolini in front of the house, and threw stones at Cavalier Bracciolini?

Have they heard it said that there were other persons accompanying Cavalier Mariotto?

In the battle of the interrogatories, Fabrizio is losing ground. Against Politi's litany of "truths" about his scandalous behavior, Fabrizio countered with lame denials and ineffectual questions about the bias of defense witnesses. With no new evidence to support his original charges against Mariotto, he is reduced to repeating them, as if repetition will make them more credible. Faced with the Cellesi's damning account of his behavior, he has been forced to take the defensive. In his new set of interrogatories he flatly denies everything alleged by the Cellesi and rehearses the accusations he had made in his original deposition.

But in this weakened hand there is one new card—the honor card. And Fabrizio attacks with it as forcefully as he can. Should an honorable knight seek to insult or fight another knight over a *puttana*, a whore? Should one who claims to be both honorable knight and good Christian try instead to persuade his father to give the woman up? A rhetorical question, and, given that Fabrizio continues to insist he has not made love to Chiara, risky. Worse, it follows the course set by Ser Giovanni: making the case turn on a matter of honor. With Fabrizio's unwitting help, Politi's interrogatories are working a reverse alchemy, transmuting plaintiff into defendant and accused into accuser before the very eyes of the court.

TWELVE

Peacemaking II

> Then come to us, gracious Peace; grasp the corn-
> spike in thy hand, and from the bosom of thy
> white robe let fruits pour out before thee.
> — Tibullus

Since the last round of exchanges between Captain Lanfredino and Jacopo Cellesi on 24 May, peacemaking seems to have ground to a halt. But in November Mariotto's trial began, and Fabrizio was called to Pisa to repeat his charges in a hearing before the Santo Stefano commissioners. At the same time, the peacemaking process was resumed.

Fabrizio Bracciolini to the council of Santo Stefano, 17 November 1578:

My Most Illustrious Signori and Respected Patrons

I was cited here by your illustrious lordships' delegate, the signor commissioner, to make peace or truce with Cavalier Mariotto Cellesi. Obeying at once, my procurator appeared [for me], I being indisposed. On my behalf he replied that I was most ready and willing to make peace; but the other side would not accept, insisting on making a truce for 2,000 scudi [saying that] this is what your illustrious lordships ordered on the basis of the determination made by the magnificent lords of the Pratica Segreta. [My procurator] replied that the said lords would certainly not have ordered this without a determination from your illustrious lordships, and that we knew very well that the said lords of the Pratica had ordered my relatives to the fourth degree to make a truce with Captain Lanfredino for 1,000 scudi.

Moreover, these relatives went to their lordships and freed themselves from the obligation to make a truce. Where matters stand now I don't know; I do not believe anything has been decided since I have not been summoned for anything except by your illustrious lordships. In all justice, then, I ask you for your favor, to demand from me only what is possible and what I am able to do. The local statutes specify that one can only be constrained to a truce for a sum that is within one's means. I will always be fully obedient to do that or whatever I can. I repeat to your illustrious lordships, as I have previously written to the former commissioner whom you delegated to make peace or truce, that I have nothing but my commenda and about half my wife's dowry. Those may serve you in the interest of truth. But if you do not allow me to pledge my commenda for a truce, I don't know what I am to do to find any [other] security. Nowadays—and it has always been so, as I understand—nobody wants to make a guarantee for payment by someone who does not have the means.

Wherefore, my lords, I beg you to permit me to pledge my [commenda], especially since your lordships know that I established it entirely out of generosity, not because I was lacking a quarter or two [of noble blood], which would have prevented me from applying for or receiving this uniform. If you grant me this I will be able to procure the security and make the truce for the normal amount for cavaliers. If your illustrious lordships do not think I should pledge my commenda, at least instruct the signor commissioner to note carefully what I possess and to see that the truce is made according to the laws and statutes. As I said, the other party is not satisfied to make a generous peace.

With this I will close, humbly praying you to have pity for me and consider the reality of the situation I find myself in. I am certain that as you are most just you will have compassion and that you will not want my blood, but what is possible.

For this I will be in your perpetual debt.

Your servant Fabrizio Bracciolini

Positions appear substantially unaltered in the six months since the last exchange: The Cellesi still seem to be setting the bar higher than Fabrizio can jump (nothing more is heard of Mariotto's quixotic gesture of a truce for 25 scudi) and Fabrizio continues to plead poverty and again offers to pledge his commenda. But in another quarter, the wind has shifted: at the Palazzo del Podestà in Pistoia, Bartolomeo Panciatichi has become commissioner after the expiration of Cosimo de'Pazzi's term. The new commissioner seems less disposed to tolerate any more foot-dragging by either side and shows less sympathy for Fabrizio's financial plight than did his predecessor, who was the father of Fabrizio's best friend. He has also replaced Attriano, the suspect notary, with Messer Dionisio Faberio di Gello of Arezzo.

Commissioner Bartolomeo Panciatichi to the council of Santo Stefano, 18 November 1578:

Most Magnificent and Illustrious Signori,

By Evangelista, public messenger of this court, I have had Cavalier Fabrizio Bracciolini notified of the reply of Cavalier Mariotto Cellesi. I have sent to his house everything your illustrious lordships commissioned me to send; nor have I failed to repeat faithfully what each of them has testified, as per your orders.

As for constraining them to make the truce, they do not want to make a peace bond for 2,000 gold scudi, the amount I set on orders from the Magnifica Pratica.[1] I have sent two orders to appear to Cavalier Fabrizio under penalty of 100 scudi and other punishment at my discretion. First he sent word he was sick and that he could in no way make a truce for such a high amount because he had nothing besides the value of his commenda and his wife's dowry and that he wanted to appeal to the illustrious council. Then he sent word that he was riding off.[2] I did not want to make any concessions to him although he did not give me a chance to say so. As I could tell your lordships, I have been very lenient with him.

Here I have found out that the Magnifica Pratica ordered my predecessor to constrain the Bracciolini and Cellesi to make a truce with each other to the fourth degree for a bond of at least 1,000 scudi. The two agreed between them to prevent that from happening, so my predecessor said they should make the truce for 500 scudi. Bracciolini would have done it for that amount, just as he would today, according to someone who has spoken to him. But the Cellesi procurators do not want to do it for a sum less than 1,000 scudi.

Please let me know what you want to be done and whether, if Bracciolini doesn't appear, I should take further action against him. If he weren't a cavalier I would know what to do, but I will do what I am ordered by you and the illustrious council without delay. As I've said, I would not intervene in this without a mandate. This is all that occurs to me to say in reply to yours of the twelfth, received on the twenty-sixth.

Bartolomeo Panciatichi, Commissioner

Commissioner Panciatichi is evidently a man who speaks his mind. Not only does he accuse the two powerful families of conspiring to defeat the efforts of the authorities to bring about a peace, he is also outspoken about the special treatment Mariotto and Fabrizio have had as knights of Santo Stefano. The council responds by giving him the summary order he seeks.

The council of Santo Stefano to Commissioner Bartolomeo Panciatichi, 28 November:[3]

Signore, from your letter to the signor grand prior and the signor grand chancellor, we see what has taken place in the matter of the pending truce between Cavaliers Fabrizio Bracciolini and Mariotto Cellesi. As we are resolved that this be concluded, we would like you, immediately, signore, by a functionary of your court, to order the said Cavalier Fabrizio to obey what has been commanded, informing him that today

Cavalier Mariotto Cellesi for his part has made a truce promising not to give offense to the said Cavalier Bracciolini for a period of three years under bond of 1,000 gold scudi and telling the said Cavalier Bracciolini to do the same. This we have already written and ordered to your predecessor and have repeated to you in three letters from the above-mentioned signor grand prior and grand chancellor, stating that the said Cavalier Fabrizio should give such security to your court as you determine. A true copy of the agreement on security should be sent at the expense of the said cavalier. We await your report on the entire matter. That is all; we offer our good wishes in everything.

Given in Pisa, at our residence, 21 November 1578[4]

The combined pressure of the new commissioner and the council of Santo Stefano seems to have been effective. Both parties now agreed to a truce of 1,000 scudi.

Commissioner Bartolomeo Panciatichi to the council of Santo Stefano, 29 November, 1578:

I did not fail to present at once to Cavalier Fabrizio Bracciolini your command received on the twenty-first by the messenger Vangelista. [Cavalier Bracciolini] appeared before me giving many excuses, saying that he had not obeyed for any other reason than that he had been unable to do so. Finally, today he made the truce and promised not to give offense to Cavalier Mariotto Cellesi for three years with a bond of 1,000 scudi, paid into the treasury of this most illustrious religion, and he presented guarantors who, I am informed, are reliable. My knight has personally drawn up official papers for all of it, a copy of which will be included here.

Bartolomeo Panciatichi

Pleading poverty and faced with the court's displeasure, Fabrizio has managed to convince his reluctant relatives to furnish the entire sum required of him.

The truce between Fabrizio Bracciolini and Mariotto Cellesi, 29 November 1578:

In the name of God, amen. Year of the Incarnation of Our Lord Jesus Christ, 1578, indiction the seventh, 29 November, in the pontificate of Gregory XIII and the reign of His Most Serene Lord Francesco I de'Medici, grand duke of Tuscany. Done in the city of Pistoia in the palace and residence of the lord commissioner at the desk of his knight assistant, in the presence of [names of witnesses] personally appeared Magnificent Signor Fabrizio, son of Messer Francesco Bracciolini . . . ready and willing to conform to orders and decrees of the most magnificent and illustrious cavaliers of the Council of Twelve . . . made a truce with the magnificent lord Mariotto, son of Captain Lanfredino Cellesi . . . promising not to offend or cause to be offended Cavalier Mariotto, either with arms or in person for a period of three years under bond of 1,000 gold scudi to be paid to the treasury of the said Order of Santo Stefano . . . his guarantors promise to pay . . . as follows:

Leonetto, son of the late Guglielmo Bracciolini of Pistoia, 325 scudi;
Giovanni, son of the late Lorenzo Bracciolini of Pistoia, 325 scudi;
Magnificent Signor Cavalier Jacopo, son of Battista Cellesi of Pistoia, 200 scudi;
Signor Filippo, son of the late Filippo Forteguerri of Pistoia, 150 scudi. . . .

I, Dionisio Faberius di Gello of Arezzo, public notary . . . and at present knight assistant to Bartolomeo Panciatichi of Florence, commissioner of Pistoia

One truce does not make a peace, however. As we learn from Fabrizio's rambling interrogatories of 8 December, the struggle for public opinion continues.

Extract from Fabrizio Bracciolini's interrogatories of 8 December, 1578, before the commissioner of Pistoia:

Item, [Fabrizio] says that he did not commission his brother-in-law Cavalier Jacopo Cellesi to write or do anything about peace with the said Captain Lanfredino. . . . If his brother-in-law wrote or did anything, he did it without the knowledge of Cavalier Bracciolini. And if he did write or do anything he did it as an intermediary . . . he also says that when [Mariotto's] procurator offered peace to the court, Cavalier Mariotto had already seen the official testimony of the witnesses because this had been repeated and made known in Asdrubale's case in episcopal court. So if [Mariotto] wanted to make peace, it was to offset suspicion from whatever was damaging to him in that testimony. And as for Messer Giovanni [Politi's] response to the offer of peace (saying that he would accept it as soon as Cavalier Bracciolini admitted the facts), [Cavalier Fabrizio] says that the truth is as he said in his deposition and that if [Messer Giovanni] wanted to make peace he could have done it as easily as making peace in court customarily is. He also says that Messer Giovanni proposed that condition because he wanted to have a reason to reject the peace, just as now he is really rejecting it, knowing the court will not make peace on those conditions any more than it allowed a truce for a bond of 25 scudi.

[Messer Giovanni] says he wants to give satisfaction but the fact is he refuses.

And there the matter was left to stand. A three-year truce has been made, but there is no record of further negotiations toward a permanent peace, nor is there any record that a peace agreement between the Cellesi and Bracciolini over the Holy Thursday affair was ever made. The impasse was due to each family's demand for a moral concession by the other and its refusal to make such a concession in its turn. Neither side spelled out the details of what it expected from the other. Did Captain Lanfredino want Fabrizio to admit that he had seduced Chiara, or only that he had paid court to her, violating the trust and friendship of the Cellesi family? In his interrogatories, Fabrizio continued to insist that he had not made love to Chiara; did he expect the Cellesi to vindicate him on that charge? Or was he after an admission from them that he had fought bravely against unequal odds in the via S. Andrea? Perhaps they were unable to reach an agreement because they were themselves unclear what they wanted, other than that "the world" should acknowledge that all virtue was on their side. And to achieve that prize, each party manipulated the proceedings with surprising ease, frustrating the authorities' efforts to restore and protect public peace.

THIRTEEN

Fabrizio

> To lose one's good name and to squander one's
> inheritance, whatever role you assume, is terrible.
> What difference does it make whether you have
> to do with a matron, a maiden or a prostitute?
> —Horace

Giovanni Politi's interrogatories present the court with a scenario in which the events of Holy Thursday—the sudden flash of naked swords in the street—dissolve back into an eight-month melodrama of intrigue, seduction, and scandal. In Politi's version, the defendant Mariotto Cellesi is a peaceable knight who reluctantly takes up arms to vindicate family honor. The real culprit is the plaintiff Fabrizio, who has betrayed the trust of the Cellesi and shamed them before the eyes of the world, bringing righteous vengeance upon himself. To support this reading, Politi has chosen his witnesses carefully. The sixty-five names on his list include none of the eye witnesses of the fight in the via S. Andrea. For the most part this is a roster of Pistoians who had watched and gossiped as Fabrizio conducted his brazenly open courtship of Chiara. Politi's list includes prostitutes, servants, a bath attendant, *sbirri* of the night watch, a barber, two grocers, artisans, three schoolmasters, merchants, notaries, men of property, and gentlemen of leisure—a long and impressive list designed to show that "everyone" in Pistoia knew about Fabrizio's misbehavior with Captain Lanfredino's woman.

For what Politi wanted, however, barbers and prostitutes made less convincing witnesses than merchants and gentlemen. In the event, out of his roster of sixty-five names, Politi summoned only seventeen to testify. Apart from the *sbirri*, these were almost exclusively Pistoians from the middle and upper ranks of Pistoian society—citizens of the more solid sort. The seven women on the list included the only eye witnesses to the alleged intimacies between Fabrizio and Chiara, yet none of them—servants and prostitutes all—were called. Clearly it was not so much the facts of the case that Politi wanted his witnesses to discuss as their moral judgment on it. The issues, as Politi presented them, were family loyalty, chivalry, and honor, and such values were the business of men, especially men of a certain standing. Their views would carry the most weight with the judges. As well as being respectable and male, those called (again, excepting the *sbirri*) had more than a casual interest in the affair of Fabrizio, Chiara, and the Cellesi and knew a good deal about it. Some were Cellesi and Bracciolini kinsmen and friends who had served the families as go-betweens, would-be peacemakers, and givers of advice, while even those less directly involved were well acquainted with the principal actors in the drama and had closely followed its course.

Questioning of Politi's witnesses had been delegated to the court of the commissioner of Pistoia by special magistrates Vaini and Vivaldi. On 27 November, Bartolomeo Panciatichi, Cosimo de'Pazzi's successor as commissioner, began hearings. Over the next several days, the seventeen witnesses were called and "diligently examined on the articles *[capitoli]* produced on the part of Cavalier Mariotto and on the interrogatories of the opposing part." All said they knew Fabrizio well ("from the time he was born"; "since he was a boy"; "for twenty-eight years—since he was able to tell right from wrong") and to a man—and all, as noted, were men—all avowed they were on good terms with both families, and specifically with Fabrizio.

Asked what they thought of Fabrizio, each gave a favorable reply: "he considers Cavalier Bracciolini to be an honorable knight"; "he regards him to be a man of honor—a gentleman." But in three of these appraisals, we might detect a shade of equivocation: "he considers [Cavalier Fabrizio] to be a person who would do what seems best for himself";[1] "he regards Cavalier Bracciolini to be what he is, he leaves it at that";[2] "he knows Cavalier Fabrizio to be a gentleman *[homo da bene]* and to be what he is."[3]

Witnesses were led through the details of Captain Lanfredino's domestic history (about which all were well informed): the captain's long liaison with Chiara; their cohabitation in his house in the Cellesi compound; Lanfredino's provision of a little house for her in the Campo S. Francesco, where she lived "on his food and drink";[4] the two children born of this connection—Dianora, now "about fifteen," sent to the *suore* of the Convent of S. Caterina di Pistoia with a dowry of 400 scudi, and Raffaello, now "about twelve," privately tutored and lately presented as a candidate for the Order of Santo Stefano with an offer by the captain of a commenda of 5,000 scudi; Mariotto's anger over what he and his brother believed was their father's favoritism for the two illegitimate children and his falling out with Lanfredino. All this, witnesses declared, was "public report and knowledge," known, as one said, to "all Pistoia, or the major part," or, as another put it, "the majority of the men of the city of Pistoia."

"All Pistoia" and "the majority of the men of the city" were more than mere figures of speech, for what all men knew—"common knowledge"—the law accepted as fact. If not *all* Pistoians knew the Cellesi's business, many did—and knew the business of the Bracciolini and of other neighbors as well. *How* they knew is revealed, to some extent, in their responses, since the interrogatories required witnesses to say how they had come by the information to which they testified. From these responses we can learn something about the ways and function of gossip in Pistoia.

In some instances the original source of gossip about the scandal was the Cellesi themselves: Simone di Filippo Battifolle Panciatichi, for one, said it was the captain who told him about his quarrel with his son. Nor were Lanfredino's business associates and notaries closemouthed. Two of the principal sources of gossip about the captain's affairs were Ser Giovanni di Jacopo Fabroni, who had worked for him for years, and Ser Benedetto Catani, who had worked in Captain Lanfredino's house "day and night." Others were Lionardo Visconti, who had been in the captain's house and "many, many times" observed what went on there, and Vincenzio Bracciolini, a regular in the Cellesi household and an important intermediary between the two families. None of the witnesses tell how they knew such facts as the size of Dianora's dowry or Raffaello's potential commenda, probably because this was the kind of semipublic information easy to come by and therefore taken for granted; a man's expenditures for dowry and benefices were a measure of his prestige, and in matters of prestige Captain Lanfredino was never one to miss an opportunity for self-advertisement.

All the avid Cellesi-Bracciolini watchers denied knowing whether Fabrizio had actually slept with Chiara, although Politi tried to get them to say this had taken place (their refusal to claim more knowledge than they had increases the credibility of their testimony on other matters). As to what transpired in Chiara's "little house" on Prato S. Francesco, much of the information originated with Chiara herself and was carried by a different set of informants to a different audience. Although Chiara had fought unsuccessfully to keep her suitor's identity from the court and then steadfastly refused to admit that Fabrizio had gained her bed, she had been less discreet in front of her servants. To a certain extent this was unavoidable. From the beginning, when letters and then gifts were being exchanged, Chiara had had to take others into the conspiracy, if not someone to help her read the letters from Fabrizio that Mariotto had seized from her closet, then very probably someone to help her write her replies.[5] Unable to move about the town freely, she had had to rely on serving women as message carriers and go-betweens, and servants were on hand when she let Fabrizio enter, first her house, then her bedroom. To fra Bartolomeo, her confessor, she turned over Fabrizio's gift of a golden heart for safekeeping at S. Francesco. To a few others she confided intimate details of the affair. Battista di Battista Cellesi, a prime gossip who was a nephew of Captain Lanfredino and related to the Bracciolini as well,[6] testified that "he has understood from Chiara herself that he [Fabrizio] sent embassies to her and used to come to her house at night." And Sforzo di Chiarito was a frequent visitor who knew what was going on and warned her that she was courting trouble. So, if the Cellesi household was at the center of one information circuit—one that was largely male—Chiara's little house at the Prato S. Francesco was at the center of another, both male and female.

A third stream of gossip issued from the palace of the bargello. Walking their rounds about the city, shining their lanterns into the Cellesi compound, fetching Chiara from the captain's bedroom and conducting her to the commissioner's court, the officers and *sbirri* of the bargello's *famiglia* picked up some of the latest and juiciest details of the scandal. Besides, if Caterina is to be believed, the son of Luca del Pierino Rossi, lieutenant of the bargello's guard, was a friend of Fabrizio, and had gone masquerading with him on the night of Carnival. Another member of the bargello's staff, the *sbirro* Francescone, was the host of the Carnival party at which Fabrizio

danced with Chiara. No sense of professional reticence seems to have operated to restrain the police from gossiping. Freely they told other citizens
what they knew about the scandal. When witnesses were asked how they
knew about Chiara's flight from the house of the captain and about Fabrizio's nocturnal serenades in the Cellesi compound, several replied that they
had heard these things from Lieutenant Luca del Capitano Pierino Rossi or
from his *sbirri*, or both.

   With three separate but overlapping circuits of information connecting
the Cellesi compound and the little house on Prato S. Francesco to the community, it did not take long before the reports of the affair of Fabrizio and
Chiara had arrived and were chewed over at the places where Pistoians
gathered—the public squares and city gates, the churches, and the inns and
shops *(botteghe)*, in particular the *bottega* belonging to the avid gossip Simone Talini. When Simone was asked to give the source of his information,
he usually replied that he heard it in his own bottega. It was in the botteghe
that details of the scandal were also heard by, as they told the court, Girolamo Perfedi, Battifolle Panciatichi, Lionardo Visconti, Nofri di Ser Donato
Politi, Anibale Fioravanti, Giuseppe di Piero Fabroni, and others—a dozen
or so men whose names occur repeatedly as informants in the Holy Thursday affair. Other key informants were the grocer Agnolo *(pizzicagnolo)*, the
bellmaker Agnolo *(campanaio)*, and the barbers Giuseppe di Nello and Master Lodovico. On his way home, the carpenter *(legniuolo)* Jacopo Chiti saw
the young gentlemen of Pistoia gathering to greet friends and snub enemies
at Lodovico's, and also, apparently, at an adjacent tavern. Alessandro del
Capitano Giovanbatista Bichi and the workers in his *fabbrica*, a shoemaking
factory, used to see Fabrizio walk around and stand near Chiara's house at
various times of the night and day, and they saw (once? often?) "a Genovese
woman" go to Chiara's house, then come out and talk with the cavalier. One
day his workers told Bichi, Giovanni Fabroni, and others that they had seen
Chiara running off to the house of Biondo, located near the factory.

   People-watching and gossiping seem to have been a pastime indulged in
by Pistoians of every stamp. At the center of a constantly renewing supply
of information, shopkeepers were impresarios of news, key agents in the
exchange and circulation of gossip, with access to more sources and to more
incoming and outgoing carriers than almost any other kinds of townspeople, with the possible exception of the police.[7]

Simone Battifolle Panciatichi said the place where he had heard so much talk of Fabrizio's courtship of Chiara—of the letters, embassies, and vigils— was the Porta Vecchia, or Old Gate (which we already know by its official designation as the Porta Lucchese).[8] As Simone recalled, this had been at the beginning of Lent, and a lot of young men were there. Another gathering place for Pistoian *giovani* was the Piazza, or Prato, of the Church of S. Francesco. Chiara's "little house" was on the north side of the prato, near the cemetery that extended toward the Porta al Borgo, so strollers in the green park of the piazza were well placed to observe Fabrizio's amatory coming and goings. Lionardo Visconti, for one, had seen Fabrizio at the Prato S. Francisco "many, many times during the day and at every hour," as well as having heard about his courtship of Chiara from others for more than six months before the Holy Thursday incident. "Many times, by day and at any hour whatever, whenever Chiara was staying at S. Francesco in the house set up for her by Captain Lanfredino, Giuseppe Fabroni saw Cavalier Bracciolini by the house; he would stand still or walk about as he chose. . . . This went on for more than six months."

Whether passing by or strolling about the Prato S. Francesco, one could not only see Fabrizio near Chiara's house but even hear him broadcast his defiance: Nofri di Ser Donato Politi reported that "many times, during the past December, if he remembers correctly, he heard Cavalier Fabrizio Bracciolini in the Prato S. Francesco say, 'If anyone asks for me tell them you've seen me here; I'll be here until the Ave Maria,' and one time I heard him [say it] in the Canto Bracciolini."

Alessandro Bichi: "One day, it was the sixth of Carnival, if he remembers accurately, as Cavalier Fabrizio was passing the Porta Vecchia there were a lot of young men there, particularly Piero Tolomei, Meo Buonaiuti, Stefano Panciatichi, Simone Battifolle Panciatichi, Sandro Finugi, Cecchino del Cappellina, the witness, and many others, [and Fabrizio] said 'Anyone who wants me, I'll be at the Prato S. Francesco; I'll stay there; I'm there often enough so that anyone who wants me can find me there; I'm not afraid of any toughs'—and other words to that effect."

In December, Mariotto, returning from galley service, began hearing the gossip about his fellow cavalier's attentions to his father's woman. When Mariotto confronted him, Fabrizio denied he was pursuing Chiara and protested his friendship and respect for the captain. Mariotto chose to accept Fabrizio's word and rejected family efforts to get him to intervene: "Let the matter [of Chiara] alone; that's my father's business," he told Battista Cellesi. Mariotto was a peaceloving man, so Politi claimed in his interrogatories, and witnesses agreed: "Quiet, and one who minds his own business and goes out of his way to make peace and resolve difficulties; he was even known to calm other men who had been fighting."

Someone less partisan than Ser Giovanni Politi or his carefully selected witnesses might have been tempted to make an aside here: perhaps Mariotto's peacemaking was selective; a peasant suspected of poaching Mariotto's hare could expect the difficulty to be resolved by a beating, while resentment, rather than a peaceloving nature, we recall, had been Mariotto's explanation for his reluctance to take up his father's quarrel with Fabrizio. He had been too angry with his father for favoring Chiara's two bastards over himself and Teodoro, especially in a matter involving the interloper Chiara. At any rate, Mariotto's ready acceptance of his denial seems to have emboldened Fabrizio to ever more egregious behavior, setting himself on a collision course with the increasingly embarrassed and outraged Cellesi family.

Before Lent was over, Fabrizio gained entry to Chiara's little house at Prato S. Francesco, and there—if Mona Francesca (Ceccha) del Bagno was to be believed—he graduated from heartsick suitor to triumphant lover. Shortly afterwards, furious at reports of Chiara's Carnival escapade, although as yet uncertain of her infidelity, Captain Lanfredino locked her up in his house. Fabrizio then transferred his nocturnal vigils to the Castel Cellesi itself, signaling his contempt for the captain's impotence (and perhaps for Mariotto's inaction, too) by singing and playing underneath the Cellesi windows. In his interrogatories, Fabrizio improbably claimed that these antics had nothing to do with Chiara or the Cellesi but were an innocent diversion, declaring that the Cellesi houses were situated in a public piazza where people could pass day and night. In a strictly technical sense this was true, witnesses agreed, but as Simone Battifolle Panciatichi pointed out: "This is not a common street; there are no other houses there but those of the Cellesi; you can pass that way but it isn't usual, and there are hinges at the sides [of the entrances] so they can put up gates closing the Piazza off [to street traffic] if they want to."

Jacopo di Bartolomeo di Bastiano Cellesi lived near the Castel Cellesi:

"People who want to can pass through Piazzetta de Cellesi in front of Captain Lanfredino's house, but at night they usually do not do so unless they're going to the houses of the Cellesi." Yes, Jacopo had heard the racket from his house—"many, many times last year in the nighttime, and particularly one night of Passion Week, although he couldn't remember what day it was precisely; he heard several people singing and playing in the Cellesi enclosure, particularly in front of the house of Cavalier Mariotto, or of Captain Lanfredino; "they're next to each other," but he didn't know who they were nor could he make out the words; he was in bed and did not get up to see.

With Fabrizio openly serenading Chiara in front of her patron's residence and with "all Pistoia" observing and reporting every move, the captain was becoming frantic to restrain her and to end his humiliation. Peaceloving or not, Mariotto could no longer ignore what was going on not only under his father's window but under his own as well. Fabrizio's friends were well aware that the matter was coming to a head. About a month before the Holy Thursday incident, Vincenzio Bracciolini told Giovanni Fabroni that he and other members of the family had warned Fabrizio to leave off his affair with Chiara because it would lead to trouble, but the cavalier had no regard for their warnings. Vincenzio also told Battista Cellesi and Francesco Perfedi that about two weeks before the fight, in front of the communal school, he had warned Fabrizio not to walk in front of Chiara's house lest trouble arise, "and he [Fabrizio] laughed and jeered at me." Vincenzio urged Battista to try to intervene. (Poor Vincenzio was caught in the crossfire between the two families. After the fight had taken place he visited the captain, who was ill in bed, only to be chastised by Lanfredino because he "had not shown any sign of friendship in the matter." "I don't know what to tell you," Vincenzio replied, "except that I begged Cavalier Bracciolini time and again. Finally I prayed to him with my arms stretched out in the form of a cross to leave off this business. He answered that he didn't need a tutor and that I should go say my paternosters or read my breviary.")[9]

To Cellesi-Bracciolini watchers, an explosion seemed imminent: "About eight days before the quarrel and fight between Cavaliers Mariotto and Fabrizio," said Lionardo Visconti, "it was feared that something scandalous would happen between them, seeing that they weren't greeting each other as they used to do, and people were watching, expecting that at any moment they might fight." Lionardo's testimony was echoed by Simone Battifolle Panciatichi, Battista Cellesi, Giuseppe Fabroni, Nofri Politi, Alessandro Bichi, Ser Giovanni Fabroni, and Fabio Cellesi, each naming others with whom they had watched and together with whom they had felt the tension of the two cavaliers as they passed each other in cold and unaccustomed silence—the feeling between them having become "aggravated," as Ser Giovanni Fabroni put it.[10]

Everyone watched them intently—"as soon as they were seen in the street," said Giuseppe Fabroni—and followed them, expecting to see a fight at any moment. Alessandro Bichi confirmed this: "From Palm Sunday on, the Cavaliers Fabrizio and Mariotto didn't salute each other as they used to do, and when people saw them some of them watched them and some followed them to see." "All Pistoia" gossiped, watched, and shadowed the two antagonists in the street, framing and explicating the action like a chorus in ancient Greek drama.[11] The constant, relentless, presence of spectators breathlessly awaiting a fight made it difficult for either man to back away from a showdown and still keep his dignity. Besides, Mariotto could no more resist playing to his audience than Fabrizio, whom we have already heard defying his critics and boasting that he would fight anyone who sought him out. Mariotto, too, according to Alessandro Bichi, began to talk about fighting, declaring that "he intended to draw against Cavalier Fabrizio Bracciolini as soon as he was sure of the discourtesy that he had done to his father."

Not all bystanders were content merely to watch and wait and dog the two cavaliers' footsteps in the street. Some talked and exchanged views with the actors, and, like the ancient Greek choristers, stepped in and out of the drama, taking a more direct part in the action by pressing the players to play their parts. Simone Battifolle Panciatichi was one of these: "Many times he saw Cavalier Fabrizio Bracciolini going and standing there [at Chiara's house], and on one of those days he was passing by there with Cavalier Mariotto and he said to him, 'Cavalier Fabrizio wants to make it with your stepmother,' and Cavalier Mariotto replied to the witness, 'I don't believe it; I talked to him about it and he told me that he's after another woman who lives nearby, and that he'd respect him [my father] and wouldn't do such a thing, on his honor.'"[12]

Likewise the shopkeeper Simone Talini: "One day during Carnival, finding himself with Cavalier Mariotto in his bottega, [Simone] jokingly asked him 'What's going on with your stepmother?' meaning the said Chiara. And the cavalier replied, 'Why do you ask?' Whereupon Simone answered, 'Because I hear she's making love with Cavalier Fabrizio Bracciolini.' And Cavalier Mariotto replied, 'It's not true,' [saying] Cavalier Fabrizio had told him he was making love with another woman who lives nearby."[13]

In explaining to the court why he had sought Fabrizio out to fight, Mariotto did not mention these painful conversations. A chivalric knight ought not to have to be prodded by his neighbors to take up arms on behalf of his family's honor. But how that coarse teasing must have rankled! To hear his father's whore (as he now called her) mockingly referred to as his stepmother was bad enough, but to hear from others what he had refused to admit even to himself—that Chiara was cuckolding his father with Fabrizio, a family friend and fellow cavalier—must have been more than Mariotto could bear. Could Battifolle Panciatichi and Talini have expected otherwise? Was not their teasing sure to shame and enrage him? Were they merely amusing themselves and their friends at Mariotto's expense? Or, by pricking Mariotto with the sharp truths he had been dodging since December, did they intend to goad him into action?

Politi's interrogatories were designed to demonstrate what "all Pistoia" thought about the behavior of Fabrizio and Mariotto. Naturally, Politi wanted answers favorable to his client, so his questions invited witnesses to register their disapproval of Fabrizio's conduct—to say that, as he himself put it, it was "sinister and evil, untoward and shameful, contrary to every obligation of reason and civility, and scandalous"—and to approve the response of Mariotto, a peaceful and quiet knight, who had acted justifiably and appropriately: "Any gentleman soldier and honorable knight whose father is powerless to revenge himself for an injury done to him is obligated by his honor and the code of chivalry to defend and repay the injury to his father. Otherwise he will be held an unworthy cavalier."

Fabrizio could not afford to heap ridicule on the code of honor appealed to by Mariotto. As a *gentiluomo* and fellow cavalier of Santo Stefano, he professed to live by the same rules; but he could try to hoist Mariotto by his own petard, by arguing that Mariotto's sense of honor was defective, his action un-Christian. The irregularity of Captain Lanfredino's relationship with

Chiara, together with Mariotto's championing of it, was a weak spot in the armor of chivalry with which he justified his behavior on Holy Thursday, and Fabrizio directed his thrust right there, charging that in taking up arms in vindication of his father's dishonorable union, Mariotto dishonored himself as well. "Should an honorable knight fight over a *puttana* (a whore)?"[14]

If this seems to us a brazenly hypocritical question to be asked by the man—himself married and a father—who for eight months had courted this same *puttana* day and night as his lady love, and who, according to his cousin Vincenzio, had repulsed Vincenzio's efforts to persuade him to stop courting Chiara by mocking him as a breviary-reading, paternoster-prattling meddler, Politi's witnesses nonetheless treated it seriously. But their responses could not have given Fabrizio much satisfaction.

Simone Battifolle Panciatichi: "An honorable knight would fight another knight over a whore depending on circumstances; in his judgment it was an honorable thing to do, according to circumstances as he already said. . . . If he had a father who was incapacitated and had been wronged he would fight for him and defend him. . . . He knows this because he's wellborn and he believes that every person of honor would do the same . . . in this city and in every honorable place . . . whenever the occasion called for it . . . and by all men of honor."[15] As to the Christian alternative suggested by Fabrizio: "It's a good thing to try to get one's father to leave his concubine and this witness would do it, but if he were living with a father who was crippled while his concubine was misbehaving, he would do for him what his father would do for himself if he were able.

Lionardo (who went by the nicknames Nardino and il Bonzetta—which may refer to a kettle) Visconti was characteristically ambiguous: "It seems to me that they fought over a whore and that the quarrel between these two cavaliers arose over a whore. He [Lionardo—the interrogatory uses the third person] doesn't know whether it is honorable and appropriate for an honorable knight to go fight someone over a whore, because he knows nothing about dueling." Still, Nardino thought that "every gentleman soldier and honorable knight whose father is powerless and crippled and suffers a wrong is obligated to repulse that wrong to his father and express resentment on his behalf. If he did otherwise he would not be held to be an honorable knight. . . . It's honorable and the work of a good Christian to get his father to leave his concubine, but it's right to take offense on behalf of a father's honor on account of insults to a concubine . . . that's all he knows about it."

Battista Cellesi believed it was a question for the experts: "He believes that this is a case of a duel, so it doesn't belong to this witness to give a judgment on it."

Simone Talini had no such reservations. "He believes that an honorable knight is obliged to fight with another knight over a whore for whatever wrong is done to her or to a father who is incapacitated . . . it's permissible in every respect for a cavalier to fight over a whore or for any other case in which he is injured. In Sicily and Naples he has seen cavaliers fight over matters connected with whores."

Giuseppe di Piero Fabroni thought an honorable knight would fight another knight over a whore when there were important and pressing matters at stake. Giovanni di Jacopo Fabroni was more emphatic: "Every honorable knight, when an injury was done to him over a whore or over anything else, would fight another knight. And he believes that an honorable knight is allowed to fight another knight over a whore or for any other reason so long as it is in a just cause."

Girolamo Perfedi was only slightly more cautious: "He doesn't believe that an honorable knight should fight another knight on account of a whore without good reason."

Similarly Fabio Cellesi: "To fight on account of a whore is appropriate in the right circumstances."

But to Francesco Mannani of Bagni di Lucca, Politi's last, and socially least, witness,[16] debates on chivalry were as remote as questions of theology or physics. "He is a simple person, Francesco protests, he doesn't know what honor is, what it isn't, because he is a bath attendant and doesn't have anything to do with these punctilios."[17]

This latest exchange in the battle of interrogatories clearly favored Mariotto. His counselor had parried Fabrizio's thrust and delivered a sharp counterblow: almost to a man, Giovanni Politi's witnesses approved Mariotto's action in defense of the Cellesi honor, turning aside Fabrizio's appeal to Christian conscience. Struggling to retake the high ground, Fabrizio returned to his original contention that Mariotto had attacked him without provocation or warning, betraying their long-standing friendship. On the

very day before Holy Thursday, he claimed, he had been exchanging pleas-
antries with Mariotto and other friends. Giannozzo Pazzi, his companion-
about-town, would, he was sure, corroborate this. Unfortunately, Giannozzo was unavailable (confined to Elba for some transgression of his own
or, perhaps, sent out of the way by his father, the former commissioner?)
and the deposition Fabrizio had requested of him is nowhere to be found in
the record. Without it, Fabrizio had only the statement of a passer-by, the
carpenter Jacopo di Lorenzo Chiti.

Called on 3 December, Chiti acknowledged that he frequently saw Messer
Giannozzo de'Pazzi and Cavalier Fabrizio together, but he saw them only
during the day; he did not go out after dark. On Holy Wednesday he had
been drinking in the shop of Matteo del Borgo. Passing by the fishmonger's
shop on his way home, he saw Messer Giannozzo, Cavalier Fabrizio, and
Cavalier Mariotto in Maestro Lodovico's barbershop and tipped his biretta.
Yes, Chiti affirmed, Maestro Lodovico's shop was a meeting place for young
noblemen, both friends and enemies. It was about fourteen paces from the
bargello's headquarters, adjacent to the commissioner's palace and to the
houses of the Bracciolini. Fabrizio's doorway was visible from there. On that
day, all the shops in the neighborhood were open and people were at their
doorways. "It seemed to me they [Fabrizio, Giannozzo, and Mariotto] were
joking; two of them were seated, but I didn't notice which."

Chiti's equivocal testimony was unlikely to help Fabrizio erase the image
of the two glowering cavaliers silently passing each other in the street, an
image previously etched into the court's memory by Nardino Visconti, Simone Battifolle Panciatichi, Battista Cellesi, and so many others.

The next move was Politi's. Brandishing a thick new sheaf of interrogatories, Ser Giovanni took aim at Fabrizio's story of the Holy Thursday attack
itself, for although the testimony of Fabrizio's own eye witnesses had rent
the fabric of his original deposition, enough of it remained to be seriously
damaging to Mariotto. These remnants Politi now moved to strip away.
After that he would stitch together a version more suitable to the figure of
Mariotto as honorable knight.

Ser Giovanni launched his attack on Fabrizio's story by alleging a pattern
of witness-tampering. Polita, Maria, and the others were called upon to disclose how they had been alternately cajoled and bullied by Fabrizio and his

allies to support his deposition, then threatened with humiliation, prison, even the rack, if they dared to change their initial stories. In particular (the interrogatories alleged) Fabrizio had told them not to say that Mariotto and his allies had called out to him before attacking, and he promised "to do something good for them" if they corroborated his story that Tonio had been present at the fight and that Asdrubale and two soldiers had taken part in the attack. And afterward, did Cavalier Fabrizio not summon one of them and say, "Go on, get out, you didn't want to say that Tonio di Nardino was there," and did this witness not say, "It's enough for you that I said that Asdrubale jumped on him, too?" Moreover, did not Fabrizio warn them to keep from mentioning that he and Giannozzo, the son of the former commissioner of Pistoia, were inseparable?[18]

This was not the first time, nor the only way, Ser Giovanni intimated, that Polita and Maria had been at the disposal of the Bracciolini. What business, he asked, did Vincenzio Bracciolini have with them that brought him to their house almost every day and night? Could they have been unaware that Vincenzio was blood cousin to Cavalier Fabrizio and that he was heir to Fabrizio's commenda [in Santo Stefano]? Wouldn't they carry out "any kind of service" for love of Cavalier Fabrizio, and in fact had they not done so? And before they were summoned by the court, did Vincenzio not ask them to say that Asdrubale, Cavalier Mariotto, Tonio di Nardino, and two other soldiers ganged up on Cavalier Fabrizio? Was it not true, as Vincenzio Bracciolini boasted, that he had had both Polita and Maria? And what of the boasts of both Cavalier Fabrizio and Messer Giannozzo Pazzi that they, too, had used Polita sexually?

Lest witness-tampering and collusion were not enough to undermine Fabrizio's charges, Politi had one more arrow to fire off from his quiver of interrogatories. Having previously elicited from some of his seventeen witnesses' testimony that Fabrizio and the court notary were friends, he now brought a new allegation into play: as they gave their statements, he asked, had Polita, Maria, and the others not observed that the notary was writing down things they had not actually said?

Ser Giovanni was now ready to float his own version of the fight. From their vantage point in the doorway of S. Andrea (his next series of interrogatories asked), could the women not see that when Cavalier Mariotto said "Draw!"

or "Grab your sword!" he was face-to-face with Cavalier Fabrizio just beyond the well opposite the Visconti house? And as soon as Cavalier Mariotto said "Draw!" to Cavalier Fabrizio, did they not see Fabrizio turn back
on the same street from the direction he had come—about two stone's
throws? Did Cavalier Mariotto not run after him striking at him as far as the
door of S. Andrea? And, after retreating, did not Cavalier Fabrizio turn, and
as he did so, with his sword in his hand, was he not wounded in the face by
Cavalier Mariotto? At this point, with Fabrizio defenseless, his head bare,
sword down, hand to wounded nose, too dispirited to call for help from bystanders, did the witnesses not agree that Mariotto could have killed him
had he wanted to do so?

Had Maria not deposed in the vicar's court that she had only been able
to see two swords in the air and had seen Cavalier Fabrizio with his hand on
his nose? Had Sandra not deposed the same, and admitted that she neither
saw, knew, nor recognized Cavalier Mariotto or Asdrubale? A fair fight, face-
to-face, one-on-one, with a particularly chivalric outcome? Politi's interrogatories turned the charges against his client on their head. But it was one
thing to assert that Fabrizio had tried to suborn Polita, Maria, Camilla, and
the others, another to prove that they did not see what they said they had
seen—one thing to allege witness-tampering, another to prove that perjury
had been committed to support a fabricated story.

Neither Polita nor Maria could be moved. "I've been examined twice,"
said Polita, "once in the [commissioner's] palace and once in the episcopal
[palace], and I told the truth; I wasn't afraid and I'm not afraid of being
punished." Warned, she said, "I told the truth the first time and the second
time and again now; I wasn't threatened or bullied by the judge's former
notary. He told me to say the truth of what I had seen. When you read me
what the notary wrote, I'll know whether that is what I said. No one sought
me out before I was examined and nothing was said to me by anyone."

Mona Maria was equally steadfast: "I can't say anything but what I said
the first time. I'm not afraid of anything. [I] wasn't bullied or threatened;
[the notary] asked us what we saw and we told him." No, no one tried to
examine her before she was summoned, and Cavalier Fabrizio never spoke
to her. "Neither Cavalier Fabrizio nor anyone else sought me out for anything either before or afterward. I wasn't there [at the fight] at the beginning; when I arrived they had finished and at the stairs of S. Andrea I saw

bare swords in the hands of Cavalier Mariotto and Asdrubale. I didn't see when Cavalier Mariotto wounded Cavalier Fabrizio in the face nor when he confronted Cavalier Fabrizio and I didn't see anyone at the well in the direction of the Church of S. Francesco." She had been examined twice and she always said the same thing in the same way and she wasn't afraid at all.

No, said Polita, Vincenzio Bracciolini does not frequent her house and has nothing to do with her or her mother. She knows he is one of the Bracciolini but that's all she knows. Nothing alleged in Politi's interrogatories was true and she knew nothing other than what she had said. Maria concurred: "She's never seen Vincenzio Bracciolini in her house and he has no business with her nor with her daughter. She knows he is of the Bracciolini clan (*casata*), but that's all she knows. If Vincenzio or others boasted that they had had her, they did not tell the truth—but she didn't know what to say about Polita before she was married. That's all she knows."

Having extracted no admission of wrongdoing from either Polita or Maria, the court now read back to each of them in turn their statements of the preceding March. Here some of Politi's allegations against the court notary found their mark.

"Everything [in the transcript] was as she had said," Polita insisted, with one exception:

She did not say that Cavalier Fabrizio had been struck before he drew his sword, although she did see Cavalier Mariotto and Asdrubale strike two or three times with bare swords, and at the last Cavalier Fabrizio putting a hand to his face and backing off. And Cavalier Mariotto went toward the house of the Pappagalli and Asdrubale followed, and Cavalier Fabrizio walked off, his head hanging down. She did not say that she saw Asdrubale talk to Cavalier Fabrizio, but that all three were holding weapons and all the rest of the examination is true, point for point.

Nor did she hear [Mariotto say] "Draw!" While she was on the stairs in front of S. Andrea, she saw all three with naked swords in hand and saw Cavalier Fabrizio put his hand on his face, just as she had said. At this Cavalier Mariotto looked at him and went off toward S. Francesco. Yes, he could have killed him if he had wanted to; there wasn't anyone else near the well [to come to his rescue].

No one else attacked Cavalier Fabrizio. At the stairs of S. Andrea there were Cavalier Mariotto and Cavalier Fabrizio with drawn swords and Asdrubale with a bare storta in his hand, but she only saw Asdrubale strike out, not wound, Cavalier Fabrizio. All three had their swords out and were mixing it up but she didn't see who hit Cavalier Fabrizio.

Mother Maria also noted some discrepancies between her original testimony and the notary's record. She did not see Cavalier Mariotto and Asdrubale wound Cavalier Fabrizio, nor strike at him. "We did say that we saw them and I in particular said that I saw Cavalier Mariotto and Cavalier Fabrizio with swords in hand on the stairs of S. Andrea and Asdrubale with the scimitar and they were all swinging them around in the air and we didn't see who struck or wounded Cavalier Fabrizio. But I did see him all at once put his hand to his face and move away and go off with his head down and Cavalier Mariotto looked at him and got his cape and went off. But I didn't pay attention to Asdrubale. This is the truth and it's what I said last time."

Even the flighty Camilla stood by her initial testimony. "I'm not afraid and I told the truth and I wouldn't take anything back; what I said once I'll always maintain." No one had sought her out to question her before she received the summons of the court. Cavalier Fabrizio told her nothing, nor had anyone else said anything to her. She had been examined three times, once by the court of the last commissioner, once in Florence, and once by the vicar of the bishop, and she said the same thing each time—just what she had seen. She did not hear Cavalier Mariotto say "Draw!" She did not remember if Cavalier Fabrizio turned back. She was at S. Andrea when Cavalier Fabrizio was struck on the face by Cavalier Mariotto. He attacked Cavalier Fabrizio just above the well toward S. Andrea—no, S. Francesco. That's all she knew.

But Camilla's reexamination did yield some damning testimony against Ser Attriano, the notary. Yes, the judge's former notary threatened to put her in prison and bullied her, but despite that she had told the truth. When her testimony was reread to her, she said everything in it was true—except that she did not see the son of Nardino il Bonzetta come out of his house.

With Luca Pazzaglia, Fabrizio's most reliable and impressive witness, Politi's allegations made no headway. Luca denied that he had been frightened or threatened and insisted he had told the truth—he would always tell the truth because that's the right thing. He had no information, either about the notary, or Messer Giannozzo de'Pazzi or Cavalier Fabrizio; he minded his own business. He had not been approached by anyone before his first examination and the notary had written down what he said. He had been examined twice, once by the judge's former notary, once by the vicar of monsignor, and he told the truth in the same way both times.

Luca had not been able to judge the respective positions of the two cavaliers (in the fight) because he had turned his back to them. He had heard some words but could not make out who said them or what they said. "It was true that after these words were spoken, the Cavalier [Bracciolini] turned back the way he had come and had gone about two stone's throws, and that Cavalier Mariotto ran after him striking him until they were opposite the door of S. Andrea, and it's true that when Cavalier Fabrizio turned with his sword, Cavalier Mariotto gave him the blow in the face. The place where Cavalier Mariotto attacked Cavalier Fabrizio was at the door of Piero Calosi, and Cavalier Fabrizio was wounded in front of the Church of S. Andrea, a little distance away.

Yes, Cavalier Mariotto could have killed Cavalier Fabrizio had he wanted to because Fabrizio was wounded in the face and had his hand on it. There was no one else at the well in the direction of S. Francesco who could have gone to Cavalier Fabrizio's rescue. That's all he knew."

When his initial testimony was read to him, Luca confirmed all of it, saying that Cavalier Fabrizio had drawn his sword at the stairs of S. Andrea and, in turning with his sword in hand, Cavalier Mariotto's blow struck him in the face.

Politi had his greatest success with ten-year-old Rinaldo di Alidonio, the last of the eye witnesses to be reexamined, on 8 December. He had no fear of being punished, Rinaldo declared; he would tell the truth. Yes, he was threatened by the former notary of the judge and bullied about being put in prison, but he had told the truth then and would tell it now. Before Rinaldo was summoned to testify, Cavalier Fabrizio called for him and asked him if he had seen the fight and he replied that he had and had heard Cavalier Mariotto say "Draw!" and strike a blow from behind. The cavalier [Fabrizio] told him not to say that he heard [Mariotto] say "Draw!" "And he asked me if I'd seen Tonio del Bonzetta and I said that he wasn't there, and the cavalier told me to say [Tonio] had thrown a stone and he threatened [me, saying] that if I didn't I'd be put in prison and be cudgeled." When Rinaldo's earlier testimony was read to him, he said it was true, except that Cavalier Mariotto did say "Draw!" to Cavalier Fabrizio and that although he did not see Asdrubale strike blows, he was holding a storta. Then Luca Pazzaglia had passed, and Rinaldo did not know who tipped birettas to whom. All the rest was true, as he had first testified.

. . .

Now that Politi's witnesses have been examined, and the eye witnesses re-examined, by Commissioner Bartolomeo Panciatichi in Pistoia, the special commissioners of the Order of Santo Stefano allow Mariotto and his procurator to appear before them in Pisa to sum up their defense. On 6 December, Politi leads off. He appears, he says, not with the intention of offending Cavalier Fabrizio, but only to defend his client—a formulaic disclaimer after which he launches into a blatantly ad hominem attack.

Everything Cavalier Bracciolini claims in his deposition and in his testimony in court against the defendant has been a calumny. The Magnifica Pratica has concluded that he suborned witnesses and that he falsely accused Antonio Visconti. The vicar of Pistoia has concluded that he wrongly accused the priest Asdrubale, while the injuries and grievance he has caused to Captain Lanfredino and his son have been proved by the testimony of his own relatives and the evidence of letters in his own hand. He has been shown to be a boaster and a liar; is it believable, as he says in his deposition, that if he were attacked from behind by five men without being able to draw his sword he would have fled toward his attackers, in a direction where there was no one [to help him], as he himself admitted? Is it believable that being attacked and struck by five men he valorously (as he claims) escaped from their midst unhurt, or that finally turning around to match blows with all of them he was wounded only by a single blow in the face, or that he called them to come back to fight?

The truth, according to Politi, is that his client met Fabrizio face-to-face and called upon him to draw his sword, that Asdrubale alone, unarmed, stood by. Indeed, if Fabrizio was holding his nose with his left hand and leaning on his sword to support himself with his right, his eyes covered with blood, how could he have called out to his client to fight? Instead, why did he not, since they were in mid city, call out for help and justice?[19]

The truth, moreover, is that Bracciolini set in motion an ugly inquest on the basis of a prejudicial deposition taken by less than neutral officials[20] and suborned witnesses to give false testimony. [Fabrizio] even tried to block the conclusion of a peace agreement, while Cavalier Mariotto has always been ready to accept a peace, on condition that Cavalier Bracciolini admit the falsity of his accusation and agree not to offend his client or his father any more. For these reasons, both in his deposition and in his appearance in court, Cavalier Fabrizio has been entirely a stranger to the truth; he has disturbed the peace and quiet; his client, for reasons altogether just, called upon him to fight and wounded him in the manner of an honorable knight.

· · ·

Availing himself of the opportunity to have the last word, Mariotto followed Politi with a statement of his own. "It is not correct," he said, "to say that an honorable knight shouldn't fight for a woman."

He [using the third person] fought for all the reasons he gave in his deposition and demonstrated in the processo, as would any cavalier who does not measure himself with a Corfù compass or does not leave his women in the care of other men.[21] His adversary has woven a tissue of negations, which he, Mariotto, will unravel:

It is incorrect to say that the sentence [in the trial of] of priest Asdrubale is not valid, because he [Fabrizio] didn't make counterarguments against it. In the processo, [Fabrizio's] counterargument that priest Asdrubale is a man of evil life who was obliged to repay four years of income in excess of 700 scudi that he had received from the parish church was [judged] without merit. . . .

It is not correct to say that the sentence of the Magnifica Pratica [dropping the charges against Tonio Visconti and Captain Lanfredino] is irrelevant, because trials before supreme and royal magistrates especially commissioned by His High Lordship [the grand duke], and imprisonments that result therefrom, enjoy extraordinary and exquisite credibility.[22]

However, Mariotto continued to argue, considerably less than exquisite credibility should be given to the proceedings of the court of the commissioner of Pistoia. Maria di Giovanni Lombardo and her daughter Polita were not worthy of belief, because they were, and continued to be, "persons of public evil life and reputation and infamous women." Rinaldo d'Alidonio ought not to be admitted as a witness nor even questioned, because he was a minor. Camilla di Piero, the saddle maker, was infamous and had been punished as a falsifier. Besides, all four of these witnesses were suborned by Fabrizio and his cousin, the priest, as had been established by the hearings of the Pratica Segreta and of the vicar of Pistoia. When they were examined by those judges, all four gave different, confused, and contradictory replies, pretending they could not remember and admitting that they had told lies in favor of and by the subornation of his adversary and of the court of Pistoia. [At the same time] they unanimously deposed that they had not said what the notary had written down.

Next Mariotto took aim at Luca Pazzaglia. Self-confident, Mariotto's social equal, Luca was the only eye witness whose story remained unshaken and uncompromised, and his was the testimony most damaging to Mariotto. Until this moment, no one had dared impugn his truthfulness, but

Mariotto had much to gain and little to lose. "No credence should be given to what Luca Pazzaglia said in his testimony because monsignor [the vicar] of Pistoia did not do so.[23] . . . [Luca] is the sole witness who is doubtful, variable, and uncertain in his depositions, one from the other . . . and he is believed to say what is favorable to Bracciolini and unfavorable to [Mariotto]. He has not been cited as a corroborating witness by any of the other witnesses."

After this blithely inaccurate characterization of both Luca and his testimony, Mariotto takes up Fabrizio's declaration that he knew of no reason for the Holy Thursday attack and that he and Giannozzo de'Pazzi had been talking and joking with Mariotto in Lodovico's barbershop only the day before the attack. This Mariotto flatly denies: he had neither seen the two at Lodovico's or even passed or stopped there during all of Holy Week. Never mind that Jacopo Chiti said he had observed him together with Fabrizio from his place in the Canto de' Bracciolini; nobody should believe the confused and lying testimony of innkeepers;[24] they have to attend to the comings and goings of their customers, while all around them is the confusion created by the young men who hang about in those places.

In alleging misconduct by the Pistoia commissioner's notary, Mariotto brings into the open what had previously been only hinted at—the suspicion that the Pistoia investigations were tainted not only by Fabrizio's alleged efforts to suborn witnesses but by his friendship with some of the investigating officials: "*all* the other proceedings before the court of Pistoia . . . those proceedings should not have and ought not be given any credence whatsoever because of the great familiarity of that court with Cavalier Bracciolini and because of the private interest that the court manifested in the case." By "the private interest" of the court, Mariotto is pointing the finger not just at the notary who received whispered messages from Fabrizio's servant, but also at that man's superior, former Commissioner Cosimo de'Pazzi. The commissioner's son Giannozzo, we recall, was Fabrizio's companion-about-town and participated in the serenade at the Cellesi compound. Had the allegedly dishonest notary been acting on the orders of the commissioner in tampering with the record? Did Messer Cosimo have anything to do with Giannozzo's timely removal to Elba?[25] Mariotto did not need to prove his allegations or to explain just how the commissioner may have tainted the *processo*; it was enough to indicate that "the suborning and intimidating of witnesses" and "the special familiarity and interest" of the Pistoia officials were the reasons that had moved his father to petition the grand duke for a change of venue for the processo, and that the change was granted. The grand duke's concession spoke for itself.

In summary, Mariotto declares, "Bracciolini has proven nothing of what he deposed or said or denied, save that he was wounded. On the contrary, everything his own witnesses have said has proved to contradict him and serves as a reproach to what he has stated." Mariotto asks the commissioners speedily to absolve him or at least reduce the penalties of the offense, seeing that he was entirely justified in fighting Cavalier Bracciolini.

Mariotto rests his case, but not before submitting a thick dossier of orders, notices, testimonies, letters, and interrogatories, as well as the decisions of the magistrates civil and ecclesiastical, that for many months had been accumulating along the triangular route between Pistoia, Florence, and Pisa—the material that makes up the great part of our documentation for this story.[26]

Most of this material we have seen. A few of the items in Mariotto's checklist have disappeared, including "supplications and letters sent to His Most Serene Highness by Captain Lanfredino to make Raffaello, son of the said Chiara, a commendatario of Santo Stefano and the sketch of the site and description of the place where the quarrel arose." Neither of these losses are serious, however, since we have information about them from other quarters. It would have been helpful to have had the missing items described as "all the laws, ordinances, statutes, and articles pertinent to this case that are helpful and profitable to [the defendant]"; they would have allowed us to see what Messer Giovanni Politi considered the legalities pertinent to his case. Without them we have had to make our own way through the laws of Pistoia and the Tuscan state. It would have been a rare treat to look into the little box where Chiara stored Fabrizio's gifts, to see and hold the golden heart and her other treasures. But we can hardly be surprised that these, the only pieces of evidence with any material value, have long since disappeared.

More precious than laws and golden hearts, however, is the last item Mariotto now offers in evidence, a more devastating wound to Fabrizio's honor than any inflicted by Cellesi swords and what may have been the ultimate weapon of Mariotto's defense. This is the packet of letters between Fabrizio and Chiara, the letters Mariotto has found in Chiara's closet.

FOURTEEN

Love Letters

> Don't tire of paying court; her love through
>   homage will increase.
> And gallant service, when well done, will never
>   fade or cease.
> Though it is slow, it's not in vain; love never fails
>   in this.
>
> —Juan Ruiz

Under questioning by Secretary Conti in May, Caterina and Ceccha revealed that they had carried letters between Fabrizio and Chiara, and Chiara herself reluctantly acknowledged that this was true. At the same time, we learned from Mariotto's story to the magistrates that he had snatched some letters from their hiding place when he ransacked Chiara's belongings. They remained out of sight, however, until the final day of Mariotto's trial, when with a certain dramatic flair he produced a packet of six letters. Undated, they do not tell us when the affair began, but they show Fabrizio initiating the courtship and pursuing Chiara with his characteristic "importunity."[1] Chiara's response is reserved but far from dismissive. Since the letters end before Fabrizio literally battered down the next to last barriers of Chiara's resistance, climbing over her garden wall and bloodying himself on the doorposts of her house in the Prato S. Francesco, we do not know whether there had been others. In any case, the six letters we have confirm in the lovers' own words the affair both of them denied so adamantly in court.[2]

1. Fabrizio Bracciolini to Chiara:

O solitary letter of my secret suffering, God grant you the felicity he gave the Trojan exile when he placed his brother Cupid in Elissa's bosom secretly and victoriously![3]

Take the road to the summit of all my good, which you alone in all the world know. And may you [i.e., the letter] be fortunate in obtaining a favorable reply.

O Chiara, my soul, o most precious, may your heart not wonder at my unexpected letter; it is moved by the great love I bear you, which binds and overwhelms me. I have been born into the world only for you, to serve you.

This, o my soul, is a secret virtue from heaven, a gift to man—to love a creature as gentle, honest, wise, and beautiful as you. And it has been given to me that I may serve you very secretly. I beg you to allow me to speak to you secretly under whatever circumstances you want, so that I may serve you in person. I pray you do this; I love you so faithfully and have loved you and regard you my goddess on earth. I promise you by the God I adore that I'll never want anything but what you may command. I'll be faithful to you unto death, secretly and obediently, as long as I am able to move and have my powers, and I will spend my life serving you. So, my sweetest, grant me the favor of speaking to you and write me to tell me when and how and at what hour you will graciously allow me to speak with you. Do not worry about giving me any amount of trouble because anything I have to do for you, no matter how exhausting and difficult, will be so easy and simple. Always, I say, I will be faithful and obedient to you. I'll be your shield and defender and do anything to serve you, even if men have to die [for it]. O Chiara, my goddess, if you knew how long I have wept for love of you while steadfastly keeping you from knowing. Be assured that I will die in loving service to you and that I am dying now, that I cry out yet remain silent. Naked and trembling I burn in the hot fire and die in spirit and in flesh. Joy abandons me and suffering embraces me. I grieve for one who has never offended me and I put my trust in one who has never known my hopes. *Fear of certain martyrdom accompanies my suffering. Faithful as Orpheus though I am,[4] I remain alone. Yet, if I keep silent I'll get no answer. Though I want to reveal my passion, your fear makes me keep it secret.** O how many times have I said, blessed am I if you receive one of my letters and accept it humanely and if you reply kindly to my request, granting me those favors that lift me up into the company of the blessed.

With this I will end. Only remember to keep the secret and do not confide in anyone; indeed, when you write me, tell the woman who carries [the letter] that you are writing to say that you cannot do what I want you to do, that it's inconvenient and that you don't want to do it. In this way no one will know our business and our secrets. Keep in mind that you have never had anyone who loves you and wants you more than I. I beg you, make some great test for me to see whether I am telling you the truth or lying, as so many do nowadays to achieve their desires. I entreat you in the name of the God I adore, in life and in death I will always be faithful to you and will always be with you to defend you and honor and love you, and with this I kiss your delicate hand, recommending myself to you with all my heart, awaiting a kind and happy reply. Burn this letter. May God protect you and give you every contentment and happiness.

From your most felicitous lover
C.B.,[5] who loves you more than himself

...

2. Fabrizio to Chiara:

Sweetest soul, never was a pilotless, rudderless ship, bereft of sails, so adrift, lost and abandoned on the waves as I felt I was when told by my faithful messenger that you were afraid I was pretending and that Vincenzio[6] got me to do this because he is your enemy. O my highest good, o Chiara my life, if only you had been present there in hiding to see the expression on my face when I was thus wounded again! O my cruel fate! O pitiless heavens! O fortunate the virile seed that *never germinated!**[7] Fortunate, too, the mother's milk that turns to poison, and most fortunate those of you for whom the cradle becomes a tomb. O most happy he who has been shielded from the flame of love! I found myself in such a state that it mattered not whether I lived or died, especially knowing that I willingly made myself your subject *and that you have to let others tell you what to say.**[8] O Chiara, dear heart, remove this wicked thought! If ever I am disloyal to you or betray you may God's wrath extinguish for me and deprive me of the splendor of the sun and moon; let every elemental power be against me, everything I have be cast into filth, and a cruel dark prison become my dwelling place while I become food and drink for wild lions. But if I am faithful and loyal and remain so and live for you with all my powers, will you not grant me a single paragraph in reply so that I may speak to you of my hopes? Have mercy and pity for me for I am wretched. The light of your eyes has made me your subject; may they take pity on the burning lover, and with gentle and reassured mind look on me your devoted lover and *on my supplication.**[9] Believe me, a lesser spectacle would have brought Mithridates to the side of the Romans, Masinissa to the Carthaginians, Achilles to Fabius, and Philip to Nicia.[10]

Grant me, Chiara, my lady, a brief audience to hear of my great suffering; hear my sighs; look at my sad face; consider my altered color; note my sad heart; look with amazement, how my body and mind are ready to serve you, and as my patroness be generous to me. Here amidst your glory, here will be your immortality if only you let me speak to you. What harm, what bad thing can happen to you? I am your faithful, vigilant nighttime guard, magnanimous and desirous of showing you the greatness of my spirit. It is my duty to maintain your good reputation and well-being. O dear heart, both my contentment and my disaster, present and future, are up to you. If in your goodness you accept me I will live a happy life, if you decide otherwise I will resolve to search out a place where almost no sunlight enters to accompany me as I unhappily live out my life.

Ah, don't be less worthy than those ancient demigoddesses who preferred to be deprived of all their well-being and happiness rather than abandon their lovers. Madonna Chiara, I am your prisoner; I confess it and I beg you to grant life to me just as they do who are unable to refuse the supplication of an enemy. As I have told you many times through the woman who carries my messages, if you don't believe me, test me, command me to do some great thing, then you will see whether I have lied or told the truth. Ah, don't believe what you've heard—that I am doing this for some other person who wants to hurt you.[11] Remember, I am a gentleman and have always shown myself to be so, and sooner than cause you the least harm, I would choose death. Enough, I do not want to write any more because my eyes no longer see for weeping. Pardon me if you find it hard to understand this because of my spirit and trembling hand and continual sighs. If you do not help me you will soon know of my end. With this I will stop writing, all disconsolate, awaiting your decision. That will determine whether I live or die. O if you knew with how much love and faith I write you would believe and would remove from your breast all caution and fear and you would be persuaded to console me and I would be for you as long as I had life. For the love of God, I pray you, let me have two words with you and then test me and bind me any way you wish and I will be gentle as a puppy. With this I kiss your hand, praying that both of us may be consoled.

By the faithful lover who loves you more than himself,

C.B.

Burn this.

3. Chiara to Fabrizio Bracciolini:

To My Most Gracious and Kind Signore,

Signore, you write that you wish to speak with me and you have also spoken to me personally about everything that you have written.[12] Therefore I can't fail to write these few lines in order not to appear discourteous to your lordship. I must ask pardon not to be able to give you the reply that I ought and that your lordship deserves; I tell you I do not have the opportunity to speak with your lordship, but I will make the effort to hear what your lordship wants to say to me, if not at night then in the daytime. If your lordship cares to wait for the opportunity, as soon as I can I will try to speak with your lordship. I will end with this, praying that the Lord keep you in felicity and giving you infinite thanks for the offers you have made me.

Your most faithful servant,

Chiara, in Pistoia

4. Fabrizio to Chiara:

Behold, kind goddess, some of the wounds you give me.[13] *I, your servant, can do no less than draw for you as best I can my spirit as it is graven in my flesh.**[14] And because I do not want to give you cause, by some mischance, to think I am less faithful to you than a saint and because I am concerned for the greater security of our affairs, I wanted to reply to your kind and consoling letter and tell you to drive away every suspicion and fear that you may have. Believe me, as I have drawn it for you, so it is in my body—and much more. Ah, my supreme good, make proof, make proof whether I am telling the truth or lying; send me to a place where my life will be in danger, and if I do your bidding it will be a sign not that I love, but that I adore you and never will deceive you. As for what you tell me—that I should be patient and wait until you have an opportunity to speak with me either by day or by night— I am infinitely grateful. To such a generous and kind spirit one never wishes to be discourteous, therefore receiving such grace I can call myself one of the happiest of faithful lovers. I tell you I will obey you always and be ever ready and watchful for your summons, so, my sweetheart, seize whatever opportunity seems good to you. I will always be ready at whatever hour, always, day and night, at your command. So that you do not forget the boon you have promised me, I am sending my picture; I have cast a spell and transformed myself into it so that it can remind you of me and implore you to talk to me.[15] Please keep it until I appear before you, and look at it now and then to see how gentle and humble it is, meaning that you are to have pity and not think of how far away I am forced to be from you, but keep your promise faithfully. With this I will end, so as not to bore you with a long letter. *Only I will try to persuade you that for the trifle that I have to say to you, you grant me more time to see you than just a morning here, a day there. If not it will do me no good to see you at all.**[16] If you knew how I suffered the other day when I went to the captain's house![17] It is so hard, but let's not do anything foolish.

O hope of mine, what have you done to me that there is so much love and fire for you in my breast? Now, come, you must comfort me and not despise me, your faithful servant. You have promised what I so ardently requested. I must hope that you are happy, and with this I close—praying for your every felicity and content-ment, humbly I kiss your delicate hands. I commend myself to you as your gentle and faithful servant.

By your most faithful slave,
C.B., who loves you more than himself

5. Fabrizio to Chiara

My sweetest and highest good,

If I were to write you how much pain and torment I had yesterday when I re-ceived such a cruel message and the returned portrait, a whole ream of paper would not suffice and you would believe I was crazy. But then I was helped and comforted by love, an exemplary protector for those who serve him faithfully. You sent me your former servant Caterina, whom I entreated, almost in tears, urging that if I get a chance to speak to you she must keep it secret for your good and that of others, and I had her swear it and promise to die rather than say anything. She will be helpful to me because she pitied me the state I was in. I told her how I burned with love for you, so I am hopeful. I did this because it is necessary to make use of her as mes-senger in order to get news reliably and because I need to communicate a great, deep secret that I hope will be acceptable to you. On her return from you, she told me that I should look for a place and write you about it and you would speak with me there. I know plenty of places. The best is outside the Porta al Borgo in the Val di Brana, going up by way of the Specchio.[18] Let me know when you want to come there; I'll get ready and be there alone and you will see me for sure and be able to follow me from a distance. But, my soul and love, it would be better and more secret for me to come to talk to you at night at ten or eleven o'clock or whenever you think best, because nobody is around in the street then; we could talk without any suspicion or fear. But you do what is best for you, and don't worry, life of mine, I do not want anything of you but what you command of me. I leave everything to your judgment, knowing you are wise, and if you have compassion for me, your faithful one, you won't lack for a way to console me. Anything connected with you and whatever you want done for you will be welcome and acceptable to me. With this I'll close so as not to bore you, awaiting a kind and happy response, and I humbly kiss your hands, my sweet soul, and pray you may have every happiness and desire.

Your faithful lover, C.B., who has put all his hopes in you

6. Fabrizio to Chiara:

My Dearest One,

I am so tormented by the inconvenience of Maria's departure that I have decided to send you these lines, pretending to Maria's son that it is a letter to his mother to ask her to return, and that he should show it to you to see that it's all right with you, and tell him to bring it back to me and I will send it to her. Tell him not to say anything. In this way, sweetheart, I'll be able to let you know the hour. I beg you by the great love I have for you that you write me and tell me what I should do to know when you want me to speak with you. We should manage secretly so that not too many people know our business. I assure you, it pains me so to have lost *the convenience of [Maria's] services** that I'm beside myself. Keep in mind, my dearest, that I am like a prisoner who is constantly waiting for a reprieve and is consumed by impatience and hope. So I won't speak to you of the pain and passion I suffer as I wait to talk to you. My life and my death are in your hands. With this I kiss your hand, remaining always to serve you most faithfully and praying for your every content.

Your faithful lover, C.B., whom you command completely

Fabrizio repeatedly warned Chiara to take no one into her confidence, and to burn the letters. But secrecy was impossible. Both Fabrizio and Chiara relied on messengers and go-betweens for the conduct of their business, and the constant presence of servants and inquisitive neighbors and friends eventually widened the circle of gossip. Fabrizio's warnings to Chiara not to share the contents of his letters with anyone suggest that he thought she could read them well enough without help. We do know—since Secretary Conti required her to demonstrate it—that Chiara could write a little, and since reading was generally the more readily acquired skill,[19] we may infer that she could also read a little. If so, she would have been atypical: few peasants and even fewer women could read and write in sixteenth-century Italy, even though its literacy rates were higher than those of most countries.[20] It seems that her letters to Commissioner Pazzi and the Pratica Segreta were written by Fabrizio, although she may have told him what she wanted them to say.[21]

Even if Chiara had more reading and writing skills than the average poor mountain woman, it is unlikely that they were adequate to cope with the inflamed rhetoric and pretentious classical references of Fabrizio's love letters. To whom would she have turned for help in making sense of his messages? Someone in the Cellesi household may have come to her aid, although, apart from servants, she seems to have had few friends there. Servants carried her messages, but probably had even less skill in reading and writing than she did. The most likely candidate for the role of ammanuensis came from outside her domestic circle—fra Bartolomeo, of Chiara's parish church of S. Francesco, who, as her confessor must have been privy to her secrets. It was to fra Bartolomeo she turned when she needed a place to hide Fabrizio's gifts. By agreeing to keep them for her, the friar became at least a passive accomplice in the illicit love affair. (Had he already compromised himself more gravely by helping her write a reply to her married suitor—underwriting, so to speak, her violation of the seventh and tenth commandments? In the absence of evidence, we should give fra Bartolomeo the benefit of the doubt and assume he played only the lesser, if not altogether innocent, role— cousin to the kindly blundering Friar Laurence of Shakespeare's *Romeo and Juliet,* rather than to the slippery and venal fra Timoteo of Machiavelli's *La Mandragola.*)[22]

One way or another, then, alone or with help Chiara read Fabrizio's love letters. With what mixture of bewilderment, pleasure, and misgivings did she read them? She was obviously aware of the dangers, and in the only letter to Fabrizio we have from her, she was demure and cautious. Still, she agreed to try to meet with him. Courtesy required her to reply, she said, employing the formally polite tone and style indicating she was sensitive to the social distance between them. Yet she did not protest that Fabrizio's attentions were inappropriate, and she does not appear to have been flustered by the advances of so great a signore. If Fabrizio's constant reminders that he was a gentleman and his pose as her would-be champion strike us as the vain posturing of a street-corner cavalier, Chiara gives no hint that *she* finds him ridiculous. Perhaps seventeen years of living with such an aggressively class-proud signore as Captain Lanfredino Cellesi had prepared her for Fabrizio's High Renaissance style of self-presentation.[23]

Chiara was vulnerable. For some time before Fabrizio appeared on the scene, Captain Lanfredino had been mistreating her, and lately he was threatening to cast her into the street. That must have made it harder for her to resist Fabrizio's love talk. Armed with his gentleman's education, at ease in a culture of stylized courtship and seduction, and a practiced womanizer, Fabrizio had tested his weapons in many an amatory campaign. When he addressed Chiara as "goddess," praised her gentleness, beauty, and wisdom, lamented his secret suffering while chastising her cruel indifference, and when he begged her to make some great test of his loyalty and service so he could prove his love for her, she may have thought he was speaking out of the inspiration of his heart; she could hardly know he was using the highly stylized language of a long tradition in which such protestations were the de rigeur ingredients of courtship.

With insincere letters and sweet words mined from this or that book, men always try to deceive women, complained a sixteenth-century Roman gentlewoman.[24] The reigning epistolary discourse of gentleman lovers derived from Petrarchan poetry and, farther back, by way of Andreas Capellanus and the Provençal troubadours, to Ovid. Whether Fabrizio had read any of these authors we are unable to say; at the University of Pisa he had spent a great deal of his time playing football. But to be able to employ the language of polite love, he need have read no more of Ovid or of Petrarch than today's college graduate needs to read of Freud in order to become familiar with the terminology of psychoanalysis, or of Marx to use the language of dialectical materialism. Like ours, this was an age of textbooks offering a smattering of knowledge on many subjects without the effort and pain of systematic study.[25] With Renaissance letterwriting coming to be recognized as an art governed by its own conventions and rhetorical strategies, letters were anthologized, analyzed, categorized, and codified in model-books and manuals for professional secretaries and literate amateurs.[26]

Although one contemporary expert complained that lovers' letters "are like their thoughts, such a mishmash of undigested, incompatible, and implacable feelings that it would be impossible to chart them,"[27] a stream of love-letter books had already been finding a ready market from about mid-century. In *Il segretario*, Francesco Sansovino counsels a lover who wishes to write a seductive letter *(inhonesto, feminile, lascivo)* to his lady love to follow this routine: first the lover should praise her person, her virtue, status, and—most important—her beauty; next he ought to seek her good opinion by demonstrating—with due modesty—his own status or rank, and to describe his ardent love and willingness to die for her; then he must beg his beloved to love him as he loves her, a love divine rather than human, and give an example of such a love from the past; finally, he should warn her that her life will end cruelly if she does not return his love, and impress upon her that all his honor and well-being depend on her.[28]

We can imagine Fabrizio trying to recall Sansovino's four steps as he composed his letters to Chiara. From Alvise Pasqualigo's *Lettere amorose* he could have absorbed the habit of calling Chiara "my soul" and "cruel lady," and learned the tactic of declaring he would die unless she granted him a private meeting. Even the plot of Pasqualigo's epistolary novel resembles the Holy Thursday scenario: servants carry messages, gifts of jewelry, and talismanic portraits and locks of hair; the lover parades in front of his beloved's house and enters secretly when the count, her husband, is away; they dance together at a ball; the count becomes suspicious and provokes jealous scenes, forcing his wife to sleep with him; the lover is attacked in the street—and one of his assailants even storms out of a nearby house. Only at this point do art and life part company: in Pasqualigo's novel, the lover stands his ground and drives off his attackers, and the lovers manage to continue their affair for years. All the while, the letters continue (536 all told). In one, the lady describes the ecstasies of their lovemaking: "Ah, poor me, while I lay in your arms not only did every part of my body enjoy all the pleasure we mortals are capable of feeling, the delicious effect was so satisfying to each of my senses in turn that all of them rejoiced. Again and again I called myself happy, so truly complete was my bliss that I was convinced the immortal gods envied it."[29]

Pasqualigo gave his heroine noble birth and sophistication; Chiara, with neither, could not have described her pleasure so eloquently. Culturally, she was closer to the female mistress Ferrante Pallavicino had in mind when he warned writers of love letters to avoid "a style too elevated, because the women to whom you are writing may not find it easy to understand. Critics will remind you that the warp of a love letter should consist only of familiar feelings; its woof, of clear ideas, such that match the female understanding."[30] Fabrizio, in his elaborately histrionic letters, made no such concessions, and Chiara, with her limited literary compass, must have found it hard to follow his convoluted similes and make her way through the thicket of his syntax. His references to classical mythology and Roman history must surely have bewildered her (as, indeed, some of them have mystified me).

But perhaps the very inaccessibility of Fabrizio's rhetoric made his letters all the more effective: barely initiated into the mystique of the printed word, Chiara must have been dazzled by this seemingly virtuoso display on her behalf, valuing the letters as much for what they represented as for what they said. In her increasingly desperate circumstances, they seemed to offer an opportunity for the freer life she imagined and longed for. Rather than destroy the letters—or return them, as she did Fabrizio's portrait—she took great risks to keep them.

"Behold, kind goddess, some of the wounds you give me. I, your servant, can do no less than draw for you as best I can my spirit as it is graven in my flesh." These opening words of one of Fabrizio's letters to Chiara (#4 above) are accompanied by an ineptly drawn figure scratched in the margin of the page.[31] A man with a faceless, oval-shaped head, the outline of a heart on his clumsy torso, and a huge, erect, dripping penis stands with legs apart and feet chained to a kind of grounded anchor. His arms are stretched out in a supplicatory gesture inviting attention to his sexual plight as he looks toward an outline of a notional disembodied vulva suspended in space. Readers suddenly encountering this crude image of blatant, impersonal lust are likely to find the contrast with Fabrizio's soulfully chivalric rhetoric jarring—like spying the cloven hoof underneath the devil's disguise in one of those moralizing prints so common in the late Middle Ages. Such coupling of unbuttoned libido and high-flown sentiment offends current aesthetic, and perhaps moral, sensibilities. But while none of the letter books I have seen mention it, the illustration of love letters with erotic sketches seems to have been an acceptable and fairly common practice in Fabrizio and Chiara's time.[32]

Fabrizio's drawing of himself in a letter to Chiara.
Reproduction of the microfilm copy shows the MS
background, but it blots the details in the drawing.
My copy of the drawing is closer to the original.

It is doubtful that Fabrizio himself perceived any disharmony between word and picture. The text accompanying the sketch is in the same worshipful, even religious, vein as his previous letters; Chiara is still his "kind goddess," and the wounds she has given him are as much spiritual as physical. This phallic self-display seems neither to be straining to shock her nor confessing a guilty lust, but demonstrating that his body is as much a vessel of his "saintly" devotion to her as his spirit—and to remind her, with some exaggeration, that she has promised to reward both. To judge from Chiara's subsequent behavior, she was neither surprised nor offended. She returned Fabrizio's portrait, as he complained in his next letter, but this was from fear of discovery rather than indignation, and together with the others she kept the letter with its erotic drawing. She continued to reply to his messages and exchange gifts, eventually admitting him to the little house in the Prato S. Francesco, where the affair apparently proceeded to the consummation she must have foreseen and did little to prevent.

FIFTEEN

The Verdict

The trial of Mariotto Cellesi is inching toward its conclusion. With Mariotto's presentation in evidence of the love letters and gifts he has rested his defense and it is time for the two special Santo Stefano commissioners appointed by the Council of Twelve to deliver their findings and make their recommendations.[1] In their rehearsal of the testimony there is little new; we have long since become familiar with the charges and countercharges as we followed the processo's windings between Pistoia, Florence, and Pisa.[2] But the way they read the evidence, the conclusions they drew from it, and what they—distinguished cavaliers and high-ranking officers of the Order of Santo Stefano—made of the moral and chivalric issues raised by the Holy Thursday affair are of the highest interest.

Grand Prior Eneo Vaini flatly dismisses as unproven Fabrizio's claim that he had been attacked from behind and struck by five men: "Bracciolini's own witnesses testify that . . . no one was there or arrived there but priest Asdrubale." He also rejected Fabrizio's allegations that the attack was "traitorous":

In the processo it is proved that the said Cavaliers did not greet each other and that for the previous eight days they were expected to fight and people followed them to see it . . . by his own witnesses it was proved that [Mariotto] told him to draw and that as soon as he heard these words he turned back about two stone's throws on the way he had come. . . . That Asdrubale and Tonio had sallied out of the Visconti house and joined in the attack is likewise unproven; the door of the house was closed the whole time and Asdrubale has already been absolved [by the vicar] for lack of proof, while Antonio was absolved by the Magnifica Pratica, it having been proven that he was not at the scene of the fight during that entire day.

For Commissioner Vaini, Fabrizio's claims to have fought back valiantly and to have tried to fight on despite being wounded are patently false: Instead of calling Mariotto to fight, "it was proved by his witnesses that he immediately let his sword down to the ground and leaned on it while he held his nose with the other hand, and that if Cavalier Mariotto had wanted to he could have killed him."

As for Fabrizio's allegation that there were two other armed men among his attackers, this (we learn at last, although not how it was done) has been investigated and disproven. "It appears," said Vaini, "that no others were ever there. And in the presence of the signor castellan [of the fortress], he [Fabrizio] withdrew his accusation against the said two soldiers." (Whether these are the two soldiers from the fortress who accompanied Mariotto and Asdrubale through the S. Marco Gate on Holy Thursday, the commissioner does not say.)

After dismissing Fabrizio's charges against Mariotto, Vaini levies a series of harsh judgments of Fabrizio's behavior, some details of which we learn for the first time:

He sent letters in his own hand via procuresses to the captain's house as well as gifts and his picture, and . . . many, many times at night he came to the Cellesi enclosure and in front of the doors of the said Cavalier Mariotto and Captain Lanfredino played, sang, yelled, called out, and made other signs and did other disreputable things. . . .

[Fabrizio] denies that he suborned witnesses, although . . . his suborning of witnesses was proved. . . . He denies he was warned [saying] that he could not have been warned because he never harassed the said Chiara, although . . . warnings by his relatives and by the said Cavalier Cellesi have been proved.

And further he denies that the letters were written in his hand. While the present dispute was pending, he disguised his handwriting in letters to your illustrious lordships; nonetheless, in the processo before your illustrious lordships, they were proved to have been written in his hand by comparing and juxtaposing them with other letters and writings he had written and sent years ago to the most illustrious council that are now in the chancellery. Furthermore, in Chiara's processo before the Magnifica Pratica, they were proved [to be his] by the recipient. . . .[3]

Lastly, on behalf of Cavalier Cellesi . . . it ought to be considered whether any credence is to be given to the proceedings or to the witnesses heard against him and his father in the court of Pistoia . . . given the familiarity of that court with Bracciolini and the court's personal interest in the case. [Here Vaini is referring to Giannozzo de' Pazzi's relation to the commissioner.] For this reason, His Most Serene

Highness removed the said case from the said court and assigned it to the Magnifica Pratica, as he also did the processo against Antonio.

For these things proved, deduced and noted in the processo, it can and should be concluded that the causes that moved the said Cavalier Cellesi to call out the said Cavalier Bracciolini to fight as a knight of honor were innumerable—that he was, so to speak, pulled by the hair—and that notwithstanding Cavalier Bracciolini's counterarguments and statements, nothing at all of this, either in his deposition or from his evidence, has been proved, but indeed the contrary case has been proved by his own witnesses. . . . Therefore the said Cavalier Cellesi ought to be absolved or at least the set punishment be reduced.

"Pulled by the hair by knightly honor"—an awkward image, but a welcome dash of feeling in the bland broth of the commissioners' officialese. Commissioner Vaini's report resolves all doubts about the course of events on Holy Thursday in Mariotto's favor. Not even the solid testimony of Luca Pazzaglia moves Vaini to accept that Mariotto and Asdrubale had set upon Fabrizio from behind or that they gave him virtually no chance to defend himself. Insisting that Mariotto had behaved honorably as a gentleman and cavalier in "calling out"—not "attacking"—Fabrizio (Vaini chooses the language of the duel of honor rather than that of the street fight), he concludes that Mariotto should be exonerated or given a light sentence. Vaini clearly believes Fabrizio to be a liar and a scoundrel whose misdeeds, listed here in detail, earned him the revenge he so weakly resisted.

Grand Chancellor Benedetto Vivaldi is equally severe in detailing Fabrizio's transgressions. In essence, he endorses Mariotto's self-justification and his account of the fight:

We can conclude that Captain Lanfredino, father of Cavalier Mariotto, took no part in this business—that is, in ordering the fight—and that Antonio del Bonzetta did not help the said Cavalier Mariotto in the fight. . . . And even if Asdrubale was there with Cavalier Mariotto, it is not proven that he was armed. . . .[4] Also it is not proven that Cavalier Fabrizio had any other wounds but in the nose, which Cavalier Mariotto admits to having given him.[5] Nor is it proven that the said Cavalier Mariotto hit Cavalier Fabrizio from behind or before the said Cavalier Fabrizio drew his sword. This is as much as we are able to report to your most illustrious lordships.

Unlike Vaini, however, Vivaldi makes no recommendation for sentencing. The case now goes before Santo Stefano's Council of Twelve, who will pronounce sentence.

SIXTEEN

The Sentence

In determining the sentence, the Twelve relied on the findings of the two commissioners, but they refused to be diverted from the legal issue of Mariotto's guilt by the moral issue so prominent in the commissioners' reports. The main question for them was not Fabrizio's dishonorable behavior, but whether Mariotto was guilty or innocent. Reporting to the grand master of the order, Grand Duke Francesco I himself, the Twelve referred to Fabrizio's behavior only as much as was necessary to establish Mariotto's motive for the Holy Thursday attack. Vaini's recommendation to acquit, they rejected.

Most Serene Highness:

We have seen and considered the inquest and processo against Cavalier Mariotto Cellesi of Pistoia that charges that [here they repeat the charge in detail and refer to Mariotto's defense]. . . . But in his deposition, Cavalier Mariotto says that encountering the said Bracciolini . . . he told him he had not behaved as a cavalier or as a gentleman and at the same moment they drew their swords and began to strike each other and Bracciolini was wounded in the nose. . . .

Therefore it is our opinion that for the injurious words, referred to above, spoken by the said Cavalier Mariotto to Cavalier Bracciolini, Cavalier Mariotto should be punished, in conformity with chapter 23 of the prohibitions and penalties, with a punishment of the *quarantena*.[1] Granting him the benefit of his confession, in conformity with the third declaration of the general chapter of 1575, this is reduced to two *settene*. For the serious wound referred to above, he is to be punished with four months of incarceration in conformity to the chapter-general of 1566, number 36. Giving him the benefit of his confession in accordance with the chapter-general of 1569, first declaration, this is reduced to three months incarceration, all of which is of course subject to the most excellent will of Your Serene Highness, to whom may the Lord God grant long and most happy life.

From Pisa, 23 January 1579[2]

. . .

To gauge the severity of Mariotto's sentence, we need to understand the penalties set in Santo Stefano's constitution and to compare his sentence to others in similar cases. The settena was a week-long course of penance, consisting mainly of confinement to quarters, fasting, and taking "the discipline" (ritual whipping by a Santo Stefano chaplain while kneeling before an altar in the order's church). Santo Stefano imposed it on their knights for such relatively minor infractions as avoiding sacred service and talking out of turn in meetings. The quarantena, or forty-day penance, was meted out for more serious transgressions—to cavaliers who disrupted sacred service or usurped the seat of a superior during mass or failed to return an official document to the order's archive. Harsher punishments included confinement in the order's prisons, loss of seniority, and expulsion—"the ultimate and gravest punishment."[3]

Imprisonment in the sixteenth century was more likely to be used as a means of temporary restraint than of punishment, to keep suspects and important witnesses, or to hold convicted culprits while they awaited sentencing. But the order is using imprisonment as punishment, setting prison terms for numerous crimes of verbal and physical violence—two months for "lightly" offending another cavalier during litigation before a Santo Stefano tribunal, or four months if the insult were grievous; six months for spilling the blood of a slave or one of the prior's serving staff. Murder was punished by life imprisonment; so was impersonating a cavalier of the order. Unlike the fearful *segrete* of the Florentine bargello or the infamous dungeons of Venice, the *carceri*, or prisons, of Santo Stefano, designed primarily for gentlemen, were to be as comfortable as the cavaliers' regular quarters at Pisa.[4]

The constitution of the order regarded violence between its knights with special gravity. A cavalier who wounded another in the nose or mouth and drew blood was to be expelled from the order; if he struck but missed, he could expect a quarantena.[5] Duels were anathema. "If a cavalier challenges another cavalier to a duel, either by [sending him a] card, through a third person, or verbally, and the other accepts . . . even if the spilling of blood is slight, both are to be irrevocably expelled and perpetually imprisoned. If there is no effusion of blood, they are to lose as much seniority as the grand master and the council decide. If one calls another out and is not accepted, the challenger is to lose at least three years seniority."[6]

If the council had gone by the book, it might have expelled Mariotto for shedding Fabrizio's blood or, if it chose to regard his challenge as a duel, condemned him to life in prison. Against this theoretical standard, then, his actual punishment seems particularly mild. But the elders of Santo Stefano allowed themselves considerable leeway in applying the disciplinary provisions of the order, and, so far as I know, never expelled a knight, much less sentenced one to life imprisonment or death, for fighting a duel. We may recall the case, a year earlier, in which Cavalier Giovanni Fioravanti, of a distinguished Pistoia family, confessed to giving the lie to our own Fabrizio Bracciolini and wounded him in the resulting sword fight. The council sentenced Fioravanti to six months in *carcere,* with another two months *confinato* outside Pistoia as well as two years' loss of seniority. In this case, a ducal rescript increased the confinato from two months to two years, specifying Elba as the place of exile.[7] Two years earlier, Cavaliers Flaminio Colleschi da Palaia and Onesto Onesti da Castiglione were convicted of fighting, but as neither was wounded they were sentenced to a "normal" punishment of a quarantena apiece. Since they had confessed and made peace, their sentences were reduced to a sentena. In this instance, the grand duke approved.[8]

Mariotto's sentence of two sentene and three months in prison, then, was not harsh by the standards of his order. Neither was it trivial. By accepting the version of the Holy Thursday fight most favorable to Mariotto—namely, his own—the Twelve were acknowledging that he had drawn his sword in obedience to a code they all shared: a knight was obliged to punish the violator of his family's honor. Still, the Twelve's sentence also recognizes that chivalry has its limits—or, rather, that its claims might be at cross-purposes with the aims of the order and of the law. Individually and privately, they may have agreed with Commissioner Vaini, but, as the council noted in an order of 15 December, 1564, their founder Cosimo I had expressly charged them with the responsibility of seeing that the knights of Santo Stefano fought the Turks, not each other. By giving the order criminal jurisdiction over those same knights, Cosimo had also charged it with the responsibility of seeing that they kept the public peace.

As grand masters of the order and as sovereign princes, the grand dukes routinely reviewed all judicial decisions of the Twelve. Francesco I approved the sentence of the Twelve in the case of Mariotto Cellesi. What he would have done if the Twelve had absolved Mariotto completely we can only speculate, but ducal rescripts increasing the severity of sentences were common—far more common than the reverse.

SEVENTEEN

What It All Means

Any closed world has its fascinations.
—Anthony Lane

The explosion of violence in the via S. Andrea on Holy Thursday was over in seconds with the bloody slashing of Fabrizio Bracciolini's nose. The processo it set off dragged on for many months, with magistrates of four jurisdictions in three cities amassing and sifting heaps of testimony, much of it repetitive, evasive, muddled, devious, or contradictory. Why did the confrontation take place? Was it a fair fight or a craven assault? Who had taken part? How had they acted? From his bed of pain, Fabrizio charged that Mariotto Cellesi and four henchmen, instigated by Captain Lanfredino Cellesi, had "traitorously" and without provocation set upon him from behind and run away when he called after them to stand and fight. Mariotto told a different story: he had challenged Fabrizio on behalf of his gout-ridden, cuckolded father and fought him face-to-face and singlehanded; then, instead of killing him, he put up his sword. Fabrizio surely exaggerated the number of his attackers and the gallantry of his defense. Just as surely, Mariotto put a face too chivalric on a fight that smacked more of Robert Dallington's back-alley ambush than of the duel doctors' refined contest of honor.

Both stories were self-serving and unreliable. But it was essentially Mariotto's account of the affair, not Fabrizio's, that prevailed in the courts. The Pratica lords in Florence dropped the charges of assault against Tonio, and for lack of evidence exonerated Captain Lanfredino of instigating the attack. The two unnamed armed men had been questioned and exonerated. When Vicar Cespi absolved Asdrubale in the episcopal court of Pistoia, Mariotto remained the single defendant still under charge, and after his case was heard by a special commission of Santo Stefano, the Council of Twelve sentenced him to a shade more than token punishment.

To the modern reader of the trial documents, it may seem that justice miscarried. Vicar Cespi, Asdrubale's judge, had his own agenda, and this did not include serious consideration of the charges. Asdrubale's exoneration was an important precedent for Mariotto's trial. The reports of Commissioners Vaini and Vivaldi were blatantly partial to Mariotto and help explain his light sentence. Fabrizio was at a disadvantage in not being represented by a procurator. A counsel of Ser Giovanni's quality would have avoided Fabrizio's tactical errors, made more of his wounds, emphasized the strong evidence for Asdrubale's participation, and probed the conflicting testimony on Tonio Visconti's movements on Holy Thursday.

For the people involved in this sixteenth-century drama, however, the trial over the incident in the via S. Andrea was about other things—about friendship, honor, gentlemanly obligation, and family solidarity. The truth of what Mariotto did to Fabrizio on Holy Thursday was bound up with the truth of what for many weeks Fabrizio had been doing with Chiara Fioresi in the little house in the Prato S. Francesco. Both truths carried with them a heavy burden of honor and shame. While the authorities performed—somewhat unevenly—their responsibilities to investigate and punish law-breakers, the processo, especially the trial of Mariotto, became a moral contest in which each man fought for exclusive occupancy of the high ground. This is the contest Fabrizio lost.

With "all Pistoia," including its police,[1] gossiping about Fabrizio's flagrant courtship of Captain Lanfredino's concubine, his complaint against the Holy Thursday attackers began to go off the rails from the start. Even as they took down his deposition, the officials had to have known that Fabrizio was feigning ignorance about the incentive for the attack. As early as 25 April, less than a month after the cavalier was wounded in the via S. Andrea, Secretary Conti named him, during the examination of Chiara, as the woman's lover. Still earlier, Captain Lanfredino must have whispered the name Fabrizio Bracciolini into the ear of the grand duke when he gave his reasons for a change of venue. So Fabrizio's complaint, especially against Mariotto, was doubly tainted, not only by the scandal of his affair with Chiara but also by the lies and omissions of his testimony to the police officials—lies he repeated in court.

Procurator Giovanni Politi skillfully exploited his advantages. His parade of witnesses—some relatives of Fabrizio, some friends, no admitted enemies—provided the materials for a devastating picture of Fabrizio's scandalous and provocative behavior, showed Fabrizio to be untruthful and at the same time put Mariotto's act of vengeance in a better light. Disapproval of Fabrizio's behavior leaches through the concluding reports by Commissioners Vivaldi and Vaini to the Twelve. With the details of his persistent courtship of Chiara, his boasting and defiance, his reckless serenading in the Cellesi compound, his suborning of witnesses, and his repeated prevarication, the reports read more like an indictment of the plaintiff than a condemnation of the defendant.

In the grand duchy of Tuscany, as I have already noted, the inquisitorial system prevailed; judges were investigators, prosecutors, and examiners all in one; they questioned witnesses, rendered verdicts, and pronounced sentence, and they were subject to no review other than by the higher authority that had given them their commissions. This was true of all the magistrates and high officials who served as judges in the Cellesi-Bracciolini affair—not only the officials of the grand duke of Tuscany, but also the commissioners and the Twelve of Santo Stefano, who answered to their grand master, and the representatives of the vicar of Pistoia who served his bishop. If inquisitorial magistrates were less representative of the community than juries, they did not, as we have seen, insulate themselves from public opinion. We noted the repeated references to what the public knew ("all Pistoia knows") and the obligatory questions about the source and nature of each witness's testimony. Much of the information that fed into the verdicts came from witnesses relaying what they had learned from others through informal and often overlapping information networks that connected a much larger number of community members than appeared in court.

As well as investigating what "all Pistoia" *knew* about the Holy Thursday affair, the judges heard, thanks to the prompting of the interrogatories of both sides, what a cross section of the respectable community *thought* about it. ("Does the witness not think he has acted honorably in the affair, Fabrizio dishonorably?") The commissioners of the Twelve must have considered the question appropriate, since they admitted it into the proceedings, put it to Politi's seventeen corroborating witnesses, and used some of the language of the interrogatories in their written verdict. By invoking Christian morality for a counterjudgment on Mariotto's conduct, Fabrizio hoped to beat the defense at its own game; instead, he succeeded in throwing away the advantage owing to him as a victim. With his interrogatories to Mariotto's witnesses he skated on the edge of admitting what he had previously denied—that he had courted Captain Lanfredino's concubine—and this assured the victory of Politi's strategy: from that point on, the issue of Mariotto's allegedly criminal attack would be overshadowed by the issue of gentlemanly honor, and the justice of Mariotto's action would inevitably be weighed against Fabrizio's provocation.

Few of the Pistoian burghers who were being asked to express their opinion on the matter could pretend to expertise in questions of chivalry. Merchants, business agents, artisans, tavern keepers and shopkeepers for the most part, they carried no swords and fought no duels. Nardino il Bonzetta, Battista Cellesi, and Francesco Mannani made a point of this, disclaiming any knowledge of the punctilio of *duello*, of aristocratic codes of honor, and the formal roles of private combat between gentlemen. Nevertheless, the knightly commissioners of the Order of Santo Stefano did not object to these non-noble witnesses sitting on a virtual court of honor, deliberating matters of chivalric behavior.

For their part, Pistoian townsmen, even il Bonzetta and Battista (but not Francesco, the lowly bath attendant from Bagni di Lucca), did not hesitate to say that Fabrizio's conduct was intolerable and Mariotto was justified in fighting him to defend the honor of his family. It would seem, then, that a man did not have to be noble or carry a sword to pronounce judgment on gentlemanly conduct. In this respect, the hearing and its outcome might be surprising if we were to accept the class distinctions of contemporary duel theorists and other writers on status and manners as a guide to late-sixteenth-century society. The mixing of servants, sbirri, and cavaliers at dances and masked balls may have been exceptional, a traditional Carnival subversion of social boundaries, but the easy familiarity with which shopkeepers and taverners talked to Mariotto about the Cellesi's private business suggests that among Pistoians of the middle and upper ranks at least, the social arteries had not yet hardened as much as sixteenth-century ideologues, professional snobs, and some twentieth-century historians have asserted.[2]

It was, then, not so much the known facts of the Holy Thursday incident as the perception of its social meaning that dominated the course of Mariotto's trial and without a doubt strongly influenced its outcome. In a sense, there were two trials, one within the other: officially there was the deliberative *processo* in which magistrates examined the charge of assault against Mariotto Cellesi—the trial proper. Morally, however, Fabrizio was in the dock with Mariotto, and a forum of Santo Stefano knights and Pistoia burghers was being asked to decide which of the two antagonists had the right in a matter of family honor and Christian morality. The result of this trial within a trial was a victory for Mariotto; for Fabrizio, it was a humiliating exposure of ignoble behavior.

In the official trial, the Twelve upheld the letter of the law; they punished Mariotto for taking violent retribution in his own hands and disrupting the public peace. Yet their punishment of the defendant was mild and their criticism of the plaintiff (or Commissioners Vaini and Vivaldi's criticism, which the Twelve accepted as the basis of their sentence) severe, because, according to the code known variously as *cavalleria, duello,* or simply the obligations of *onore* that governed the inner trial, it was the duty of a gentleman or knight to draw his sword against a fellow gentleman and knight who had outraged his family. Giovanni Politi's tactic of asking Pistoian townsmen for their views on the Holy Thursday affair succeeded brilliantly. By choosing his witnesses from among the friends, relatives, associates, and neighbors of both the Bracciolini and Cellesi, Politi shrewdly forestalled potential objections about the bias of his sample. Besides, it is doubtful whether Politi could have found any sizeable group of Pistoians, whether nobles or burghers, who would have condoned Fabrizio's defiance of the obligations of friendship and public decorum or denied Mariotto's right to punish him for it.

In one way Fabrizio was lucky. Despite the judges' willingness to believe that he had attempted to bribe and suborn witnesses (and perhaps succeeded), conspired with the commissioner's notary to falsify the record, and given false testimony about his relations with Chiara, he came out of the Holy Thursday affair with no more than a wounded nose and damage to an already equivocal reputation. As a cavalier and noble, he was in no danger of having to endure the torture of "the rope" or the more burlesque punishment of *l'asino,* in which the culprit, wearing a miter on his head and a sign around his neck proclaiming him to be "a false calumniator," was led astride an ass through the streets of Pistoia on market day "as an example to those who are always brazenly making false accusations."[3] As a knight of Santo Stefano, Fabrizio could claim immunity from any penalties the civil courts might wish to impose on him, but he was subject to the discipline of the order. For giving false testimony or for accusing a fellow knight of a serious crime that he could not prove (i.e., that he was ambushed by five men rather than challenged fairly by one), he was liable to be expelled from the order.[4] But Fabrizio was neither expelled nor disciplined.

In the absence of any documentation of it in Santo Stefano's usually meticulous records, it seems unlikely that the commissioners even deliberated on his culpability. Neither do they seem to have considered punishing him for violating the order's rules against sexual misconduct, although here the evidence was overwhelming. We can interpret their inaction in several ways. They may have felt, *malgré* Commissioner Vaini, that the evidence of subornation and bribery was sketchy and inconsistent and depended upon the testimony of witnesses who changed their stories. Besides, if the lowly status of Polita, Maria, and Camilla and the youth of Rinaldo counted against them when testifying against Mariotto and Asdrubale, the same applied to their reports that Fabrizio had bribed and threatened them. Even less conclusive was the hearsay allegation that he had colluded with the commissioner's notary or with the commissioner himself. As to his sexual misconduct—which also violated the order's rules—"all Pistoia" knew of his "importunate" courtship of the captain's concubine, but as to whether he and Chiara had actually slept together, there was only the word of a prostitute against the combined denials of the principals. The commissioners' cautiousness in matters of evidence speaks well for their standards of legal and judicial procedure; their standards for marital fidelity and sexual propriety seem to us somewhat less demanding. However, we should not underestimate how powerful in their scheme of things was Fabrizio's punishment by public shame.

Gossip, writes Patricia Ann Meyer Spacks, "provides groups with means of self-control and emotional stability. It circulates both information and evaluation, supplies a mode of socialization and social control, facilitates self-knowledge by offering bases for comparison, creates catharsis for guilt, constitutes a form of wish-fulfillment, helps to control competition, facilitates the selection of leaders, and generates power."[5] The Holy Thursday incident could have been her proof-text.

Politi's witnesses included the most avid observers of the Bracciolini-Cellesi affair and its most active gossips. More than disinterested spectators watching an exotic plot unfold on some distant stage, they were supporting players and chorus in a real-life drama. Trading the latest titillating bits on the wooing of Chiara, circling Fabrizio as he strutted about at the Porta al Borgo, goading the reluctant Mariotto by teasing him about a despised "stepmother" who made a cuckold of his father, following the two cavaliers in the street, Pistoians nudged the action along toward its climax. Some of the reasons for wanting to see the two men come to blows must have been banal enough: an itch for excitement, self-righteousness—perhaps, too, admiration and envy of this dashing cavalier whose escapades they had been watching for years. None of these motives precluded the need to see a wrong righted. Few norms were as deeply ingrained as the barriers of honor and pride that men raised around their families and their women. Three score years earlier, Niccolò Machiavelli had advised the prince that if he wanted to avoid being hated by citizens and subjects, he should keep his hands off their property and their women.[6] It was a typical piece of Machiavellian wisdom, based on long observation, and it was still relevant, for subjects as well as for princes, in 1578. In the Holy Thursday affair, burgher and gentiluomo found common ground in endorsing forceful retribution against one of their number who had repeatedly violated that taboo.

Not only did Fabrizio break the rules, he also challenged the social consensus that enforced them: should an honorable knight who was also a good Christian, he asked, come to blows over an offense received on account of his father's concubine? Ought not a good Christian try instead to persuade his father to punish his concubine, or, if she became the occasion of an offense, to abandon her rather than fight on her account? The question was awkwardly framed, and, considering what had brought him into court, Fabrizio was not the most suitable person to ask it. Nevertheless it was a vital point, and it touched on an old problem: the manly virtue that demanded the spilling of blood in the cause of personal honor translated into the Christian sins of anger and pride.

To counter the violence of Christian against Christian, some of the sixteenth century's leading humanists, most notably Erasmus and Juan Luis Vives, revived the medieval paradigm of the *miles christianus,* the Christian knight who dedicated his sword to defending the faith and protecting the poor and weak; but outside the imaginary realms of literature, that ideal made little headway.[7] By contrast, the secular religion of honor was as ardently lived as it was solemnly professed.[8] A noble, and many a would-be noble, carried its code along with his sword as a badge of identity, and while it may be that few duels actually followed the increasingly elaborate rules of the duel doctors, and that more duels were talked than fought, dueling over questions of honor caused so much mayhem in sixteenth-century Europe that it was repeatedly forbidden by governments and condemned by the church. The Tridentine decree condemning duelists also condemned anyone who supported them—rulers who granted them a closed field, duel seconds, even spectators.

But while the hostility of church and state may have had some surface effect, it did not strike at the roots of the problem: in a society obsessed by maintaining *la bella figura* and formed by a culture that glorified violence, men would constantly be on guard against insults to their honor and they would find ways to fight. By outlawing the formal public duel with its rules of fair play, authorities may even have given a new lease on life to the less respectable kinds of fights it was meant to replace: Robert Dallington's back-alley ambushes and the rowdy, no-holds-barred clashes that Italians called *duello a la macchia*—clandestine hedge fights.[9] Many in government were members of the elite class that claimed the duel as its right, while princes who shut the front door against dueling often let it in at the back. Tuscany's Grand Duke Cosimo I is a case in point: while he forbade dueling, he sometimes gave the green light to Tuscan nobles to fight so long as they did it outside his territorial jurisdiction. Five years before the Tridentine decree, Cosimo himself served as an expert on duel protocol at the request of one of the rival parties. The year was 1559 and the request was made by none other than Captain Lanfredino Cellesi, who had challenged his cousin Piero Gatteschi for impugning his honor in a quarrel over money. Cosimo had submitted a written *consiglio* supporting Lanfredino's point of view in the dispute and allowed it to be published together with the opinions of other princes and prominent men on both sides.[10]

In a good example of the prevailing ambivalence about chivalric and Christian codes of morality, the same Duke Cosimo who closed one eye when regarding dueling among his more prominent subjects was responsible for one of the few successful reincarnations of the *miles christianus* ideal when he founded the Order—the *Religione*—of Santo Stefano in 1561–62. Dueling and other forms of violence among the cavaliers of Santo Stefano was forbidden and severe penalties were enumerated. Young nobles would not fight each other: the order was designed to give young nobles the opportunity, instead, to win honor and glory by making common cause against the enemies of Christendom, notably the Turks.

The order was in many respects an effective instrument of Tuscan foreign and military policy and brought great prestige and influence to the Medici dukes as champions of Christendom in the era of Counter Reformation. Its mission to be a school of Christian knighthood and an agent of social control, however, was inherently compromised. By revitalizing the link between nobility and military service and exalting the old knightly virtues, the grand dukes also gave a new lease on life to the notion that chivalry was untenable without an accompanying right to private violence. We need look no further than the Holy Thursday affair to see that Santo Stefano's cavaliers still claimed vendetta as an obligation of honor and a right of gentlemen, although it is more surprising to have found that their claims had broad support among their non-noble compatriots. Not only did the Medici dukes foster the code, they also sanctioned the means: Santo Stefano knights had special privileges to carry weapons even as the state repeatedly denied the privilege to others.

Against such deeply and widely rooted values, Fabrizio's belated, self-serving, eleventh-hour appeal to Christian morality made little headway. Almost to a man, Giovanni Politi's witnesses affirmed that a Christian knight was obliged to fight over his father's whore (as most chose to call her). Most of them advanced their opinions tentatively and with qualifications, as though they were feeling their way across difficult and unfamiliar terrain; it was not every day that ordinary citizens were pressed to map the boundaries of the divergent codes by which their world was governed. Practical men, for the most part, whose Christian piety ran more to comfortably routine observance than to anguished introspection, they did not, in the normal course of things, have to decide between the religion of forgiveness and peace and the religion of honor and vendetta. They replied to Fabrizio's questions with varying degrees of certainty, ranging from shopkeeper Simone d'Antonio Talini's unqualified advocacy of knightly combat "on account of a whore or for any other offense" to the more common and more cautious opinion of Nardino il Bonzetta and his friends, that a Christian knight might resort to arms "depending on circumstances" and only after he had tried peaceful persuasion. With different degrees of assurance, but a high degree of unanimity, this segment of the Pistoian community, confronted with a choice between gentlemanly pride and Christian humility, came down on the side of pride. In their concluding opinion, the Twelve of Santo Stefano did not reject this view. On the other hand, though they were cavaliers sworn to follow the ideal of the *miles christianus,* they did not, any more than Pistoian townsmen, pretend that there was an easy solution to this old rivalry between a religion of honor and violence and a religion of charity and forbearance.

A swaggering antihero pays court to the mistress of a rich and gouty old nobleman. Ignoring the inevitable consequences, he parades in front of her house, writes her frenzied letters of undying love, sends her a clumsy priapic drawing, and serenades her under the window of her crippled patron, whom he also mocks and belittles. Set upon in the street by the old man's son, he suffers the indignity of an almost-severed nose—figurative chastisement of the more troublesome private appendage forever leading him into temptation.[11] His overblown story of being attacked from behind by five assailants begins to unravel when his eye witnesses fail to confirm it and disclose his attempts to bribe and bully them. The details of the scandalous courtship emerge; the love letters are read by the court; the boasting and deceits are minutely chronicled. The son of the wronged man acknowledges that he smote the seducer on behalf of his family's honor and, to general approval, he receives the mildest sentence the code of his order allows.

Thus the story of the Holy Thursday affair retold as Renaissance comedy, with Fabrizio Bracciolini as Andreini's il Capitan Spavento and Shakespeare's Sir Toby Belch fused into one.

"Seduction may be baneful, even tragic, but the seducer at his work is essentially comic," writes Elizabeth Hardwick.[12] But this was comedy with a sober, even darker, side. To Chiara, the woman in the case, it was a disaster. Had Chiara been a great lady we might be able to tell her story as a chivalric romance: the unhappy heroine, in the power of a rich old man who abuses her, is courted by a dashing young cavalier; she resists at first, but then, flattered by his ardor and assured when he vows to serve her as her own true knight, she ignores all warnings and takes him as a lover. Discovered, she tries valiantly but unsuccessfully to shield him as well as herself. Ungrateful, and untrue to his promises of protection, he abandons her to face, alone, the wrath of her patron.

But Chiara was no lady. A poor, powerless mountain woman, living with one man while married to another, was not a proper subject for a tale of knightly *cortesia*. Still, she was neither servile nor weak: she rebelled more than once against the meager possibilities life offered her. Not that her choices were prudent or safe; at least two men exploited her feelings and her need for security; but if men selfishly used her, she also dared to use them and to discard them—though she could be bravely loyal, too. Married young and taken by her husband to Rocha del Corneto, a hamlet even higher in the Apennines than her own Lizzano Matto, she had found her way to the city, whether to improve on the hard pastoral life of that remote place or to rid herself of an incompatible husband, or both, we cannot say; nor do we know if she went off with Captain Lanfredino or met him after she had abandoned il Morino.

Whatever the personal circumstances, Chiara's flight can be seen as part of a historic demographic pattern, the centuries-old movement of villagers from the mountains and countryside to the town. These were the men and women who had populated renascent Italian towns and cities, offering their strength and skill for workshops and militias, their ambition and restless spirits for the spectacular achievements of the High Middle Ages and the Renaissance.[13] The sketchy information about individual migrants does not allow us to say how many among these multitudes were runaway wives (doubtless a relatively small number) nor how many became the kept women of rich townsmen, with houses and servants of their own (surely an even smaller number). In these respects, Chiara's case is atypical, but it does tell us what was possible, and this makes it precious. Chiara's union with the captain was irregular, adulterous, and, according to local statutes, illegal, but no one, not Chiara's abandoned husband, not the authorities, had been willing to defy her powerful patron by challenging the arrangement.

With the passage of the years and the birth of two children acknowledged and provided for by the captain, the relationship seems to have taken on a measure of legitimacy, at least in the eyes of the townspeople; but Chiara's situation could never have been easy. She was resented by the older Cellesi children, who saw her as putting her two bastards ahead of them, and she seems to have been isolated from the relatives and friends who made up the captain's social world, relying on servants for companionship. Still, she had come into a degree of luxury far beyond what she could have dreamed of in Lizzano Matto—her own house, servants, jewels—the captain let her lack for nothing, as she was to tell Fabrizio; as long as she continued to enjoy her protector's regard, her situation was secure. Unfortunately, as Lanfredino grew older and enfeebled by gout, he became violently jealous and began to threaten and beat her. Perhaps she gave him cause for his anger: we recall the affair of the earrings and Lanfredino's rage when she refused to tell him who had pawned them on her behalf. According to her testimony to Commissioner Pazzi and Secretary Conti, Captain Lanfredino had been abusing her for some time before Fabrizio Bracciolini entered her life. In her late thirties or early forties—that is, well past her prime by the standards of her time[14]—she must have been gratified by the attentions of this younger, ardent cavalier. But she was warned about Fabrizio and put him off for months. Perhaps she was weighing the advantages and disadvantages of the alternatives: on the one hand, a protector who was rich but aging, generous but suspicious and abusive; on the other, an ardent and dashing nobleman who sent her gifts and promised to be her true knight but who had a scandalous reputation, shaky material prospects, and a wife and two children. She must have realized Fabrizio would not abandon his family (not to mention his wife's dowry), brave the fury of the Cellesi, the penalties of the law, and the displeasure of his superiors in Santo Stefano to go off with her. But she had too few defenses against his amatory rhetoric. So she took the plunge, allowing Fabrizio into her house, her bedchamber, then, in all probability, into her bed.

Chiara's story does not have a happy ending. She was sent back, probably to live in poverty, with a cuckolded husband. The freedom she had reached out for eluded her. But that this ignorant woman from Lizzano Matto should have aspired to freedom at all and that she should have articulated it as a single life, without lover, patron, or husband, was itself a victory of imagination over destiny. Was Chiara exceptional in her ability to imagine—and even pursue—alternatives to the roles society tried to assign to her? In looking for an answer, a more famous case of another sixteenth-century peasant woman comes to mind. Six hundred crow-flight miles to the west, at Artigat in the Pyrenees, Bertrande de Rols was living with her husband, Martin Guerre.[15] Twenty years earlier—about three years before Chiara took up with her rich patron—Bertrande had begun living with a man who claimed to be her long-lost husband, although she must have suspected, and soon knew, that he was an imposter. After three happy years together in this "invented marriage," the real Martin Guerre improbably showed up and denounced the trickster who had usurped his identity, his wife, and his property. Although she seems to have loved the false Martin, Bertrande abandoned him to the gallows and begged her husband's forgiveness, pretending she had been duped. The real Martin grudgingly took her back, and husband and wife made their peace. In this way Bertrande was able to preserve the things that meant most to her—honor, her son's inheritance, and her position of respect in their tightly knit community—at what private emotional cost only she could say.

What has been described as Bertrande's "shrewd realism about how she could maneuver within the constraints placed upon one of her sex"[16] might be said of Chiara as well, although Chiara, perhaps because she had fewer social and material assets to begin with, was readier to defy convention and less successful in achieving a tolerable equilibrium. To be sure, two "individual villagers who tried to fashion their lives in unusual and unexpected ways"[17] do not add up to a trend, but they should make us curious to see if we can find other independent-willed Bertrandes and Chiaras among "the people without a history."[18]

Readers who have followed this story must have found Chiara's lover ridiculous and faithless (as I did) and cheered on the agents of his discomfiture. Probably they laughed, or at least smiled, at the nature of his punishment. A strutting, boastful, bullying cavalier whose conquests are all in the wars of Cupid has little claim on sympathy if he receives his comeuppance. Claiming the rights and privileges of noble birth and Christian chivalry even as he rides roughshod over the responsibilities such assets entail, he can hardly be surprised to hear sounds of cheering when he is unhorsed. Fabrizio is so perfect the stage scoundrel that we may fool ourselves into endowing the agents of his nemesis with more virtue than they deserve. His seduction and abandonment of Chiara was as shabby as it could be, but arguably no worse than her treatment at the hands of the Cellesi. A less irascible, more intro-spective person than Captain Lanfredino might have reflected on his own responsibility for hounding Chiara into the arms of another man; instead, he self-righteously thrust her out of his house. For that matter, his son Mari-otto, for all his much-vaunted gentlemanly honor and peaceful nature, was no kinder; the chivalric code that obliged knights to protect defenseless women, did not, it seems, cover this particular woman. Although he resented Chiara's presence in the Cellesi household and quarreled with his father over his preference for her bastards, it was Mariotto who pursued her when she ran away and persuaded her—with false promises—to return. As he ex-plained to his judges, he was honor-bound to put aside personal differences on behalf of his family; Chiara's welfare was obviously not a consideration. Neither was her privacy. In his belated rush to vindicate his family's honor, he searched the little house on Prato S. Francesco and confiscated the love letters, then strode across the square to the church; there, he claimed, he found the treasure trove Chiara had given to fra Bartolomeo for safekeep-ing. Whether the friar resisted we are not told; in any case Mariotto took them. (Perhaps fra Bartolomeo knew about the hunting incident in which Mariotto gave a peasant a beating for not handing over a disputed hare.)

With the masters of his order and his fellow Pistoians conceding Mariotto's right to punish Fabrizio for offending his father, one kind of justice was served. Honor and knightly obligation were satisfied; community norms were upheld, family solidarity maintained. The kind of justice we associate with sovereign governments, in which states claim the sole responsibility to maintain peace and order, was not so well served, although the practices and attitudes that would ultimately make that form of justice predominant were beginning to take hold in institutions and minds. In fact, one can see in this case the tension between the two.

It should not surprise us that such values as feminine chastity, family honor, and the obligations of knighthood still counted with sixteenth-century princes, even as they struggled to establish sovereign states. Adultery, concubinage, sexual license, and disregarding judicial summonses were all condemned in the sixteenth century, either by city statute, ducal decree, the laws of the church, or a combination of those authorities. Yet none of the principals in the Holy Thursday case were called to account for these misdeeds, although they were plainly culpable. Like the hedgehog, the judges in the Holy Thursday case knew One Big Thing and ignored the fox's many Small Things. Concubinage, adultery, a belated response to court summons were not insignificant, but in the scale of things, Small; a gentleman's reputation, and that of his family, were still Big. Whatever the advance of state power, whatever the hold of Christian sexual morality, the bonds between men were still based on honor; the sacred unit to be defended was the family. Today, we might generally agree on leaving sexual sins and offenses against honor to the fox, but surely most of us would assign an offense against the judicial system to the hedgehog. Family, religion, and personal status are important in ways beyond counting, but today the guarantors of public order and social cohesion are primarily the state, the courts, and the law.

EIGHTEEN

And Then What Happened?

26 July 1579:

Cavalier Fabrizio Bracciolini makes an outright gift of furniture and furnishings to his wife Camilla on behalf of their daughter Ludovica. He declares that he has consumed one-third of her dowry of 4,000 scudi and "made use of" the other two-thirds. He pledges the return to Camilla of goods equal to the amount of the dowry.[1]

Fabrizio and Mariotto go off to war.

Fabrizio Bracciolini to Grand Duke Francis I:

Fabrizio Bracciolini, cavalier of the order and most humble servant and vassal of Your Most Serene Highness, humbly begs that he may be graciously permitted to take part in the war campaign that is being prepared. I remain forever obliged and pray the Lord God may protect and increase Your Highness's felicitous well-being.[2]

A ducal rescript, dated 30 August 1579, reads: "Let it be granted without prejudice."[3]

From the August 1579 entry in the chronicle of the Florentine Giuliano Ricci:[4]

There were huge preparations for the enterprise . . . organized on behalf of the Spaniards, although no one knew where it was going. Everyone loaded as many ships as they possibly could. . . . The Italians and Germans embarked at La Spezia, the Spaniards at Barcelona, while the mass of troops was supposed to embark at Maiorca or Minorca. No one knew who the commander was. Africa was believed the destination. . . . [Embarcation] at La Spezia was set for August 25 for the troops of Colonel Prospero Colonna. He sent three Florentine captains . . . also a son of Captain Lanfredino Cellesi of Pistoia, Sig. Cesare da Montauto, and others. . . . The troops of these captains were to embark at La Spezia and some had already been sent there, but they were not accepted by the Genovese and were sent back. They say the Genovese did not want the massing of the troops in their territory, fearing dissension among them. Signor Don Pietro de'Medici, although for many days expected from one hour to the next, never came. If he went at all, it must have been by a different route.

From the unpublished chronicle of Piero Ricciardi of Pistoia, 20 September 1579:[5]

Signor Don Pietro Medici, brother of the grand duke, was made general in command of ten thousand foot soldiers by His Catholic Majesty for the campaign of the king of Portugal. Among the colonels created by Signor Don Pietro was Signor Prospero Colonna, who created many valiant captains, among them Cavalier Mariotto, son of Captain Lanfredino Cellesi. The same day they came to Pisa to embark from Livorno. Having appointed the young nobleman Bastiano Sozzifanti his standard-bearer, Captain Mariotto made a handsome entry into Pisa this evening. May God grant him good fortune. In truth, Signor Prospero's soldiers are the strength of Italy. It is being said that a more handsome and richer body of men has not been seen for a long time.

Report (undated) of the death of Mariotto:

Now began to be felt the effects of this war undertaken at such expense and with so much trouble. They intended to have men ready in Spain for the opportunity that would come with the death of the King of Portugal, but there are few there and few to come because they have been left without funds, at sea at the mercy of wind and wave, to die of deprivation and hunger. One of their ships was wrecked on the coast of Denia,[6] and Captain Mariotto Cellesi of Pistoia died there with his whole company. [From the chronicle of Giuliano Ricci, undated entry, "Wrecks and losses at sea."][7]

Ricciardi's chronicle records in an entry for 12 November 1580:[8]

The only ones who suffered in this war were the poor Italian soldiers, some of whom died of sickness, some of hunger because they didn't get their provisions, and a lot who were killed by the Spaniards. Captain Mariotto Cellesi died with almost all his soldiers, few of whom [?] returned.[9] This is the way it usually is with Pistoians; such is their good fortune that—during my lifetime, anyhow—whenever they've gone on campaign not a soul has returned.

A letter from Asdrubale Cellesi in Podenzana to Jacopo Tonti, 22 January 1581, accompanies a repayment of 100 scudi borrowed by Mariotto Cellesi.[10]

A letter from Marchese Alessandro Malespina in Podenzana to Captain Lanfredino in Pistoia, 10 April, 1581, reports having been informed by "Messer Asdrubale and other soldiers" that Mariotto, of happy memory, had received money at La Spezia from Messer Giovanni Biassa, relative of the marchese, enabling the company to make the voyage to Spain.[11] Apparently, Mariotto and his company had been at La Spezia awaiting a ship to take them to Spain when orders came transferring them to Pisa. Asdrubale must have accompanied Mariotto to Spain and upon his return visited Podenzana, a fortress seat of Mariotto's relatives, the Malaspina, near the mouth of the Magra River, on the Versilia coast of the Tyrrhenian Sea.

The preceding year, Captain Lanfredino had changed his will.

Addition to the will of Captain Lanfredino Cellesi, 16 April 1580:[12]

To Raffaello his natural son, whom he acknowledges and has always held, maintained, and acknowledged as such, born to him and his concubine Chiara, daughter of Domenico, he leaves the usufruct of a house for his lifetime but no longer, to revert to his [Lanfredino's] heirs, located in Cappella S. Michele, presently occupied by Lionardo Melocchi, in the locale called Garighera fra Fabri . . . [and] a property with a house and all its legal rights and appurtenances, cultivated land, and vineyards, in Casale, on this side of the Stella[13]. . . [and] a farm [podere] in Ferruccia[14] of eleven coltre . . . [and] four wooden beds, four palliassess [saccones], four fustian mattresses and eight of wool, with six pair of linen drawers [lintrorum—underwear?] and three of canvas, sixty napkins [mantiluzzos] stupeos [of linen?], and the same number of sheets, three bombazine covers, and others for a maidservant, and four pillows, which should all be new, all to be given to him at the end of his twentieth year.

He asks his heirs to rear and govern the said Raffaello and treat him just as well as he, the testator, himself would do, under pain of deprivation of their inheritance, and by the same token orders the said Raffaello to be submissive and obedient to his brothers just as he would be to the testator himself, with the stipulation, charge, and obligation to the said Raffaello never to associate with, or to receive in his house, or in any manner to live with Donna Chiara, his mother, because of her evil life, wicked morals and speech, lest she be a cause of the ruin of the said Raffaello and like a pit of perdition to him. . . . In order to avoid any scandal on account of Chiara, if Raffaello does anything counter to [the testator's wishes in this] his guardians may deprive him of the aforesaid legacy and of all property the testator leaves to him.

As guardians of Raffaello for the necessary period, he appoints Francesco di Piero Cellesi and the magnificent cavaliers Mariotto and Teodoro, sons of the testator, to whom he especially entrusts the said Raffaello, and most especially to Ippolita (wife of Mariotto).

Item, in the event that his son, the magnificent and valorous Captain Mariotto, cavalier of the Religion of Santo Stefano, who has left for Belem [in Portugal] does not return or predeceases the testator (which God forbid), in his absence the said testator duly appoints his daughter-in-law, wife of the said Mariotto, mistress of the household and of the property in usufruct and of all property and goods bequeathed to him at present . . . because he [Lanfredino] knows the said Ippolita very well and has great confidence in her goodness, honesty, and observance of the law.

A son is born to Ippolita and the late Mariotto.[15]

Saturday, 28 May 1580:

By the grace of God and in loving memory of Captain Lanfredino [Mariotto must be meant here; our Captain Lanfredino is still alive] Cellesi, this morning between the hours of 5 and 6 a son was born to 'Polita, daughter of Jacopo di Domizio Canciliere [and] wife of the said Cavalier Mariotto, who named him for Mariotto's father. He was presented for baptism by Anton [*Giovanni* is ruled out] Francesco Ghondi, current commissioner of Pistoia [blank] wife of Giovanni Centi [blank] and was baptized in the Duomo. Together with his sister Giulia he was christened on September by Monsignor Abios.o [*sic*]. They both [i.e., the two children] have had roseola.

12 March 1581, Francesco Franchini Fiscale of Pistoia to [Piero Conti?], secretary of the grand duke.[16] (A few nights earlier, Simone Battifolle Panciatichi had been attacked and clubbed by two men.)

[Panciatichi] denied the event to the court, which, it seems to me, most people do here. . . . Simone has certain differences with Captain Lanfredino Cellesi about monies given and owed, and, as a man who has a loose tongue both by nature and habit (which is characteristic of this place), he had been going around saying that Captain Lanfredino is a tyrant, a dog, that he ought to be hanged, and other things of the sort. Someone heard this and said he told Teodoro, the captain's son, about it, and maybe this is true, and maybe it is Teodoro who [beat] him. But Simone said he did not recognize who did it. . . . I left [Simone] at liberty.

I know these things from a secret source and they cannot be proved, so I am just informing the secretary of the matter. I would have issued a *levare l'offesa* but thought I should first write to your eminence to let you decide.

More evidence of Teodoro's involvement in the beating must have come to light. On 4 January 1581, a Pistoia court found that Teodoro had beaten Panciatichi on the head, leg, and hand and bloodied him. Teodoro, in his defense, declared that Simone had insulted him and his father, and this was corroborated by witnesses. Nevertheless, he was ordered to pay a fine of 450 lire (about 65 scudi) and to receive two turns of the rope *(fune)*. Teodoro paid the fine but appealed the punishment of the rope. Not surprisingly, the grand duke commuted this part of the sentence to exile,[17] physical punishment being as unsuitable for wayward aristocrats as questioning under torture. His rescript does not specify for how long Teodoro was to be banished.

If Captain Lanfredino had ordered the beating of Simone Panciatichi, as secretly reported to the fiscale, it was not, so far as we know, for reasons connected to the Holy Thursday incident. But he and some of the other actors in that drama continue to behave true to type: the captain, contentious as ever, still has his detractors waylaid in the street; Teodoro, who is now the eldest son, is his instrument of vengeance; Simone, the victim of Cellesi vengeance, one of the prime gossips in the affair of Mariotto and Fabrizio, is gossiping still; but he is closemouthed when officials try to question him about the beating. Such behavior, according to Fiscale Franchini, who has been serving there for some years now, is typical of Pistoia, where people are loose-tongued "by nature and habit," but fall silent when confronted by state authorities. Franchini, who knew it at first hand, might also have been thinking of the Holy Thursday imbroglio, now three years past, in which— although that affair was infinitely more complicated—there was a similar pattern of gossip and silence.

Fabrizio, on the other hand, is still seeking revenge.

We have seen the complaint . . . against Lorenzo di Alessandro Parenti of Lucca, to wit: that in August 1581 the said Lorenzo made an agreement promising Cavalier Fabrizio di Messer Francesco Bracciolini of Pistoia that he would kill or have killed in Pistoia Priest Asdrubale Cellesi of Pistoia, that he was promised money and a reward by the said cavalier, and that while they were negotiating about the matter it came to the notice of the court and they were arrested before anything more happened. . . . With the completion of the processo in which it is shown that the details contained in the complaint are true and having seen and considered everything [their lordships] find the above named Lorenzo di Alessandro Parenti of Lucca guilty and therefore condemn him to the galleys as reasonable punishment. Subject to the approval of His Highness and to all due procedures, he is to be confined to prison *(alle stinche)* then sent into the galleys.[18]

In 1582, Captain Lanfredino tried to collect a debt owed to his late son Mariotto.

To Ser Giovanni [Politi?], 4 August, 1582.[19]

I commissioned you quite a while ago to get the person who borrowed money from my son Captain Mariotto to pay me; but you do not have to be polite to make him understand that if he does not pay me the approximately 20 scudi immediately I will be forced to proceed against him.

Captain Lanfredino refuses to pay Mariotto's debts.

To Messer Giulio del Caccia in Florence, 27 December 1583.[20]

About three years ago, at the time of Messer Domenico Bonsi,[21] I was charged by the Religion of Santo Stefano for about 12 scudi, expenses, they said, of my son Mariotto. I wrote to [Bonsi] and showed that I had neither the property nor goods of Mariotto and said that they should collect from him. Bonsi agreed and cancelled the charge. I wish you would tell this to the order. I don't want to, and am not obligated to pay the debts of my son . . . I neither am nor want to be my son's heir; I renounced [his inheritance] quite a while ago.[22]

Notwithstanding his conviction for assault on Simone Panciatichi three years earlier, in 1584 Teodoro Cellesi was readily accepted into the Order of Santo Stefano, at the age of twenty-six, characterized in his *provanza*[23] by his father as "a young man of good habits" and by an anonymous commentator as "one of the leading youths of the city of Pistoia."

We also learn from a letter of Vicar Orazio Berindelli, included in the application file, that Fabrizio Bracciolini made some comment *(intervento)* on the application. Alas, the vicar does not reveal what Fabrizio said; but when six prominent Pistoians testified on Teodoro's behalf it was duly noted in the proceedings that Fabrizio, "senior cavalier of the city of Pistoia of the magnificent cavaliers of the Order of Santo Stefano" accompanied them, although he did not speak. Teodoro's application noted that Captain Lanfredino intended to endow the order with a perpetual benefice, or *commenda perpetua*. Teodoro would be its first beneficiary and it would be passed on to future Cellesi cavaliers *(commenda padronato)*. The holder of this commenda would also be named *balì* for Pistoia; that is, chief of the Pistoia group of Santo Stefano cavaliers. The contract for establishing the Cellesi commenda was signed soon afterward.[24]

The captain's arranging for Teodoro to become balì must have been a calculated slap at his old rival Fabrizio, who was senior Santo Stefano cavalier in Pistoia.

Teodoro del Captain Lanfredino Cellesi went to Florence to receive the uniform of balì of the Religion of Santo Stefano and place 10,000 scudi in a *commenda da padronato*. He received it in the Church of the Nuns of the Crocetta in Florence, which is behind the Church of Santissima Annunziata. They gave him the Grand Cross of the Asini of Florence[25] and the balì del Martelli gave him the *stocco*, as I record here.[26]

An undated memoir of the Cellesi family provides this sketch of Teodoro:[27]

Teodoro di Lanfredino Cellesi, with the rich inheritance left to him by his father and his own abilities, was able to create a figure of great respect in the city. Besides, he married Caterina Vinta, daughter of Prior Paolo Vinta, auditor of His Highness and Florentine senator, and with this alliance he enjoyed many favors in the city. He was balì for Pistoia of the Sacred Religion of Santo Stefano and established the baliage for his house [so that it never failed to go to one of the family].[28] With his nephew Cosimo he went to Paris to serve Maria de'Medici, spouse of Henry IV, where he received many honors.

In this sketch, the term describing Teodoro's marriage to Caterina Vinta is *apparentadosi*—entered a family relationship. The betrothal contract is even more pointed: the *parentado* is not made between Teodoro and Caterina but between Teodoro and the bride's father, Paolo Vinta.[29] Clearly, the main function of such a marriage was to link two important and ambitious families. The Vinta was one of the "new" provincial families that rose to great prominence in the service of the Medici dynasty. Already, as auditor of the Riformagioni, one of the state's most important administrative officials, Paolo Vinta was to reach the very peak of ducal service when he became first secretary in 1606.[30] Although the Cellesi was the older, more aristocratic of the two houses, the alliance is clearly seen in this family memoir as a coup for them. Teodoro's bride brought him a dowry of 5,000 scudi cash and "such gifts as [Paolo] wished to give." More importantly, with the marriage came entrée into the court life of Florence ("the city") and Paris for Teodoro and his nephew Cosimo, the firstborn son of his late brother Cavalier Mariotto, now just approaching the age of thirty.

On 7 December 1587, Teodoro Cellesi wrote to Lodovico Mannelli in Florence:[31] "Captain Lanfredino my father has been in bed about twenty days, so seriously ill that the physicians have said he should not deal with any business but only concern himself to rest." Then soon afterward:

The night of 9 December 1587 at one o'clock at night it pleased almighty God to take to himself the good soul of Captain Lanfredino di Mariotto Cellesi. He confessed three days earlier after requesting a confessor on his own initiative. He took communion and had the holy oils. He made his will in 1580, dividing his estate between the balì [Teodoro] his son and his grandchildren, leaving all his moveable property in *fidecommisso* [deed of trust].

The Cellesi and the Bishop's Entry ceremony of 1599:

Sunday, the clerics and regular friars went in procession to the hospice, where Bishop Passerini and his party had spent the night. [The hospice was three miles outside the Lucca Gate.] Monsignor said low mass in the hospice chapel, and from there the clerics, followed by monsignor dressed all in white, wearing pontificals, a white mitre on his head, riding on a white palfrey decked out in white. In front of him on a white palfrey rode Messer Giovanni Battista, the chancellor and dean of the canons carrying a silver pastoral [staff?]. When monsignor arrived near the bastion of the Lucca Gate, he stopped at a street crossing where an arch had been erected at the expense of the Cellesi family, which was present. It was decorated with pictures, statues, and inscriptions. The most distinguished of the family, the Balì Teodoro, son of Captain Lanfredino Cellesi, addressed some words to him in name of the entire Cellesi family and monsignor replied very graciously. . . . Then [after the customary circuit of the city's sacred places], he divested himself of his pontificals and went to his own palace, where the Balì Teodoro again addressed him and returned his white palfrey to him. Monsignor thanked him and said the palfrey should be given to him to whom it was due—that is, the eldest of the Cellesi, who in that time was Niccolao di Piero Cellesi. The family took the palfrey to the house of Niccolao, who the following day sent her with her saddle and bridle to . . . [the recipient is omitted], while to Niccolao remained monsignor's gloves.

Several days before Monsignor's arrival, Niccolao, as the eldest, had invited the family to his house to discuss how they were to honor him and the next morning he invited the members of the family who were to greet the bishop and gave them a fine collation in his house.

Raffaello Cellesi claims a legacy:

Balì Teodoro died in 1608, at the age of fifty.[32] Later that year, on 2 September, Raffaello Cellesi, son of the late Captain Lanfredino and Chiara Fioresi, appeared before the commissioner's court in Pistoia to claim his share of his father's *banco*, both Mariotto and Teodoro now being deceased. His claim was contested by Mariotto's widow, Ippolita, who refused to surrender the keys to the *banco* in the bishop's palace or allow Raffaello to consult the account books. On 25 September the court decided that the books were to be deposited at S. Jacopo and an inventory made from them; the keys were to be held by the commissioner.[33]

In 1610, Raffaello again sued the widows of his two half-brothers for what he claimed was his share of the captain's estate. The admonition of Lanfredino that his sons were not to give Raffaello or Ippolita any difficulties about their legacies under pain of losing their own was introduced into the suit. But Raffaello was still in litigation in 1615 for what he claimed was his share—this time both he and Caterina Vinta, widow of Teodoro, being against Ippolita. I have not found any record of the outcome of the litigation.

Death notice for Fabrizio Bracciolini, 31 December 1611: "On the said day [funeral], for Captain Cavalier Fabbrizio Bracciolini with two pairs of candelabra: 2 scudi, 2 lire, 8 soldi."[34] Fabrizio lived to be sixty-six.

Death notice for "Madonna Chiara, mother of Raffaello, son of Captain Lanfredino Cellesi," 21 July 1612.[35]

Chiara must have been close to seventy at the time of her death. Evidently she had not remained in Lizzano Matto or Rocha del Corneto. At some time between 1578 and 1612 she had returned to Pistoia, for it was there that her death was recorded. Either she had left her husband again or she returned to Pistoia after his death. Was she reunited with her children? In so small a town, it would have been difficult to avoid seeing them, despite the captain's efforts to keep them apart.

Death notice for Raffaello, son of Captain Lanfredino Cellesi, 20 May 1628.[36] Raffaello would have been about sixty-four at his death.

The New and the Old

From the communal car park near the Porta al Borgo and Pistoia's medieval walls, my morning walk to the Archivio di Stato and the Biblioteca Forteguerriana regularly took me across the Piazza S. Francesco d'Assisi, down the length of the via S. Andrea, past its great Romanesque church. Halfway along the via dei Rossi, I turned left, crossing the tip of the little street still bearing the name Bracciolini, almost within sight of Fabrizio's family palace at the far end. From there it was a few steps to the library, and a few more steps around another corner to the archives.

When I had finished for the day, I retraced my route, the Holy Thursday story still replaying itself in my mind. On some days I turned into the doorway of the S. Andrea Church to review what Camilla could have seen of the sword fight as she stood at the holy-water stoup or as she came out to the front steps. Back on the street, with the friendly help of some of the neighbors, I looked (in vain) for traces of the public well in front of Tonio's house, where Mariotto had waited for Fabrizio to pass. Returning across the Piazza S. Francesco, I imagined myself one of Fabrizio's audience as he strutted and preened in front of Chiara's "little house." Sometimes I made a detour to Castel Cellesi to see if I could determine which of two adjacent houses was Captain Lanfredino's, which Mariotto's, or where the bargello's lieutenant and his *sbirri* had taken cover as they spied on Fabrizio serenading his mistress under the Cellesi windows.

This daily interleaving of documents, streets, and places primed my sense of connection to the characters and settings of the Holy Thursday story, as though Pistoia itself were prompting me in reconstructing a tiny segment of its history. On one particularly memorable day, the curtain of time seemed to draw back altogether and the past to repeat itself before my astonished eyes. Returning from a day in the archives, I saw two young men on the grassy plot between the Church of S. Andrea and the house next door—the house occupied by the family of Nardino il Bonzetta in 1578. Toe-to-toe, arms waving, voices loud and angry, threatening, they passed, as the Italians say, from words to deeds. A sudden eruption of blows, a sudden stop; a uniformed policeman (whether *carabiniere* or *vigile* I was too startled to notice; shades of Camilla and the other Holy Thursday eye witnesses!) was bearing down on them from the direction of Piazza S. Francesco. As the Law came nearer, the two slunk off down the vicolo S. Andrea, behind the Compagnia di S. Giuseppe (where Tonio Visconti had made his Easter observance of the *Quarantore*). An unpleasant little scene, and in any other circumstances one I would have tried to forget quickly, but I was elated and I thanked whatever goddess of Pistoian history had staged this time-warped reenactment of the Holy Thursday drama for me alone.

Plus ça change—cliché or not—was a maxim hard to resist after witnessing the replay of the fight at S. Andrea, yet another demonstration that violence by young men against other young men has some claim to being a biological constant. At the same time, I was aware that a historian who allows himself to muse about young men's hormonal excesses over the centuries must also be mindful of the different social and cultural frameworks in which biology does its work. Most obviously, the *look* had changed: instead of the mail jackets, vambraces, and steel under helmets worn by Mariotto and Fabrizio, the antagonists I saw in the via S. Andrea were dressed more vulnerably in flimsy T-shirts and threadbare jeans. Instead of fighting with swords and daggers, they used their bare fists. These were no noble cavaliers. In our egalitarian age, class distinctions are not so obviously signaled by differences in clothing, hair styles, and weaponry as they were four centuries ago; still, the scruffy appearance and shifty bearing of the two antagonists I watched at S. Andrea left me no doubt that they were on the lower rungs of Pistoia's social ladder—that they were, in fact, street toughs. Besides, nowadays most "respectable" citizens, unlike their sixteenth-century counterparts, tend to fight their personal battles by more peaceful means and away from the public gaze. Language makes it plain: when we "make a public spectacle of ourselves," we lose respectability (unless we are media stars, in which case we are beyond considerations of respectability).

Reasons for fighting, no less than social identities, vary with time and place. About the motives of these two modern brawlers I can only speculate. Possibly, like Mariotto and Fabrizio, they were quarreling about a woman; if so, this being up-to-date Tuscany, not archaic Sicily or Calabria, I doubt they would have had the same concern for family honor. Possibly they were fighting over drugs or money, or both. Even if they were, pride and the need for the respect of their peers must have played some part in their angry exchange, just as a craving for respect and a fear of "disrespect" play roles in the well-documented mayhem of American inner cities.

Provincial though it may still be, Pistoia, with its motor cars and parking meters, suburbs and high-rise apartment buildings, supermarkets and off-the-rack clothing stores, is a more impersonal place than it was in the sixteenth century. This came home to me acutely when I asked a businessman who rents office space at Castel Cellesi what he knew of the history of these buildings. My informant was agreeable and well-meaning, but vague, and he assured me—quite mistakenly as I learned later—that its old owners, the Cellesi, had died out a generation or two earlier. In 1578, even the street-walkers knew who Captain Lanfredino was, and a good deal more about him than that. A modern Lanfredino might be less open about his private life, perhaps less concerned about "the opinion of the world" than his sixteenth-century forebear. When I found Cellesi still living at La Magia, the old Panciatichi villa near Quarrata, I sought an appointment with Captain Lanfredino's namesake, Count Lanfredino Amati Cellesi (since deceased). I was politely turned away.

As personal identity has become less dependent upon honor and *bella figura*, so communal public space is no longer the venue of choice for social interactions, either peaceful or violent, to anything like the extent it was in 1578. When my two T-shirted, bare-headed modern cavaliers "entered fighting" like the Guelfs and Ghibellines of Max Beerbohm's *Savonarola Brown*, there was no one in the street to see them but myself; the policeman arrived after they had begun to trade blows. This was the only fight I saw during the months I spent in Pistoia; in the sixteenth century, I probably would have seen many more.[1] The intense, face-to-face life that once characterized the streets and piazzas inside the perimeter of Pistoia's old walls has, as in so many other Italian cities, been carried off, first on Vespas, then in Fiats, to the periphery, there to be transmuted into an impersonal TV-watching culture (the highest rate in Europe).

Nowadays, apart from a few feast days, Pistoia's inner city comes alive only on Wednesday and Saturday mornings, when the stalls and customers of the open-air market fill the Piazza Grande. By afternoon, the stalls and customers are gone and the great square is quiet again, barely disturbed by the men with brooms cleaning up the morning's debris. On a windy March day, the swirling paper and the bent figures of the sweepers only accentuate the emptiness of this vast anachronistic space. In the sixteenth century, the very magnitude of the piazza was functional, with a social purpose and a ceremonial grandeur; today it seems absurdly grandiose.

Haunting the city's streets and conjuring up the scenes of the Holy Thursday story has been a stimulating correlative to mining it out of texts, revealing continuities between Pistoia past and Pistoia present, and bringing home to me how much has changed. In 1578, Pistoia was no longer medieval; that is to say, no longer a wealthy, growing, self-confident, self-governing commune. With little more than half the population it had before 1348, the year of the Black Death, it was ruled from Florence, administered mainly by Florentine officials, garrisoned by the grand duke's hired troops, and increasingly integrated into a regional economy centered in the capital. More than half a century had passed since the last Cancellieri partisan had burned down a Panciatichi house or the last Panciatichi murdered a Cancellieri in the streets. Sons of the old patrician families and would-be aristocrats were increasingly drawn into the orbit of the grand duke's court, making honorable careers in the Order of Santo Stefano and the growing bureaucracy. Pistoia was part of an expansionist Renaissance territorial state under construction by a young, ambitious new dynasty. Not medieval, but not modern either. Important as these changes were, they led to few radical innovations in political institutions, to little questioning of social hierarchies or of inherited assumptions about the nature of things. Effervescent new wine was being poured into traditional old bottles, but the old vessels, give or take a few cracks, mostly held.

In the Holy Thursday case, with its tangled strands of power criss-crossing between center and periphery and its jurisdictional troika of monarchy, church, and Order of Santo Stefano, the centralizing state had to cope with its medieval heritage of divided authority. Each of the three had its own mission, its own judicial system, and its own carefully guarded prerogatives, and each shaped the Cellesi *processo* in its own way. True, two of the three jurisdictions were presided over by the grand duke, who united in his august person the rule of the Tuscan state and, ex officio, the command of the Order of Santo Stefano; but Mariotto's trial illustrates some of the difficulties this dual role could make for his highness. As an ambitious state builder, the grand duke tried to suppress private violence by repeatedly banning the carrying of weapons, outlawing feuds, and ordering his magistrates to apply promptly the compulsory peacemaking mechanisms, as well as by swift and severe punishment for transgressors. Dueling was a crime; quarrels were to be settled in the courts rather than in the streets; antagonists were bonded to keep the peace. But as the premier noble, the chief and patron of all other Tuscan *gentiluomini,* and grand commander of the cavaliers of Santo Stefano, Francesco I, de'Medici was called upon to tolerate, to practice—indeed, to promote—a chivalric code that treated those very behaviors as the birthright of Tuscany's burgeoning nobility.

Abbreviations

ACV   Archivio Curiale Vescovile, Pistoia
ASF   Archivio di Stato, Firenze
ASP   Archivio di Stato, Pisa
ASPist   Archivio di Stato, Pistoia
ASI   *Archivio storico italiano*
BNF   Biblioteca Nazionale di Firenze
BNR   Biblioteca Nazionale di Roma
BSP   *Bulletino storico pistoiese*
DBI   *Dizionario biografico degli italiani*
Fort   Biblioteca Forteguerriana, Pistoia
OSS   Archivio di Stato Pisa Ordine di Santo Stefano
Vat   Biblioteca Vaticana

Unless otherwise noted, my source for all matters regarding the Holy Thursday incident is ASP, Ordine di Santo Stefano 1757, Sentenze, a *filza,* or file, of about three hundred folio pages, many unnumbered and many others incorrectly numbered or out of order. On this and other records, see my remarks in the bibliography under "Primary Sources."

One   The Holy Thursday Incident

Epigraph: Guido Cavalcanti, sonnet 18, trans. G. S. Fraser, *Lyric Poetry of the Italian Renaissance* (New Haven, 1954), 93.

1. I have not found a contemporary description of the Pistoia ceremony. In describing Archbishop Antonio Altoviti's performance of the Holy Thursday foot washing of 1569 in Florence, the diarist Lapini says: "This was the first time the feet of poor men were washed, because it was the custom on that day to wash the feet of the cathedral canons, not of the poor." Archbishop Altoviti also gave the participants, at his own expense, two soldi, a loaf of bread, and a cap of white cloth topped with an olive garland and a white vest. Agostino Lapini, *Diario fiorentino dal 252 al 1596,* ed. Giuseppe Odoardo Corazzini (Florence, 1900), 163.

2. Forms and spelling of names often varies in the documents. Thus Bracciolini,

Braccini, Bracciolino; Raffaello, Raffaelle. I have standardized them and also modernized spelling and punctuation.

3. On the preference of Pistoia's noble families for the center, see Lucia Gai, "Centro e periferia nell'orbita fiorentina," *Pistoia: una città nello stato mediceo,* catalog of the exhibition, Pistoia, 28 June–30 September, 1980 (Pistoia, 1980), 80–83.

4. The southeast corner of the palace rose over the crossing of the *cardo* and *decumanus*—the precise center of the Roman city—on the ancient consular via Cassia. The facade of the sixteenth-century building was asymmetrical, so that the main door could open on the Piazza del Duomo. *Il patrimonio artistico di Pistoia e del suo territorio: Catalogo storico descrittivo* (Pistoia, 1967), n. 22.

A document of 1382 refers to the construction of the Palace of the Podestà (literally, Palace of Power, the Podestà being the medieval commune's highest magistrate). It stood among houses of the Bracciolini and a Mattei house formerly owned by Andrea Bracciolini. See *Liber censuum comunis Pistorii,* ed. Q. Santoli (Pistoia, 1915), 492.

At the time of the Holy Thursday incident, the Bracciolini had just sold their house and the two adjoining buildings to the educational foundation of the Sapienza, which owned a good deal of property in the neighborhood, although the family continued to occupy the palace as tenants. The other two buildings were occupied by the bargello and a shop. Lucia Gai, "Centro e periferia," 140, and illustration no. 46. The Bracciolini had been litigating over the property since 1526, and well into the seventeenth century they were still quarreling with the Sapienza and the commune over alterations. ASF, Acquisti e Doni Galletti, 266, busta 7.

5. A thirteenth-century statute forbade any tower to be built in the city or *in suis burgis,* in its dependent towns, higher than the tower of the Ildebrandi. If a tower exceeded the Ildebrandi's it was to be knocked down to that height or destroyed. *Statutum potestatis comunis Pistorii,* ed. Lodovicus Zdekauer (Milan, 1888), book 5, no. 2., p. 271.

6. The names Visconti and Bisconti are interchangeable in the documents.

7. The Visconti house was just north of the Church of S. Andrea. Lionardo, Tonio's father, bought it from the church for 215 lire (about 32 scudi). The copy of the contract I found does not give the date of sale. "Testamenti e contratti S. Andrea," ASPist, Patrimonio Ecclesiastico 543, filza 304, fol. 51v–52r.

8. In earlier days Pistoians went in procession to shrines outside the city walls to receive the Holy Week pardons. Alberto Chiappelli, *Pistoia città e terre mistiche* (Florence, 1924), 236–38.

9. An old Pistoian ordinance required solemn observance of principal feast days, including abstention from work by all *homines et personas. Breve et ordinamenta populi Anni MCCLXXXIIII,* ed. Lodovicus Zdekauer (Milan, 1891), 3.140: 143. At the diocesan synod of 1587, called to implement the reforms of the Council of Trent, Bishop Lattanzi complained that many Pistoians "forgetful of their souls . . . are not ashamed to work, buy and sell, keep their shops open, cart and haul, and do

all sorts of business on the prohibited days," but then the bishop exempts activities related to producing, buying, and selling bread, grain, meat, vegetables, wine, fish, and the like. In all, there were thirty-six feast days, not counting saints' days and Sundays, to be observed. *Decreta Diocesanae Synodi Pistorensis,* 37–39. The great swell of Marian piety following the Council of Trent tended to overshadow devotion to the saints, and the number of saints' days in the liturgy was reduced. A 1574 memorandum of the Church of the Annunciation lists nine for the year. Davide Maria Montagna, *Feste liturgiche ed altre "allegrezze" all'Annunziata di Pistoia fra il '500 e il '700* (Pistoia, 1987), 16. Pistoia's total of ninety-seven holy days (counting Sundays) is in the range of Christopher Hill's estimate of "over a 100" for the seventeenth century. Samuel Berner, "Florentine Society in the Late-Sixteenth- and Early-Seventeenth Centuries," *Studies in the Renaissance* 18 (1971): 224, n. 89.

Two   History and Comedy

1. Robert Dallington, *A Survey of the Great Duke's State of Tuscany in the Yeare of Our Lord 1596* (London, 1605).

2. As contemporaries noted, two examples: man of letters Giovanni Muzio compared service to princes and the love of ladies with theater acting. *Lettere,* ed. Giovanni Francesco Lucchi (Florence, 1590), 90–95; Santo Stefano cavalier Francesco Ferretti wrote that in dying Grand Duke Cosimo de'Medici was able to watch as in a theater the deeds of his successor. *Diporti notturni* (Ancona, 1580), dedication. See also Peter Burke, *The Historical Anthropology of Early Modern Italy: Essays on Perception and Communication* (Cambridge, 1987), 9–10. On life imitating art in Renaissance Rome, see Thomas V. Cohen and Elizabeth S. Cohen, *Words and Deeds in Renaissance Rome: Trials before the Papal Magistrates* (Toronto, 1993), 30–31.

3. See Edward Muir, *Mad Blood Stirring: Vendetta and Factions in Friuli during the Renaissance* (Baltimore, 1993), 158–59 and bibliography in n. 13, 323–24.

4. Elizabeth Cropper and Charles Dempsey told me about Tagliacozzi, or Tagliacozzo (1545–99). He was the father of plastic surgery, specializing in noses, ears, and lips. Already well known and influential on the Continent by the 1570s, he published his *De curtorum chirurgia per insitionem* at Venice in 1597. Alexander Read (1586?–1641) prescribed his methods and described them at length in *Chirurgorum comes, or The whole practice of chirurgery* (London, 1687), 645–704.

5. "Often, one man's loss was another's gain, as if honour, like matter and momentum, could be conserved." Cohen and Cohen, *Words and Deeds,* 25. Often, but not always: as Kristen B. Neuschel points out, the rules of manners and courtesy made it possible for equals mutually to sustain each other's honor. *Word of Honor: Interpreting Noble Culture in Sixteenth-Century France* (Ithaca, 1989), 206.

6. Alongside such professional duel theorists as Girolamo Muzio (1496–1576) were princes and other nobles of the highest rank who were regularly called upon to contribute written opinions in affairs of honor. See my "Fighting or Flyting? Ver-

bal Duelling in Mid-Sixteenth Century Italy," in *Crime, Society, and the Law in Renaissance Italy,* ed. T. Dean and K. Lowe (Cambridge, 1994), 204–20.

7. For one completely different reading, see chap. 14, n. 11.

8. See Thomas Kuehn, "Reading Microhistory: The Example of Giovanni and Lusanna" *Journal of Modern History* 61 (1989): 514–34, and the introduction to Cohen and Cohen, *Words and Deeds,* 25.

Three   Pistoia and the Medici State

1. "Relazione del Commissario Gio. Battista Tedaldi," 312. On Tedaldi, his career, and his *relazioni,* see Elena Fasano Guarini, "Arezzo, Pistoia, Pisa nelle note del Commissario Giovan Batista Tedaldi (1566–1574)," *Studi di storia pisana e toscana in onore del Prof. Cinzio Violante: Biblioteca del Bollettino storico pisano* (Pisa, 1991), 161–76.

2. This is the explanation favored by David Herlihy, *Medieval and Renaissance Pistoia* (New Haven, 1967). My sketch of Pistoia history owes much to Herlihy's book, as well as to Tedaldi.

3. On Pistoia's factions, William J. Connell, "Republican Territorial Government: Florence and Pistoia, Fifteenth and Early Sixteenth Centuries" (Ph.D. diss., University of California, Berkeley, 1989), chap. 2. I am grateful to Professor Connell for allowing me to read and quote from his work, soon to be published in Florence as *La città dei crucci.*

4. Reported by the Venetian ambassador. See Jolanda Ferretti, "L'organizzazione militare in Toscana durante il governo di Alessandro e Cosimo I de'Medici," *Rivista storica degli archivi toscani,* pt. 1 (1929), 248–75, pt. 2 (1930), 58–80, quoting from *Relazioni degli Ambasciatori Veneti,* ed. E. Alberi (Florence, 1841), ser. 2, 1: 73. See also Marco Dedola, "'Tener Pistoia con le parti': governo fiorentino e fazioni pistoiesi all'inizio del '500," *Ricerche storiche* 22 (1992): 239–59. I have altered the order but not the sense of the quotation by placing Pistoia last in the series of places listed by Lorenzo.

5. ASPist, Inventario 64 del Capitano di Custodia, 12.

6. According to the unpublished diary attributed to Messer Jacopo di Niccolò Melocchi, a Cancellieri leader, the February 4 attack was part of a plot to kill *la maggior parte* of the Cancellieri leaders when they gathered at the cathedral on the Feast of S. Agatha, February 4. *Ricordi* BNF, Acquisti e Doni, filza 8, fol. 8r, but the feast was February 5. William Connell's forthcoming book (n. 3 above) will give a much more thorough account of the conflict.

7. Connell, 354, citing Jacopo Maria Fioravanti, *Memorie storiche della città di Pistoia.* Lucca, 1758 (repr. Bologna, 1968), 400.

8. Deposition of Salimbene di Tomaso Panciatichi, Fort, MS Chiappelli 121, p. 74.

9. Antonio Ivan Pini, "La demografia italiana dalla Peste Nera alla metà del Quattrocento: bilancio di studi e problemi di ricerca," *Italia, 1350–1450: tra crisi, trasformazione, sviluppo* (Pistoia, 1993), 7–33. On Pistoia, see 19–21, 26–27.

10. Gai, "Centro e periferia," 85.

11. Ibid.

12. Ibid., 77.

13. Forty years earlier it was reported that the canons regular of Pistoia were infected with Lutheranism. In nearby Lucca, Lutheranism was rife among the laity. Armando F. Verde, "Il movimento savonaroliano della congregazione di S. Marco nella prima metà del cinquecento attraverso alcuni suoi rappresentanti," *Studi savonaroliani verso il V centenario,* ed. Gian Carlo Garfagnini (Florence, 1996), 254–56.

14. Lucia Gai points out that Pistoian bishops, mostly noble and predominantly Florentine, were usually nonresident, leaving their vicars in charge with excessive freedom and that local protests to the Holy See were unavailing until the apostolic visitation of 1582 and the episcopacy of Alessandro del Caccia (1600–49). "Centro e periferia," 64–65. However, as we shall see, the Pistoia synod of 1587, in the last year of Bishop Lattanzi's administration, began to implement the reforms of the Council of Trent. See ibid., 77.

15. Cosimo I was still grand duke in name, and Tedaldi's words are directed to him, although in 1564, Cosimo, after a twenty-seven-year reign, had officially transferred power to his son Francesco I. He died in 1574.

16. Since the mid fifteenth century, commissioners had been sent out as needed, but Cosimo I, seeing that "the Pistoiese have always been inclined to brawling *[risse]*" decided a single resident official would be more effective. Fioravanti, 427.

17. Arnaldo D'Addario, *La formazione dello stato moderno in Toscana da Cosimo il Vecchio a Cosimo I de' Medici* (Lecce, 1976), 224. Gai believes it was after 1547. "Centro e periferia," 94, n. 143.

18. ASF, Medici Principato, 406, fol. 12.

Four   The Cellesi

1. In 1717, out of *"pura curiosità,"* three local clergyman, Girolamo Casseri, the pievano of Celle, Padre Gian Battista Casseri, and fra Felice Cetrocchi, searched in the neighborhood of the church of Celle and found traces of the via Lombarda, one of the early mountain roads that linked Tuscany with the north. Tracing it for some distance, the three amateur archeologists identified the ruins of a bridge over the Vincio made with dressed stone, ruins of a building in which they believed iron-working had been carried on, and considerable remains of a hospice erected, they believed, by the Templars, for pilgrims. With their signed report is a drawing of the area. Fort, Raccolta B. Chiappelli, 77, fols. 525v–526r and 575r; at fol. 492, an insert with a large-scale map of the area. For more on roads through Pistoia, see Herlihy, *Medieval and Renaissance Pistoia,* 19–26.

2. On *incastellamento* and the settling of the area, see Philip Jones, *The Italian City-State from Commune to Signoria* (Oxford, 1997), 29–30, passim, and Natale

Rauty, "L'incastellamento nel territorio pistoiese tra il X e l'XI secolo," *BSP* 92 (1990), 31–57.

3. Fort, MS C 198, fol. 3r.

4. "de Victis hereticiis Predecessore que tuo incolumne preservato ex privilegio actio iteramus."

5. In most accounts of the symbolic nuptials, the bishop puts a ring on the finger of the abbess and spends the night in a convent bed she has prepared for him.

6. ASPist, Famiglio Cellesi.

7. *Cronache di Ser Luca Dominici della venuta dei Bianchi.* Ed. Carlo Gigliotti (Pistoia, 1933), 228–32.

8. "Dell' Antico Privilegio della Famiglia Cellesi d'introdurre i nuovi Vescovi in Pistoia, nuovo vescovo [*sic*] delle mal fondate pretensioni che gli *Operai* del S. Jacopo suscitarono a riguardo di tale honorificenza contro la medesima famiglia," ASPist, Cellesi 32, fasc. 4.

9. For a partial description of the entry of 1599, still dominated by the Cellesi, see chap. 18.

10. The city's preparations for staging them in 1620 are described in "Partito e Deliberazioni, 1612–28," Fort, MS E 373, fasc. 3, fols. not numbered.

11. Richard Trexler, *Public Life in Renaissance Florence* (New York, 1980), 271.

12. Ibid., 273.

13. Ibid., 273–74.

14. In a report to the Pratica Segreta by Fiscale Francesco Franchini in 1588. ASF, Pratica Segreta Pistoia Lettere 475, fol. 856v. See also G. Pinto, *Storia di Pistoia* (Florence, 1999), chap. 4.

15. "Dell' Antico Privilegio della Famiglia Cellesi."

16. Jacopo Maria Fioravanti, *Memorie storiche della città di Pistoia* (Lucca, 1758), 380–84.

17. In Mariotto Cellesi's application for admission to Santo Stefano, the cost was given as 120 scudi.

18. Baptized 25 February, 1518. This and the following birth dates are from records of baptism in Fort, MS E 342, n.p.

19. "Captain Lanfredino is a merchant of lamb fells and has a banco as a legally recognized merchant"—testimony of his agent Giovanni Fabroni in a suit against Tommaso Cellesi in 1574. Fort, MS Chiappelli 4, fol. 41 r–v.

20. By the sixteenth century, partible inheritance, short-sighted ambition, and greed had made of the Malaspina an archaic clan of petty feudators forever fighting each other with weapons and lawsuits while being manipulated by their more powerful neighbors, the states of Milan, Genoa, and Tuscany. The case of Marchese Teodoro, Giulia's father, is typical. The youngest of five sons, he was lord of a handful of fairly obscure properties and castles in the valley of the upper Magro River. Besieged and dispossessed of all his lands by his brothers and their allies, he spent

the rest of his life trying to obtain restitution. When he died, he named Angela's distant relative, Duke Alessandro de'Medici of Florence, as his executor and commended her and their two children to the duke's protection. Eugenio Branchi, *Storia della Lunigiana feudale*, 3 vols. (Pistoia, 1897, repr. 1971) 2, 238–45. Apparently Duke Cosimo I and his consort, Eleonora of Toledo, honored that charge; whether they provided Giulia with a dowry is not recorded; Branchi thought not, although her dowry of 2,000 scudi is recorded in a list of Cellesi marriages and dowries (MS Chiappelli, 77 fols. 241–42). Marriage to a Malaspina, even dowerless, was a coup for the socially ambitious Lanfredino Cellesi. How furious he would have been to read in Branchi: "It is not known who the second daughter [Giulia] married, but it was probably someone of ignoble status."

21. In 1525 members of the Grazzini family lost a suit requesting they be recognized as owners of the Cellesi property (in Cappella di S. Michele in Bonacci tra Fabbri). They claimed the Cellesi had wrongfully appropriated it from the Grazzini after renting it from them for thirty years. In 1503 the Grazzini recovered it, only to lose it to the Cellesi again in another decision of 1508. The Grazzini continued litigation over the property until 1571, when Captain Lanfredino Cellesi finally won a verdict terminating the case in his favor. Fort, MS Chiappelli 121, fols. not numbered.

22. On Captain Lanfredino's conviction for murder many years earlier, see my "Fighting or Flyting?" (see chap. 2, n. 6), 210, n. 8.

23. Fort, MS Chiappelli, Capitolo 11, fol. 34v. The document is undated, but from its context the date can be determined as 1574. Fabroni's reply is on fol. 40r. Giovanni Fabroni, about fifty-three years old at this time, worked for the captain as a business agent. He died in 1586 of a fever after a two-week illness. Lanfredino mentioned him in a letter: "I note [his death] because he was manager here *[al ghoverno]* for many years." Fort, MS Chiappelli, 133, fol. 100r.

24. Mariotto was baptized on 22 November 1558 (ASPist di S. Jacopo, Registri dei battezati 1112, fol. 67). He was accepted by Santo Stefano in 1571, when he would have been only 13. (ASPOSS Provanze 617 no. 33). However, he does not seem to have commenced active service until about five years later.

25. His name appears on a 1575 list of cavalieri who had been on two galley voyages but had not yet completed their seniority. ASF, Miscellanea Medici, 135, fol. 179. In December 1578 he returned to Pisa from another voyage (see chap. 11 for his statement in his processo).

26. Mariotto appeals for relief from the *confinato* in ASP, OSS, Zibaldoni, 457, nos. 76 and 93; the beating charge in ASP, OSS, Informazioni, 390, fols. 135r–136r; 179v. The rescript in ASP, OSS, Suppliche 155, no. 440, fol. 1344.

Five   The Bracciolini

1. See Niccolò's letters expressing friendship and anti-Medicean sentiments to Filippo Strozzi as late as June 1537, just weeks before the decisive battle at Montemurlo. ASF, Carte Strozziane, ser. 3, 95 Copia Lettere, fol. 106r–v. I owe this reference to Lorenzo Polizzotto. Niccolò's biographer in *DBI*, 13: 639–40, says that Filippo Strozzi offered him half a million ducats to come over to his side, but that he refused.

2. This being so, the absence of books in the sixteenth-century Bracciolini inventories studied by Lucia Gai is surprising. There was a luxurious collection of clothes, furniture, tapestries, and jewels, and a few painted reliefs and plaster images. "Centro e periferia," 104, n. 402. By contrast, Nicola di Cosimo Fabroni had in his library seventy-eight *libri vulgari*—books in Italian—including works by Aristotle, Cicero, Apian, Valerius Maximus, and Diodorus Siculus, among the ancients, and S. Antoninus, Girolamo Savonarola, Bembo, and Ariosto, among the moderns, as well as a Vulgate Bible. See BNF, MS Rossi Cassigoli 237, fols. 51v–52r.

3. See Fabrizio's proofs of nobility presented in 1563. ASP, OSS, Provanze 612, fol. not numbered. Francesco was alive at the time of this biographical sketch.

4. Letters of Fabrizio Bracciolini, Francesco da Cascina, and Jacopo Maltacchini in Pisa to Camillo Cellesi in Pistoia, 26 August, 1561–9 January, 1562, Fort, MS Chiappelli 50, 1, fols. 228–29; insert 1, fol. 232; insert 6, fols. 1–3.

5. On the other hand, asked by the superiors of the order for a report on "the nobility, manner of life, and morals" of Fabrizio, Cavalier Jacopo Forni wrote, on 20 February, 1564, that both sides of the Bracciolini family were gentlemen, had never done anything dishonorable, and in addition Fabrizio's father was a doctor of laws with distinguished government service. ASP, OSS, Provanze 612, no. 41 (fols. not numbered).

Some examples of rejected applications: In 1562, Piero di Giovanni Zanchini of Florence, who claimed (dubiously) to be a descendant of such prominent noble families as the Pitti and Ricasoli, was "not accepted into the order because of unfavorable information about his conduct." Reports of his *mala vita* included a robbery and sword fights. ASP, OSS, Provanze 1056, no. 4. In 1563, Lodovico Buonaparte of S. Miniato al Tedesco was "not accepted by the order because of his incorrect conduct"; this consisted of involvement in two fights *(quistioni),* in one of which he had been wounded. Also cited against him: his grandfather had operated a spice shop. Ibid., n. 11. In 1571 Giuliano di Ruberto Pagni of Pescia, age thirty-two, was "not admitted for reproachable morals" although one of the quarterings he boasted was "the Medici of Florence." More details in ASP, Santo Stefano *Provanze* 1059, n. 10.

6. "Upper-class Pistoiese youths readily assumed as *noms de guerre* nicknames of a kind found elsewhere most commonly among peasants." William J. Connell, "Republican Territorial Government: Florence and Pistoia, Fifteenth and Early Sixteenth Centuries" (Ph.D. diss., University of California, Berkeley, 1989), 142.

7. In addition to the general exemption granted in the statutes of the order, Fabrizio's name appears in 1575 on a list of *commendatari di padronato* (holders of family-endowed benefices) exempt from maritime service. ASF, Miscellanea Medicea 135, fol. 180r. A check of attendance records for 1574 through 1580 (ASP, OSS, Zibaldoni 457, 458) does not show him in residence in Pisa during those years, although in August 1579 (after the conclusion of the Holy Thursday incident) his request to join the grand duke's military campaign was granted. ASP, OSS, Suppliche 156, no. 206, fol. 591r. Presumably this *impresa di guerra*, as Fabrizio calls it, was Francesco I's participation in the campaign of the Spanish king, Philip II, to conquer Portugal. Fabrizio's antagonist, Mariotto Cellesi, went on that expedition, as we shall see, but none of the records I have examined list Fabrizio as a combatant.

8. ASPist, Opera di S. Jacopo 1112, *Registro dei battezati*, fol. 31r. There would be at least one more son, in 1585. Ibid., fol. 38v. For the daughter, see chap. 18.

9. ASF, Pratica Segreta Pistoia Copia Lettere 497, fol. 100r–v, 102r.

10. For the charges against his servant, see ASF, Pratica Segreta Pistoia Copia Lettere 497, fol. 104r. For the suspension of Fabrizio's arms-bearing privilege, ASF, Pratica Segreta Pistoia Copia Lettere 497, fol. 104r, and for the restoration of the privilege, ASPist, Capitano, ser. 1, 15, fol. 260v. The charges of 1569 are referred to in the second round of charges of October 1573, in ASF, Medici Principato 593, fol. 50.

11. Religious confraternities, companies, or sodalities, widespread in late-medieval Italy, were voluntary organizations of laymen who dedicated themselves to particular devotional practices such as hearing sermons, penitential flagellation, the veneration of favorite saints, charity, and the staging of religious ceremonies and festivals. With a central role in the religious and public life of the towns and cities, it is hardly surprising that the confraternity was an important locus of social interaction for Italian men. For more on this, see Ronald F. E. Weissman, *Ritual Brotherhood in Renaissance Florence* (New York, 1982).

12. For some of the Florentine bans (1568, 1569) as well as others of Siena, Bologna, and so on, see BNR, Duello M 8, G quat. 1–4. For the definitive ecclesiastical ban of "the detestable practice of duels, introduced by the invention of the devil in order to accomplish with the bloody death of bodies the ruin of souls," Sessio 25, cap. 19 of the Council of Trent (1563). I quote from *Il Sacro Concilio di Trento* (Venice, 1788), 318.

13. ASPist, Capitano, ser. 8, fol. 1262r.

14. He must have had income from properties in his own name, but he would be reduced to selling some of them. For example, he sold a rental property of 6 staia in the commune of Masiano for 400 lire to Dott. Carlo Vassellini, 23 February, 1579 [80] ASF, Notarile Moderno (Bernardi), 4345, fol. 24v. In 1608 he would sell a property with an annual rent of 126 lire to the Company of Santissima Trinità for 2,100 lire, or about 300 scudi. The last payment was made in 1618 by the Piovano Bartolomeo Cellesi, after Fabrizio's death. ASPist, Famiglia Cellesi filza 3, two unnumbered, not consecutive, folios.

15. For example, he owed 125 lire to Camillo Odardi, 4 February, 1573, Odardi Ricordi BNF, MS Rossi Cassigoli 229, fol. 21v; 350 lire to Fiammetta, widow of Ludovico Bracciolini, 29 December, 1573, ASF, Notarile Moderno (Belnari) 3260, fols. 178v–79r; 6 lire to Giovanni Cellesi, 1578, ASF, Monte di Pietà nel Bigallo, fol. 5r; 300 scudi to Leonetto fu Guglielmo Bracciolini, 20 April, 1580, ASF, Notarile Moderno (Bernardi), 4345; 92 lire to Benedetta, widow of Raffaello Conversini, 16 February, 1581, ibid.; 300 lire to Madonna Maria, widow of Ser Giuliano Cattani, 21 March, 1582 [3], ibid., 4346, fol. 53r.

16. On the Bracciolini estate, see ASF, Notarile Antecosimiano 17210 (Donato Politi), fols. 250r–51v.

Six   The Order of Santo Stefano

1. *Statuti, e constitutioni dell'Ordine de Cavalieri di Santo Stefano* (Florence, Filippo Giunti, 1571). This first edition contains the original statutes as well as the additions of 1562–71.

2. Franco Angiolini, Paolo Malanima, "Problemi della mobilità sociale a Firenze tra la metà del Cinquecento e i primi decenni del Seicento," *Società e Storia* 4 (1979): 27.

3. On the part of Santo Stefano's galleys in the relief of the siege of Malta in 1565 and at the Battle of Lepanto, see Bastiano Balbiani, "Imprese delle Galere," ASF, Carte Strozziane, ser. 1, filza 145, fols. 9v, 10–12v. On Malta, see also Kenneth M. Setton, *The Papacy and the Levant, 1204–1571*, vol. 4, *The Sixteenth Century from Julius III to Pius V* (Philadelphia, 1984), 872, n. 151. In 1586 the captain of Santo Stefano's galley *S. Giovanni* refused to attack a Turkish ship. By order of Admiral Galerati (his cousin) he was strangled and his body was thrown into the sea. The grand duke approved. Bastiano Balbiani, "Imprese delle Galere," ASF, Carte Strozziane 1, 145, fol. 26v.

4. On the establishment of the order, see Riguccio Galluzzi, *Istoria del Granducato di Toscana*, 5 vols. (Florence, 1781), 2: 191–94. On Cosimo I's complex motives for founding the order, see Furio Diaz, *Il Granducato Di Toscana—I Medici* (Turin, 1987), 192–93.

Burr Litchfield stresses the continuity between the old communal patriciate and the service gentry of the grand duchy, *Emergence of a Bureaucracy: The Florentine Patricians* (Princeton, 1986), while F. Angiolini and P. Malanima emphasize the role of the order in making new nobles. "Problemi della mobilità sociale a Firenze tra la metà del Cinquecento e i primi decenni del Seicento," *Società e Storia,*" no. 4 (1979): 17–47. The distinction between old noble status and aspiring nouveaux riches may not have been as clear as these scholars seem to think. The Cellesi are a case in point, with some of the characteristics of both categories. Evidently Captain Lanfredino took his eldest son, Cosimo (died before March 1576), into the family business before Santo Stefano was available as a career option, but with the founding of the order opening up new career possibilities, he presented his two other legitimate sons for admission, as well as his bastard Raffaello. Captain Lanfredino's status as a merchant with a bottega in Pistoia was not an obstacle to their candidacy. Mariotto was accepted without the endowment of a benefice. Either the captain did not himself work in the shop, but employed others to do so, so that his hands were not sullied with trade, or his noble status and his military and civil service outweighed any such possible taint. When Raffaello was eventually disqualified, it was because of his illegitimate status, not his father's vocation.

5. See the papal privileges in the prefaces of the *Statuti di Santo Stefano*.

6. "ab omni iurisdictione, superioritate, visitatione, dominio, & potestate quorumvis Archiepiscoporum, aliorumque locorum ordinariorum apostolica auctoritate tenore praesentium ex certa nostra scientia perpetuo eximimus et totaliter liberamus." Privileges of Pope Pius V in 1562. BNF, Carte Strozziane, ser. 1, filza 244, n.n. By contrast, militia officers were allowed to settle only minor quarrels *(case leggieri)* among themselves in *il foro cavaleresco;* violent altercations were to be dealt with in *il foro della giustitia,* by the civil authorities. (Order of the grand duke in 1615, reaffirming earlier orders of 1568 and 1605), ASF, Miscellanea Medicea 130, fol. 99r–v.

Seven   The Processo

Epigraph: Quoted by Julian Barnes, *Talking It Over* (London, 1991).

1. On the Fioravanti case, see chap. 5.

2. By the thirteenth century, the public or "inquisitorial" *processus* had come to rival the private "accusatory" means of investigating and prosecuting crime in communal Italy. By the sixteenth century, the inquisitorial system was the rule. See, among others, Ettore Dezza, *Accusa e inquisizione dal diritto comune ai codici moderni* 1 (Milan, 1989); Laura I. Stern, *The Criminal Law System of Medieval and Renaissance Florence* (Baltimore, 1994). The absolute control of inquisitorial proceedings by the magistrate is emphasized by Michel Foucault, although the present case does not bear out Foucault's assertion that proceedings were absolutely secret, even to the accused himself. *Discipline and Punish: The Birth of the Prison,* trans. Alan Sheridan, 2nd ed. (New York, 1995), 35.

3. The Florentine diarist Lapini said that the style of short hair and beards began about the time of the siege of Florence, 1530. Before that, "everyone" had shoulder-length hair and was clean-shaven. *Diario fiorentino,* 96. According to a modern scholar, beards were worn only by magistrates and old men until Pope Clement VII grew a beard to mourn the sack of Rome in 1527 and was widely imitated, even among the secular clergy. Michele Vocino, *Storia del costume: venti secoli di vita italiana,* 2nd ed. (Rome, 1961), 114.

4. That is, back along the via S. Andrea to the via degli'Orafi and the Bracciolini palace.

5. Crete was frequently referred to as Candia, the name of its principal city.

6. The Church of S. Maria a Ripalta, containing the Cross of Ripalta—more accurately, the Crucifix of Ripalta—a much revered Pistoian relic, was reached by a side street that runs east from via S. Andrea, just north of the Church of S. Andrea. The church had been called the Cappella of S. Giusto until it became the repository of the crucifix carried in the famous penitential procession of 1399, called *i Bianchi*. Fioravanti, *Memorie Istoriche,* 64–65, Giuseppe Tigri, *Pistoia e il suo territorio* (Pistoia, 1854; repr. 1979), 251.

7. The storta was a short, broad-bladed sword with a distinctive double-curved shape, mainly used by marines, originally of Turkish design. Some of the witnesses refer to it as a scimitar, another form of curved sword.

8. Fabrizio uses the word *assassinato.*

9. *Campanaio* can mean either a bellringer or a bellfounder. Since Agniolo had a bottega, or shop, the second is the more likely, although it is notoriously difficult to determine whether such designations refer to occupations, names, or place of origin. See Silvia Meloni Trkulja, *I Fiorentini nel 1562* (Florence, 1962), xi, and David Herlihy and Christiane Klapisch-Zuber, *Les Toscans et leurs familles: Une étude du "catasto" florentin de 1427* (Paris, 1978), 348–49, 350.

10. *Salsapariglia* was the Spanish *zarzaparilla,* a popular medicine made from *Smilax officinalis,* a Central and South American plant of the Liliaceae family. In 1573, after suffering eighteen months with an illness described as a catarrh, Grand Duke Cosimo I was treated with salsapariglia, without success. Giuliano de'Ricci, *Cronaca* (1532–1606), ed. Giuliana Sapori (Milan, 1972), 66. The grand duke died in 1574.

11. In grafting skin on wounded noses, Gaspare Tagliacozzi advocated using well-beaten white of egg mixed with rosewater, "a little dragon's blood" (*Daemonrops Draco,* or palm resin), and *terra sigillata* (a clay-like sealer?), rolled wet over the bandaged wound. See Read, *Chirurgorum comes,* 645.

12. The term *ex officio* identifies this as a public action, initiated and conducted by the state, as opposed to the private or accusatory action.

13. Letter of 4 April, 1578. ASF, Pratica Segreta Pistoia Copia Lettere 497, fol. 167r.

14. He must mean the Company of S. Giuseppe.

15. The *Oratio quadraginta horarum, or Quarantore* honored Christ during the forty hours he lay dead in the tomb. It originated in the liturgical practice of hiding the consecrated Host in an altar in the form of a tomb. It was performed in the last three days of Holy Week as early as the thirteenth century. In the sixteenth century, it took various other forms and was widely propagated by the Capuchins. *Enciclopedia Cattolica,* 12 vols. (Vatican City, 1948–54), 10: 375–78.

16. For example, on 24 May the Pratica Segreta wrote to Messer Francesco Franchini, fiscale of Pistoia, ordering him to investigate

whether the witness [unnamed] descending the stairs [in front of S. Andrea] could have seen the cavaliers tip birettas to each other or not. For this we want and commission you to go to that place and by the testimony of your own eyes determine whether from the stairs of S. Andrea one can really see the doorway of the house of the aforesaid Nardino del Bonzetta and the nearby well. Report to us by letter to our Secretary Messer Giovanni Conti and all this without telling anyone anything and keeping it confidential.

ASF Pratica Segreta Copia Lettere 497, fol. 178r. There is no record of the assignment having been carried out. The Visconti house *is* visible from the stairs of S. Andrea, as I have personally determined.

17. The priest's given name does not appear. In the report of a pastoral visit of 1550, a Prete Jacopo Bracciolini was cited for neglecting to officiate in his beneficed chapel of S. Lorenzo in the Church of S. Giovanni Fuorcivitas. ACV, Stanza 3, R 66. On the night of 15 June, 1562, a Prete Jacopo Bracciolini (the same man?) was surprised in the act of sodomizing young Piero di Guglielmo Fioravanti against a wall in the Prato di Monte di Oliveto. He fled, was pursued, arrested, and taken to the headquarters of the bargello, but then turned over to the ecclesiastical authorities. I have found no record of the disposition of his case. Piero Fioravanti reportedly consented to the act, but since he was "under the age of 20" he received the relatively lenient sentence of fifty strokes on bare flesh. Fort, Sentenze Criminali C 259, fol. 123r.

On 11 July, 1578, a Prete Bracciolino Bracciolini petitioned the Pratica Segreta for permission to collect a debt from the vicar of the commune of Celle. ASF, Pratica Segreta Copia Lettere 497, fol. 187v.

18. *La fune*, or *strappado*, was perhaps the most common form of inquisitorial torture. Hands tied behind back, the witness was hoisted off the ground then suddenly dropped, the fall checked just before hitting the floor. This was often repeated several times. Besides causing great pain, the shock dislocated shoulders and broke arms.

Eight   Peacemaking I

1. The bibliography is vast. See the essays in *Disputes and Settlements: Law and Human Relations in the West,* ed. John Bossy (Cambridge, 1983).

2. "In the structure of the clan, solidarity and reciprocity had an essential role in the righting of wrongs. Faced with an injury committed against a member, the whole clan upheld the vendetta, which belonged to both individual and collectivity, while the offenses were blamed not only on those who had actually carried them out but on all those who belonged to the opposing family and faction." Furio Bianco, "*Mihi vindictam:* Aristocratic Clans and Rural Communities in a Feud in Friuli in the Late Fifteenth and Early Sixteenth Centuries," Dean and Lowe, *Crime, Society, and the Law,* 270.

3. ASPist, Capitano 7, 875, fol. 1298r.

4. ASF, Pratica Segreta Pistoia Copia Lettere 497, fol. 175v–176r.

5. The word used here is *casata.* Note that while the original levare l'offesa was

to include relatives to the fourth degree on both sides, subsequent orders drop this requirement for the Cellesi. Four degrees of Bracciolini relatives are ordered to make peace with Captain Lanfredino, father of the accused aggressor.

6. ASP, OSS, Lettere Originali 1369, no. 25.

7. It seems Fabrizio or someone for him had done some research in the court records.

8. ASP, OSS, Lettere Originali 1369, no. 27.

9. Entries in the archives in Pistoia, presumably by the commissioner or one of his functionaries, give more detail; the commissioner set the bond at 1,500 scudi (500 for Fabrizio, the rest for his guarantors); Fabrizio said he could offer no more than 100; the commissioner reduced the amount to 500 scudi; Fabrizio accepted, but Giovanni Fabroni said his client, Mariotto, would not do it for less than 1,000. ASPist, Capitano 7, 875, fols. 1298v–1299r.

10. Pontito was about twenty to twenty-five kilometers northwest of Pistoia. Mariotto could have sent the letter to Procurator Fabroni in Pistoia by mounted messenger, to be delivered before the time set for his court appearance, about 4 P.M. on the same day. Fabroni's willingness to produce the letter to the authorities and thus disclose his client's whereabouts suggests that Mariotto was already preparing to return to Pistoia. He did so soon afterward. See chap. 11.

11. Jacopo joined the order on 3 February, 1570, about seven months after Fabrizio (13 June, 1569) and about a year and a half before Mariotto (20 November, 1571). He was on a list, probably compiled in 1575, of those cavaliers who, although they had no commenda, had *anzianità,* or seniority, as a result of having made two galley voyages. ASF, Misc. Medic. 135, fol. 178v. As to his relation to the principals, I have not been able to determine to whom he was married or how he was related to Captain Lanfredino.

12. ASP, OSS, Suppliche 157, fol. 865r, and ASPist, Capitano, ser. 7, 875, fol. 1214.

13. See the order for the levare l'offesa and truce bond in ASF, Prat. Seg. Pistoia Copia Lett. 497, fol. 108v. A year later, on 28 July, 1578, the slave was murdered in a bizarre incident that, although not related to the Holy Thursday affair, offers an interesting vignette of domestic life among the Cellesi. Fifteen years earlier, Francesco, who was lame and blind, had taken into his care his seven-month-old cousin Benedetto di Giorgio Cellesi, who had lost both his parents (the father had died and the mother had remarried and gone to live in Città di Castello). Francesco received the slave from Jacopo Cellesi ("Cavalier Jacopo Cellesi gave me a Turkish slave from Constantinople"), no doubt to help him care for the child. As Francesco tells it in his petition to the grand duke,

> I kept the Turk in the service of myself and my family in the manner we usually keep men of this kind. Yesterday evening, the 28th of this month, when we were at table, Benedetto [now sixteen] said to me these exact words: "If you knew what the Turk did to me you'd beat him." And I replied, "When you have your own servants you can beat them." Then Benedetto said, "Look at

the bruise *[livido]* on my lips; you'll beat him for sure. Last night he came to my bed while I was asleep and he sucked on me and did this to me, then ran away." Hearing this, the Turk scornfully retorted, "You're a big liar, you never tell the truth," and more things of that kind. At this Benedetto rose from the table in a fury, seized a table knife, and struck it into [the Turk's] left breast and killed him almost instantly.

Francesco begged the grand duke to consider the boy's age and the circumstances of the killing. His brother-in-law Francesco Giovanni Bracciolini wrote the petition for him. There is no record of the grand duke's response. ASF, Mediceo Principato 713, fol. 19, 6 r–v.

14. I have not found this letter.

15. Official truce and peace documents, which are recorded in their thousands in Italian archives, do not often mention private negotiations, although I think it reasonable to assume that they were not uncommon, given the importance of the issue of honor in disputes of this kind. It is also likely that a good deal of such private communication was oral, with little committed to paper either by the principals or their mediators. In any case, the recovery of a paper trail here is unusual.

16. See my "Fighting or Flyting?" (see chap. 2, n. 6).

17. ASPist, Capitano 875, fol. 1308v.

18. Again, the language of chivalry.

Nine   Chiara

1. The commissioner's order dispatching the two officers is dated 23 March, while the commissioner's report to the Pratica is dated 22 March. Evidently the notary reversed the two dates.

2. The word I have translated as "weird things" is *bischinche.*

3. The coincidental welter of different forms of the name Giovanni seems to have confused Caterina, and I cannot guarantee that I have them correctly sorted out here.

4. On singing as a part of courtship, see Christiane Klapisch-Zuber, *Women, Family, and Ritual in Renaissance Italy,* trans. Lydia G. Cochrane (Chicago, 1985), 261–82.

5. There are two towns called Lizzano in the mountains north of Pistoia, one in Bolognese territory, formerly called Lizzano Matto, the other in Pistoiese territory, called Lizzano Belvedere. *Matto* is not in use today. William Connell tells me that Don Napoleone Toccafondi, parish priest of Lizzano Belvedere, says that *Matto* refers to a local saint and is a corruption of Tommaso. Professor Connell also called my attention to a village called Santomato, near Montale, between Pistoia and Prato.

6. One would think that the captain was in need of il Morino's forgiveness, but the text here and below indicates the opposite: il Morino seems to have committed

some offense against the captain, although this may have been a response to the captain's harboring of his wife.

7. *Ricordi del Capitano Lanfredino Cellesi,* Fort, MS Chiappelli 133, fols. 212r–213v.

8. In Pistoia, a neighborhood administrative unit was called a *cappella.* The Cellesi lived in the Cappella of S. Michele.

9. Chiara may have left her husband before she went to live with Captain Lanfredino, in which case she would have been away even longer.

Ten   Asdrubale

Epigraph: Cicero, *Laelius De Amicitia* 13, trans. William Armistead Falconer. Loeb Classical Library (London, 1923).

1. In a brief of 10 June, 1570, to the Venetian captain-general, Pope Pius V authorized the service on Venetian galleys of as many secular and religious priests as were necessary to minister to the religious needs of its soldiers and sailors in the war against the Turks. Kenneth Setton, *The Papacy and the Levant* 4: 964, citing an unpublished brief. Whether this applied to the rest of the military force in that war, and whether this is the brief Asdrubale referred to is not clear. In any case, while the pope authorized clerics to go to war, he does not seem to have sanctioned their bearing arms. Asdrubale does not explicitly claim that the pope did; neither does he say that he had actually been a combatant in the war.

2. The Ufficiali di Sanità were a kind of sanitary police. Guards of the Sanità were stationed at the city gates to supervise the passage of commercial goods and work animals to determine whether they were a threat to public health.

3. Politi's technique here is not unlike that of the lawyers who successfully defended the Los Angeles policemen accused of beating a motorist, Rodney King, in the famous incident of March 1991. The beating had been videotaped by a bystander. The defense ran the film in court, stopping the action from instant to instant. Each segment of the sequence of actions was thus isolated from the others so that it became difficult to see the beating as a whole.

4. Although a procurator is mentioned once, in all Fabrizio's appearances in court he represented himself.

Eleven   Mariotto

1. The Pistoia copyist has Coreglio. There is a village of that name in Pistoia territory, but the village meant here is Coreglia in the district of Lucca.

2. Fort, MS Chiappelli 133, fol. 208r.

3. This is the only indication that Mariotto had a bad hand. Fabrizio also seems to have had trouble with a hand prior to the Holy Thursday incident. See chap. 13, n. 16.

4. The Pratica Segreta had separated the captain and Tonio from the charge after their hearings in Florence, but they were retained on the statement of the charge that went to the council of Santo Stefano, although the order did not have jurisdiction over them. There is no mention of the two armed men Fabrizio accused in his original deposition.

5. ASP, OSS, Partiti 55, fol. 121v.

6. On the negotiations for concluding a peace pact between the Cellesi and Bracciolini, see chaps. 8 and 12.

7. The copyist of the Santo Stefano text of the interrogatories wrongly identified them as "produced by Cavalier Fabritio." They are correctly identified as Mariotto's in the Pistoia copy of the processo.

8. Chiara, in her account, gave very different reasons for her flight; that is to say, threats and confinement by the captain.

Twelve   Peacemaking II

Epigraph: Tibullus 1, lines 67–68, trans. J. P. Postgate, in *Catullus, Tibullus, and Pervigilium Veneris* (Cambridge, Mass., rev. 1950).

1. "They" refers to the Bracciolini. As the next paragraph shows, Commissioner Panciatichi was in error in believing that the Pratica ordered bond to be set at 2,000 scudi. This had been the figure set by Commissioner Cosimo de'Pazzi in his original levare l'offesa of 27 March, and the Cellesi had been insisting on this sum; but the Pratica lords said it should be "no less than 1,000 scudi."

2. I have not found this message. Fabrizio was probably riding off to Pisa to answer his summons to appear at Mariotto's trial and to conclude a truce.

3. ASP, OSS, Lettere, Missive 1325, fol. 56.

4. Ibid.

Thirteen   Fabrizio

Epigraph: Horace, "Conversation Pieces," *The Complete Works of Horace,* ed. Casper J. Kraemer Jr. (New York, 1936), 9.

1. "ha detto Cavaliere Bracciolini per persona da fare quello che li torna bene." This was sixty-year-old Nardino, or Lionardo, di Francesco Bisconti, or Visconti, the father of the accused Tonio. A man of middling means (property value of 2,000 scudi), he had known Fabrizio since birth.

2. "ha il Cavaliere Bracciolini per quello che gl'è lasciandolo nel grado che è." This was Simone d'Antonio Talini, who owned a bottega of some unspecified kind. He also said he had known Fabrizio from boyhood, was his friend, and had never quarreled with him.

3. "per homo da bene et per quello che gl'è." This was Girolamo di Francesco Perfedi, age sixty, who said he was a long-time friend of Fabrizio and had never

quarreled with him. Perfedi did not give an occupation, although he did say he had no property ("non ha niente in beni").

4. *al suo pane e vino;* literally, "on his bread and wine." For a variant of this traditional phrase, see Christiane Klapisch-Zuber and Michel Demonet, "'A uno pane e uno vino': The Rural Tuscan Family at the Beginning of the Fifteenth Century," trans. Patricia M. Ranum, in Klapisch-Zuber, *Women, Family, and Ritual,* 36–67.

5. For Fabrizio's letters to Chiara and a letter of Chiara in reply, see chap. 14, below. For another case of an illiterate woman's need to find someone to read her love letters, see Elizabeth S. Cohen, "Between Oral and Written Culture: The Social Meaning of an Illustrated Love Letter," B. B. Diefendorf and C. Hesse, eds., *Culture and Identity in Early Modern Europe (1500–1800): Essays in Honor of Natalie Zemon Davis* (Ann Arbor, 1993), 181–202.

6. "ha per moglie una nipote del Cavaliere [*sic*] Lanfredino et cugina del Cavaliere Mariotto et che è della medesima casata de Cellesi. . . . È amico del Cavaliere Fabrizio Bracciolini et il fratello di detto testimone ha per moglie la sorella."

7. "The bottega was also a basic institution of male sociability, where young apprentices mingled with older workers, and where friends met to while away the time and perhaps to drink or gamble." Michael Rocke, *Forbidden Friendships: Homosexuality and Male Culture in Renaissance Florence* (New York, 1996), 158.

8. Emanuele Repetti, *Dizionario geografico fisico storico della Toscana,* 6 vols. (Florence, 1833–45; repr.), 4, 428–29.

9. This exchange was reported by Francesco di Benedetto Mannani, who was present with Battista di Battista Cellesi. Francesco said this was at Easter, perhaps 8 April, although he could not recall the exact date. That the exchange took place after the Holy Thursday fight, in a rehash of the quarrel, is confirmed by Battista, who said it was after the fight. (Vincenzo may have been a cleric.)

10. "sendo fra di loro ingrossati gl'humor."

11. On the participation of the chorus in Greek drama, see Cynthia P. Gardiner, *The Sophoclean Chorus: A Study of Character and Function* (Iowa City, 1987), 1, passim.

12. "disse detto testimone à esso Cavaliere il Cavaliere Fabritio vi vuole negoziare questa vostra matrigna et allora il Cavaliere Mariotto rispose a detto testimone, io non lo credo perche gneme ho parlato et lui mi ha detto che attende a un altra vicina et che gli harebbe rispetto et che non farebbe tal cosa sopra l'honor suo."

13. "ritruovandosi un giorno di Carnovale con il Cavaliere Mariotto in bottegha sua burlando gli domandò, 'Che è della vostra matrigna?' intendendo detta Chiara, che detto Cavaliere gli disse, 'Perchè me ne domandate?' Et detto testimonegli rispose, 'Perchè ho sentito dire che la fa l'amore con il Cavaliere Fabrizio Bracciolini,' et detto Cavaliere Mariotto gli disse, 'Non è vero, perche esso Cavaliere Fabrizio gli haveva detto che faceva l'amore con un'altra vicina.'"

14. In the diocesan synod at Pistoia in 1587, concubinage was named as one of the sins that incurred excommunication. *Decreta Diocesanae Synodi Pistoriensis (1587).*

15. "disse sapere per essere ben nato, et che crede che tutte le persone honorate farebbero il medesimo del luogo per tutta la città et luoghi honorati. Del tempo quando si porgesse occasione de contesti disse di se et di tutti gl'huomini honorati."

16. Francesco had attended both Captain Lanfredino (at home) and Fabrizio (at Bagni di Lucca, where Fabrizio had gone for treatment of an injured hand).

17. "et che per essere persona ingeniosa che [?] non sa che cosa sia honore o no perche è bagniaiuolo et non sta su questi puntiglie."

18. "fussino una medesima cosa col Cavaliere Fabrizio."

19. "chiamare il suo principale non gia per fare quistione ma si bene sendo massime nel mezzo della Città per farlo pericolare con la justitia."

20. That is, Commissioner Pazzi's notary.

21. *compasso di Corfù:* In trying to find other uses of this expression, I had the generous help of Professoressa Rita Librandi of the University of Naples and Professor Vito Giustiniani of the University of Freiburg. I had been unsuccessful until Professoressa Librandi put me in touch with Professor Ottavio Lurati of the University of Basel, who is preparing a book on Italian sayings. Professor Lurati reports hearing the expression *compasso di Corfù* in 1988 at a Venetian wharf, where it was applied to an inferior wooden compass that gave unreliable measure—exactly the meaning of Mariotto's usage four hundred years earlier. Professor Lurati believes the expression to be a reflection of the Venetian sense of superiority vis-à-vis things connected with Corfù. The cavaliers of Santo Stefano must have picked up this saying, as they did others, in their frequent contacts with Venetians.

22. "perchè alli processi fatti avanti li supremi et regii Magistrati precedente massime [?] la commissione particulare di Sua Altezza Signoria et la carceratione si presta inaudita et exquisita fede."

23. Readers will recall that the vicar had exonerated Asdrubale of the charge that he had participated with arms in the attack on Fabrizio, despite Luca's testimony that he had.

24. Jacopo had earlier been identified as a carpenter. Commissioner Vaini, perhaps simply following Mariotto, calls him an innkeeper. See chapter 15.

25. On 10 July the embarrassed commissioner had found himself in the position not only of supplicating the grand duke on behalf of his son, Giannozzo, who six days earlier had wounded Antonio Visconti in a fight (related to the Holy Thursday incident?), but also of assuring the grand duke that he was not making excuses for his son and that, although fatherly concern had delayed his response, it had not caused him to fail in his duty to administer justice. ASF, Medici Principato 713, fol. 363r.

26. Mariotto submitted the documents in response to the Santo Stefano commissioners' order that he "produce his arguments [*ragioni*]" by a certain date. He submits the dossier as ordered, including a checklist of all the items it contained.

Fourteen   *Love Letters*

Epigraph: Juan Ruiz, *The Book of True Love,* trans. Saralyn R. Daly (University Park, Pa., 1978), 133.

1. In her study of sixteenth-century French nobles, Karen B. Neuschel (following David Sabean) notes how self was defined in the course of its interaction with others and how that characterization was then used as an explanation of behavior. Thus the behavior of someone described by the community as "contentious" would be explained in terms of that characteristic. *Word of Honor: Interpreting Noble Culture in Sixteenth-Century France* (Ithaca, 1989), 191. The frequent reference in our texts to Fabrizio's "importunity" as the motor of his behavior suggests that a similar psychology was at work here.

2. In several places in these letters I am unsure of the correct reading. I signal the beginning of each of these passages with an asterisk (*) and end the questionable reading with double asterisk (**).

3. In book 1 of *The Aeneid,* Vergil tells how Cupid, at the behest of his sister Venus, makes Dido (Elissa) fall in love with Aeneas.

4. In Greek mythology, Orpheus, mourning the death of his wife, Eurydice, spurned all attempts by maidens to gain his love. He was torn apart by the Ciconian women, perhaps in revenge.

5. That is, Cessio Bracciolini.

6. Fabrizio is probably referring to Vincenzio Bracciolini, who, as we have seen, was a friend of Captain Lanfredino and had repeatedly urged Fabrizio to stop seeing Chiara. The passage suggests Chiara regarded Vincenzio as an enemy even before the affair began.

7. "ò beati quel seme virile che mai non ha curata": Fabrizio seems to be saying that it is better never to have been born than to suffer for love as he does.

8. "et che voi haviare a vedere per altri vi habbia a tua dire."

9. "et suplica me": the text is probably corrupt here.

10. Mithridates, or Mithradates: Of several Near Eastern kings of this name, Fabrizio was probably referring to Mithradates VI Eupater, king of Pontus, who fought the Romans in Asia Minor until his defeat by Pompey in 63 B.C.

Masinissa: An ally of Scipio against Carthage. Made chief, then king, of Numidia, he remained loyal to Rome, defeating Carthage in battle in 151 B.C.

Achilles to Fabio and Philip to Nicia: these two references are obscure.

11. That others were already gossiping about Fabrizio and Chiara and had put the idea into Chiara's head that Fabrizio was the agent of one of her enemies is not surprising. A likely candidate for plotting against her would have been Mariotto Cellesi himself, who admitted that he resented Chiara's influence on his father. He and Teodoro had much to gain from her disgrace and banishment. Indeed, two Italian scholars who heard me discuss my project in a seminar were convinced that the

whole Holy Thursday incident was cooked up by the Cellesi brothers to displace Chiara and regain their father's affections.

12. "et di piu me ha detto a bocca tutte le parole che mi havete scritto." Whether Chiara means that Fabrizio has actually spoken to her in person or through an intermediary is not clear. I think the second more likely since the sense of the letter is that a meeting has not yet taken place. Or perhaps he spoke to her briefly in the street and requested a more private meeting.

13. In the left margin there is a crude line drawing. See page 133.

14. "Non ce a me suo servo di grazioso e benigno vi figuro meglio che che [?] ho [?] saputo lo spirito mio quale vi demostra nel corpo quello che v'è scolpito dentro."

15. This is my free translation of "in esso mi sono transformato acciò quello debbia ricordarvi et sollecitarvi in effetto vi parli." This must be the portrait he sent Chiara (referred to in her examination), not the crude, erotic drawing in the margin of the letter. In Fabrizio's day, the commissioning of miniature protraits was common among Europe's royalty and upper classes. Fabrizio was an almost exact contemporary of Nicholas Hilliard (1547–1619), one of the finest practitioners of the art, who worked at both the English and French courts, although I doubt Fabrizio's portrait was painted in the refined moral and aesthetic atmosphere urged by Hilliard in his unpublished MS "A Treatise Concerning the Arte of Limning"; on the treatise, see *Encyclopedia of the Renaissance* (New York, 1999), s.v. Hilliard.

16. "solo cercherò pregarvi che su questo niente che vi ho a parlare mi concediate gratia di piu che da mattina vi vegha una volta et il giorno un altra, che se questo non seguisse non ho mai beneficio non la veggho."

17. Evidently Fabrizio continues to frequent the Cellesi household as a friend of the family, even as he courts Chiara.

18. The Porta al Borgo, in the outer circle of walls, was the northwest gate of the city, a short walk from the Prato S. Francesco, hence close to Chiara's house. Today the via dello Specchio runs straight north from the gate, probably following the stream of that name that once flowed into the Val di Brana.

19. François Furet and Jacques Ozouf's discussion of the relation between reading and writing in France has wider implications: "Three Centuries of Cultural Cross-Fertilization: France," in *Literacy and Social Development in the West: A Reader,* ed. Harvey J. Graff (Cambridge, 1981), 214–31, esp. 220–21. See also Neuschel, *Word of Honor,* 108, and Burke, *Historical Anthropology of Early Modern Italy,* 112.

20. "The majority of Italians, throughout this period, must have been illiterate; some professional men, most peasants and almost all women." Burke, *Historical Anthropology,* 128–29.

21. Compare the similarities and dissimilarities regarding literacy and secrecy in the case ably presented by Elizabeth S. Cohen, "Between Oral and Written Culture: The Social Meaning of an Illustrated Love Letter," *Culture and Identity in Early Modern Europe (1500–1800): Essays in Honor of Natalie Zemon Davis,* ed. Barbara B. Diefendorf and Carla Hesse (Ann Arbor, 1993), 181–201.

22. Commissario Tedaldi's later description of the scandalous Pistoia clergy, especially of the bishop's vicar, comes to mind, although Tedaldi did not include monks and friars in his sweeping condemnation.

23. On Captain Lanfredino's public persona, see my article "Fighting or Flyting?" (see chap. 2, n. 6). On the Renaissance style of self-presentation, see, for example, Peter Burke, *Historical Anthropology,* 9–10, passim.

24. Stefano Guazzo, *Lettere amorose di Madonna Celia gentildonna romana scritte al suo amante* (Venice, 1562), 8r.

25. See Rudolph M. Bell, *How to Do It: Guides to Good Living for Renaissance Italians* (Chicago, 1999).

26. Amedeo Quondam, ed., *Le "carte messagiere": Retorica e modelli di comunicazione epistolare: per un indice dei libri di lettere del cinquecento* (Rome, 1981), 96–120.

27. Guarini, Battista, *Il segretario dialogo nel quale non sol si tratta dell'ufficio del segretario et del modo del compor lettere* (Venice, 1600), 91.

28. Francesco Sansvino, *Il segretario* (Venice, 1584), 34r–77v. He gives a sample *lettera amatoria lasciva* on 91v–92r. The first edition of this work was 1565.

29. Alvise Pasqualigo, *Lettere amorose libri III ne' quali sotto maravigliosi concetti si contengono tutti gli accidenti d'Amore* ([2nd ed.?] Venice, 1581), 344–45 (letter no. 271).

30. Ferrante Pallavicino, *Panegirici, epitalami, discorsi accademici, novelle, et lettere amorosi* (Venice, 1652), 7–9.

31. See page 133. The drawing available to us is, like the text of the letters, in the notary's copy.

32. For an erotic drawing with obscene comments in an early-seventeenth-century Roman love letter, as well as a discussion of the practice, see Cohen, in Diefendorf and Hesse, *Culture and Identity,* 181–201.

Fifteen   The Verdict

1. The commissioners filed separate reports, differing only slightly in details. One is unsigned, and since Commissioner Benedetto Vivaldi signed his, the other must be Vaini's. In the Pistoia copy of the processo transcript, both men signed their names in various places, so we know that both carried out their commission. ASPist, Capitano di Custodia, ser. 8, filza 876, e.g., fol. 1172.

2. However, we do get further evidence that Grand Duke Francesco I was not only following the progress of the case but personally stepped into it more than once. For example, besides granting Captain Lanfredino's appeal for a change of venue from Pistoia to Florence, he had ordered that members of the Bracciolini family be privately questioned about their warnings to Fabrizio to desist from courting Chiara.

3. Commissioner Vaini overstates: Chiara's hearings did not establish conclusively that Fabrizio wrote Chiara's letters.

4. Commissioner Vivaldi is technically correct, but the evidence that Asdrubale was armed was compelling.

5. While Vivaldi does not, as Vaini does, explicitly repudiate the hearings in the Pistoia court, he does so implicitly by rejecting Ser Attriano's list of Fabrizio's wounds.

Sixteen   The Sentence

1. "Any cavalier who has words with another cavalier and angrily humiliates him publicly [literally, unbuttons him—*l'harà sbottoneggiato*] and insults him is to be punished with a *quarantena*, even if he admits it or, if he says [the other] has lied in his throat, even if he regrets that he said such a thing. If he shames and disdains him by telling him he lies in his throat, he loses two years of seniority. If he defames him verbally, the council is to give the punishment it sees fit according to the quality of the persons [involved]. If he insults him by beating him with a club or stick or slaps him or beats him in some other way, he loses three years of seniority. "*Statuti, e constitutioni dell'Ordine de Cavalieri di Santo Stefano*, titolo 17, cap. 23, "Delle ingiurie."

2. The sentence is also recorded in ASP, OSS 55 Partiti, fols. 129v–130v, where it is dated 13 January.

3. See, for example, *Statuti* (1571), titolo 2, cap. 10, and ibid., Aggiunte del Capitolo Generale del 1564, 6.

4. By a provision of 11 July, 1565, four rooms were to be set aside as a *carcere* for the cavaliers, "near the place where the cavaliers' chaplain is to be." It was specified that the rooms were to be furnished in the same way as their ordinary rooms and the detained cavaliers were to be responsible for maintaining them in the same way. ASP, OSS, 45, fols. 155v, 157v.

5. *Statuti, e constitutioni* (1571), titolo 27, cap. 19.

6. Ibid., titolo 17, cap. 20.

7. ASP, OSS, Suppliche 155, fol. 134r–v (21 April 1477).

8. ASP, OSS, Suppliche 157, fol. 716r. (14 January, 1577 [8]).

Seventeen   What It All Means

Epigraph: Anthony Lane, "True Lives," *New Yorker*, 27 July 1998, 74.

1. On 4 September, 1578, Michele di Nanni da Cireglio, one of the Pistoia bargello's sbirri, was questioned, tortured, and condemned to two years expulsion from the Florentine state for having written and affixed a placard on Fabrizio Bracciolini's doorway, just under the bell. The notice does not record what the placard said, except that it began, "On the day of 20 May, 1578. . . . " It seems highly likely that this had something to do with the Holy Thursday affair. ASF, Pratica Segreta Deliberazioni 10, fol. 5v.

2. For a different perspective on social hierarchy, see Lucia Gai, *Pistoia nel secolo*

16," Incontri Pistoiesi di storia arte cultura 15 (Pistoia, 1982), 2. Gai observes that there was a "rigid subdivision of citizens into social classes that no longer communicated" in Pistoia in the late sixteenth century.

3. Two examples: (a) the tailor's servant who in 1562 accused two men of raping and sodomizing her in her employer's hallway was condemned as *falsaria* and sentenced to ride the ass as well as serve six months in the prison of Volterra. Fort MS Chiappelli, Sentenze Criminali 259, fol. 126r–v; (b) Menico di Stefano, who accused another of an unspecified crime of which he was absolved, was sentenced in 1580 to two turns of the rope. The Pratica Segreta converted the sentence to *l'asino. ASF,* Pratica Segreta Copia Lettere 498, fol. 100v. Riding the ass was a punishment for other transgressions as well, such as marriage within the forbidden degrees of consanguinity. See the case of Antonio Giuliana and Margherita di Sandro of Sambuca (in the Pistoiese mountains), 3 April, 1579, ibid., fol. 44r. No doubt *l'asino* was considered more humane than the punishment for false witness set in an old city statute: a culprit who was unable to pay a fine of 200 lire was condemned to the loss of a hand. For corrupting witnesses, the fine was 50 lire. Zdekauer, ed. *Statutum* 3.3 and 3.18.

4. *Statuti . . . dell'Ordine . . . di Santo Stefano,* titolo 17, cap. 18. Although calumny of another cavalier might be punished more lightly with a *settena.* Ibid., cap. 28.

5. Spacks, *Gossip* (New York, 1985), 34.

6. "Debbe non di manco el principe farsi temere in modo, che, se non acquista lo amore, che fugga l'odio; perché può molto bene stare insieme esser temuto e non odiato; il che farà sempre, quando si astenga dalla roba de' sua cittadini e de' suoi sudditi, e dalle donne loro" (The prince ought to make himself feared, in such a way that even if he is not loved he avoids being hated; to be feared and not hated can go very well together, and he will always manage it if he keeps his hands off the property and the women of his citizens and subjects). Niccolò Machiavelli, *Il Principe,* ed. Luigi Firpo (Turin, 1961), chap. 17.

7. Adriano Prosperi, "Il 'miles christianus' nella cultura italiana tra '400 e '500," *Critica storica/Bollettino A. S. E.* 26.4 (1989) 685–704.

8. On the duel of honor as a religion, see Billacois, 83.

9. Lanfredino Cellesi's killing of Marsili, the Bolognese noble, to which I referred in chap. 4, n. 22, was something of this kind.

10. See my article "Fighting or Flyting?" (see chap. 2, n. 6).

11. The suggestion of the symbolism of the nose I owe to Sergio Bertelli.

12. Elizabeth Hardwick, *Seduction and Betrayal: Women and Literature* (New York, 1970), 177.

13. On the revival of towns and cities, see P. Jones, *Italian City-State,* esp. chaps. 2–3.

14. In 1461 the humanist Isotta Nogarola was "old for a woman (about forty-three)": Margaret King, *The Death of the Child Valerio Marcello* (Chicago, 1994), 36. On perceptions of age in the Renaissance, see Creighton Gilbert, "When Did a Man in the Renaissance Grow Old?" *Studies in the Renaissance* 14 (1967): 7–32.

15. Natalie Zemon Davis, *The Return of Martin Guerre* (Cambridge, Mass., 1983). In thinking about Chiara's story, I have found highly suggestive Davis's search for "the ways in which [sixteenth-century peasants] experienced the constraints and possibilities in their lives" (1).

16. Ibid., 28.

17. Ibid., 1.

18. I take the phrase from Eric R. Wolf, *Europe and the People without History* (Berkeley, 1982), although he might not approve my use of it since he applies it to "the so-called primitives, people 'without history,' supposedly isolated from the external world and from one another" (x).

Eighteen   And Then What Happened?

1. ASF, Notarile moderno (Bernardi), filza 4345, fol. 46r. On the practise of wives suing for the recovery of dowries, see Julius Kirshner, "Wives' Claims against Insolvent Husbands in Late Medieval Italy," *Women of the Medieval World: Essays in Honor of John M. Mundy,* ed. J. Kirshner and S. F. Wemple (Oxford, 1985), 256–303.

2. "Well-being" is my translation of *stato,* a notoriously ambiguous word with meanings that include condition, estate, property, status, power, and state in the modern sense.

3. ASP, OSS, Suppliche 156 no. 206, fol. 591r.

4. Giuliano de'Ricci, *Cronaca (1532–1606),* ed. Giuliana Sapori (Milan, 1972), 269–70. The entry is for August 1579.

5. Piero Ricciardi, "Ricordi pubblici e di famiglia dal 1558 al 1588." Fort, MS B 146, fol. 39. The MS is a copy of the original.

6. A seaport on the Mediterranean, in southern Aragon. The island of Iviza, in the Balearics, is opposite.

7. Ricci, *Cronaca,* 294–95.

8. Ricciardi, *Riccordi pubblici,* fol. 49v. The date of this entry is as close as I can come to the date of Mariotto's death.

9. Ricciardi's meaning here is unclear. Perhaps he is saying that even of those who survived combat, few returned to Pistoia.

10. Fort, MS Chiappelli 133, fol. 73v.

11. Ibid., fol. 75v.

12. There are Latin and Italian texts (in equally bad condition) of Captain Lanfredino's 1580 codicil in ASPist, Famiglia Cellesi 6, fasc. 38, fols. not numbered. There is a Latin copy in a late-seventeenth- or early-eighteenth-century hand in ASPist, Famiglia Cellesi, filza 6, fasc. 38, fols. 1–20.

13. One of several villages by this name in the vicinity of Pistoia; the one referred to here, near the Torrente Stella, a tributary of the Ombrone, several kilometers south of Pistoia, must be Casale Guidi, or Casalguidi, named for the feudal family that dominated the area in earlier times.

14. Ferruccia, village on the right bank of the Ombrone, near the road from Florence to Pistoia, by way of Poggio a Caiano.

15. Fort, MS Chiapelli 133, fol. 223v.

16. ASF, Pratica Segreta Lettere 475, fol. 82 r–v.

17. ASPist, Capitano, ser. 1, 17, fol. 105v, 5 June, 1581.

18. ASF, Pratica Segreta Deliberazioni 10, fol. 74r. 4 January, 1582.

19. Fort, MS Chiappelli 133, fol. 230r.

20. Ibid., fol. 88v.

21. I find no Domenico Bonsi among the list of officials of Santo Stefano. A Francesco di Domenico Bonsi was accepted into the order in 1575. A Cavalier Lorenzo Bonsi was appointed special comptroller of ducal accounts in 1597. Diaz, *Il Granducato,* 303, n. 1.

22. Renouncing inheritances was fairly common practice. An intended beneficiary who did so was freed of responsibility for claims against the estate—in this case, a trifling sum. In telling the officials of the order to collect the debt from him [Mariotto], Captain Lanfredino is indulging in black humor, Mariotto having died no later than November 1580.

23. Fort, MS Chiapelli 133, fol. 212v. ASP, OSS, Provanze 637 no. 8. The cover sheet bears the erroneous date 1586.

24. For the contract drawn up between Captain Lanfredino and the order (10 October, 1587), see ASPist, Famiglia Cellesi, fasc. 43 (2 fols., n.n.).

25. The Asini were an old, distinguished Florentine family.

26. A *stocco* is a short, pointed sword. Decorated stocchi were presented by popes to princes and soldiers of the Faith. See *Il dizionario della lingua italiana* (Florence, 1990), s.v., "stocco" (2).

27. *Relazione Cronologica della Famiglia Cellesi,* Fort, MS Chiapelli 77, fol. 425v.

28. Teodoro receives more credit than he deserves. The commenda established by his father was *padronato*—that is, entailed in the family line, and the baliage was to go with it, as I noted above.

29. (7 November, 1594), ASPist, Famiglia Cellesi 6, fasc. 49 (2 copies of 2 fols., each n.n.)

30. On Paolo Vinta and his family, see Diaz, *Il Granducato,* 92, passim.

31. Copia Lettere di Lanfredino Cellesi, Fort, MS Chiappelli 133, fol. 111r.

32. Notice of his burial is given under the year 1608, no day or month. ASPist, S. Jacopo 1122, fol. 74v.

33. Fort, MS Chiappelli 108, inserts 1 and 2, fols. n.n.

34. "Libro dei morti," ASPist, Opera di S. Iacopo 1122, fol. 95.

35. Ibid., fol. 99v.

36. Ibid., filza 1123, fol. 149v.

Epilogue

1. According to impressions based on my reading of judicial records. But figures are difficult to come by and unreliable. Besides, "judicial records reveal only the history of criminal justice, not that of criminality." Andrea Zorzi, "The Judicial System in Florence in the Fourteenth and Fifteenth Centuries," in Dean and Lowe, *Crime, Society, and the Law,* 41.

Bibliographies and Works of Reference

Bongi, S., ed. *Annali di Gabriel Giolito dei Ferrari da Trino di Monferrato stampatore in Venezia.* 2 vols. Rome, 1890, 1895.

Capponi, Vittorio. *Bibliografia pistoiese.* Bologna, 1874, 1878; repr. 1971, 1972.

del Gratta, R., G. Volpi, and L. Ruta. *Acta graduum Academiae Pisanae.* 3 vols. Pisa, 1980.

Dizionario biografico degli italiani. 38 vols. Rome, 1960–90.

DuCange, Charles du Fresne. *Glossarium Mediae et infimae latinitatis.* 10 vols. Repr. Graz, 1954.

Enciclopedia Cattolica. 12 vols. Vatican City, 1948–54.

Fabroni, Angelo. *Historia Academiae Pisanae.* 3 vols. Pisa, 1791–95; repr. Bologna, 1971.

Florio, John. *Vocabolario Italiano et Inglese.* London, 1659.

Gerini, E. *Memorie storiche d'illustri scrittori e di uomini insigni dell'antica e moderna Lunigiana.* Massa, 1822.

Gori, Lidia, and Stefania Lucarelli, eds. *Vocabolario Pistoiese.* Pistoia, 1984.

Il dizionario della lingua italiana. Ed. Giacomo De Voto and Gian Carlo Oli. Florence, 1990.

Il Sacro Concilio di Trento. Venice, 1788.

Lester, G. A. *Sir John Paston's "Grete Boke": A Descriptive Catalogue, with an Introduction, of British Library MS Landsdowne 285.* Cambridge, 1984.

Levi, [Giorgio] Enrico. *Il duello giudiziario enciclopedia e bibliografia.* Florence, 1932.

Levi, Giorgio Enrico, and Jacopo Gelli. *Bibliografia del duello.* Milan, 1903.

Pacini, Alfredo, ed. *La chiesa pistoiese e la sua cattedrale nel tempo: III Repertorio di documenti (a. 1501–a.1580).* Pistoia, 1994.

Repetti, Emanuele. *Dizionario geografico fisico storico della Toscana.* 6 vols. Florence, 1833–46; repr. Rome, n.d.

Ughelli, Ferdinando. *Italia sacra: sive De episcopis Italiae et insularum adjacentium.* 10 vols. 2nd ed., Venice, 1717–22; repr. Bologna, 1976.

Vocabolario della Crusca. 6 vols. 4th ed., Venice, 1741.

Volpi, Giuliana, ed. *Acta graduum Academiae Pisanae (1543–1765).* 3 vols. Pisa, 1979.

Zacharia, Francesco Antonio. *Bibliotheca Pistoriensis.* Turin, 1752; repr. 1979.

Zupko, R. *Italian Weights and Measures.* Philadelphia, 1981.

Primary Sources

My basic source is the dossier of the case of Mariotto Cellesi in its most complete notarial copy, Archivio di Stato Pisa, Santo Stefano filza 1757 Sentenze, marked "Numero 43 Processo contro al Cavalliere Mariotto Cellesi." This copy also includes the cases of Antonio Visconti and Asdrubale Cellesi and the investigation of Chiara Fioresi. I compared this with partial copies of the dossier in the Archivio di Stato, Pistoia (ASPist), Ordine di Santo Stefano filza 1669; Atti Civili (1569–80), filza 2515, Risposte a'Partiti e Stanziamenti al Auditori Bonsi, Caccia e Cavalli, and copies in the Archivio Diocesano di Pistoia.

- Other Archival and Documentary Sources

ASF: Carte Strozziane, Medici Principato Miscellanea Medicea, Monte di Pietà nel Bigallo, Notarile, Otto di Guardia Principato, Pratica Segreta di Pistoia.

ASPist: Archivio del Comune, Capitano di Pistoia, Comunità Civica, Opera di S. Iacopo, Catasto del Granduca, Bastardello Atti Civili, Criminali, Raccolte.

ASPist: Papers of the Cellesi, Bracciolini, Cancellieri, and Panciatichi families.

Biblioteca Forteguerriana (Fort) Raccolta A. Chiappelli.

Bracciolini Papers, ASF, Acquisti e Doni 266.

Canestrini, G. "Documenti per servire alla storia della milizia italiana dal xiii secolo al xvi secolo." *Archivio storico italiano* ser. 1, 15 (1851): whole volume.

"Memorie diverse relative a Pistoia racolte dal Commissario di quella città nell'anno 1705. . . . " ASF, Manoscritti 706.

Misc. Pistoia papers of fifteenth to seventeenth centuries. ASF, Acquisti e Doni 281, fasc. 1.

Panciatichi et al. Papers. ASF, Acquisti e Doni 286.

Plans and drawings relating to the Cellesi, Pistoia, etc. ASF, Acquisti e Doni Picollelis-Ricci 185.

"Relazione della provvisione fatta; anno 1590, 1591 per la carestia." Fort, MS E 341.

- Chronicles and Diaries

Arditi, Bastiano. *Diario di Firenze e di altri parti della Cristianità, 1574–1579.* Ed. Roberto Cantagalli. Florence, 1970.
Arfaruoli, Pandolfo. "Di cose pistoiese." Fort, MS B 77.
Baldinotti, Fabio di Baldinotto. "Libro di ricordi [1556–1650]. BNF, Rossi Cassigoli, 238.
De'Ricci, Giuliano. *Cronaca (1532–1606).* Ed. Giuliana Sapori. Milan, 1972.

[Dominici, Luca]. *Cronache di Ser Luca Dominici della venuta dei Bianchi.* Ed. Carlo Gigliotti. Pistoia, 1933.

[Fabroni, Nicolò]. "Al nome di dio libro di ricordi di me Nicolo di Cosimo Fabroni" [1556–1583]. BNF, Rossi Cassigoli, MS 237.

[Fioravanti, Fioravante]. "Libro di ricordi di Fioravante di Paulo Tommaso Fioravanti dal 1544 al 1651." BNF, Rossi Cassigoli, MS 241.

Gigliotti, Carlo. *Rerum Pistorium Scriptores.* 2 vols. Pistoia, 1933, 1937.

Lapini, Agostino. *Diario fiorentino.* Ed. Giuseppe Odoardo Corazzini. Florence, 1900.

Manetti, Giannozzo. *Chronicon pistoriense. Rerum Italicarum Scriptores.* 19 Milan, 1731, 989–1026.

[Melocchi, Jacopo; attrib.] "Ricordi." ASF, Acquisti e Doni Rossi Melocchi 8.

Monaldi, Guido. *Storie pistolesi* (1340–81). Ed. Rosso Antonio Martini. Florence, 1883.

Odardi, Cammillo. "Libro de'Ricordi 1540" (1540–1626). BNF, MS Rossi Cassigoli 229.

Ricciardi, Piero. "Ricordi pubblici e di famiglia dal 1558 al 1588." Fort, MS B 146.

Settimani, F. "Memorie fiorentine regnante Cosimo Medici Duce 2d della Repubblica Fiorentina Anno 1550" 3 (1555–74). ASF, MS 128.

• Other Printed Sources

Dallington, Robert. *A Survey of the Great Duke's State of Tuscany In the Yeare of Our Lord 1596.* London, 1605.

Liber censuum comunis Pistorii. Ed. Quinto Santoli. Pistoia, 1915.

Liber focorum districtus Pistorii a. 1226, Liber finium districtus Pistorii. Ed. Quinto Santoli. *Fonti per la storia d'Italia,* vol. 93. Rome, 1956.

Machiavelli, Niccolò. *Il Principe.* Ed. Luigi Firpo. Turin, 1961.

Read, Alexander. *Chirurgorum comes, or The whole practice of chirurgery.* London, 1687.

Riforma de'magistrati et uffizi publici della città di Pistoia. (bound with *Capitoli dell'Opera di S.Jacopo della Città di Pistoia* and *Capitoli sopra l'Ofizio di Fiumi, e Strade della Città di Pistoia.* Pistoia, 1696 [British Library 8032 f.79 (1–3)].

Statuta Civitatis Pistoriensis. Ed. Lodovico Antonio Muratori. *Antiquitates Italicae Medii Aevi sive Dissertationes.* T.10. Arezzo, 1777.

Statuta Civitatis Pistorii. Florence, 1546.

Statutum potestatis comunis Pistorii anni mcclxxxxvi. Ed. Lodovicus Zdekauer. Milan, 1888.

Tagliacozzi, Gaspare. *De curtorum chirurgia per insitionem.* Venice, 1597.

[Tedaldi, Giovanni Battista]. "Relazione del Commissario Gio. Battista Tedaldi sopra la città e il Capitanato di Pistoia nell'anno 1569." Ed. Vincenzo Minuti. *Archivio storico italiano,* ser. 5, T.10 (1892): 302–31.

Tuscany, Leggi, Bande, etc. Bound sheets at the British Library.

Treatises on Honor, Dueling, and Nobility

Albergati, Fabio. *Del modo di ridurre a pace le inimicitie private.* [2nd ed.?]. Bergamo, 1587.

Alciato, Andrea. *Duello.* Venice, 1545.

Ashley, Robert. *Of Honour* [ca. 1596–1603]. Ed. Virgil B. Heltzel. San Marino, Calif., 1947.

Baldi, Camillo. *Introduzione alla virtù morale con l'aggiunta d'un trattato dell'imprese.* Bologna, 1624.

Baldo, Camillo. *Delle mentite.* Venice, 1633.

Bernardi, Antonio. *Eversiones singularis certaminis.* Basel, n.d.

Birago, Francesco. *Consigli cavallereschi circa il modo del fare le paci.* Milan, 1623.

Camerata, Giuliano. *Trattato dell'honore vero, et del vero dishonore.* Bologna, 1567.

Castiglione, Sabba. *Ricordi ovvero ammaestramenti di tutte le materie honorate che si ricercano a un vero gentil'homo.* Venice, 1554.

Castillo, Diego del [de Villa Sante]. *Tractatus de duello.* Torino, 1525.

Corso, Rinaldo. *Delle private rappacificazioni.* Venice, 1555.

[Della Valle, Battista]. *Vallo libro continente appartenente ad capitanii.* Venice, 1524.

De Vieri, Francesco detto Il Verino Secondo. *Trattato della lode, dell'honore, della fama, et della gloria.* Florence, 1580.

Di Grassi, Giacomo. *Ragione di adoprar sicuramente l'arme si da offesa, come da difesa.* Venice, 1570.

Duel miscellany. Printed collection of sixteenth-century pamphlets concerning duels and questions of chivalry. Biblioteca Vaticana Capponi, 4:753.

"Duellum," Domenicus Cardinal Tuschius. *Praticae conclusiones iuris.* T.2: 1052–55. Rome, 1605.

Ferretti, Francesco. *Diporti notturni dialoghi familliari.* Ancona, 1580.

Guazzo, Stefano. *Dialoghi piacevoli.* Rev. ed., Piacenza, 1590.

———. *La civil conversatione.* Venice, 1575.

Iacobilli, Francesco. *Le conditioni del cavaliero.* Rome, 1606.

Jimenez De Urrea, Jeronimo. *Dialogo del vero honore militare.* Venice, 1569.

Landi, Giulio. *Le attioni morali.* Venice, 1564.

Legnano, Giovanni da. *Tractatus de bello, de represaliis et duello.* Bologna, 1360; modern ed., Thomas E. Holland, Oxford, 1917.

Longiano, Fausto da. *Discorso, quali siano arme da cavalliere con due risposte l'una ad una scrittura consultato da l'Mutio: l'altra ad un consiglio de l'Alciato giovane.* Venice, 1559.

———. *Duello regolato a le leggi de l'honore.* 2nd ed. Venice, 1566.

———. *Il gentilhuomo.* Venice, 1544.

Lovino, Giovanni Antonio. *Traité d'Escrime.* Ed. "H. O." [16th century]; Paris, 1909.

Maestro Fiore dei Liberi da Premariacco. *Flos duellatorum in armis sine armis equester pedester* (1410). Ed. Francesco Novati. Bergamo, 1902.

Massa, Antonio. *Contra l'uso del duello.* Venice, 1550.

——. *Contra usum duelli.* Rome, 1554.

Mora, Domenico. *Il cavaliere in risposta del gentilhuomo del Signore Mutio Giustinapolitano, nella precedenza del armi, et delle lettere.* (Vilna, 1589).

——. *Tre quesiti in dialogo sopra il fare batterie, fortificare una città, et ordinar battaglie quadrate, con una disputa di precedenza tra l'arme e le lettere.* Venice, 1567.

[Muzio, Girolamo]. *Il Duello del Mutio Iustinopolitano.* Venice, 1551.

——. *Il gentilhuomo del Mutio Iustinopolitano.* Venice, 1571.

——. *La faustina del Mutio Iustinopolitano delle arme cavalleresche.* Venice, 1560.

——. *Lettere del Mutio Iustinopolitano.* Ed. Giovanni Francesco Lucchi. Florence, 1590.

Patrizi, Francesco. *La città felice dialogo dell'honore.* Venice, 1553.

Pigna, Giovan-Batista. *Duello.* Venice, 1554.

Possevino, Antonio. *Il soldato christiano.* Venice, 1604.

Possevino, Giovanni Battista. *Dialogo dell'honore, nel quale si tratta a pieno del duello.* Venice, 1559.

Puteo, Paris de. *Duello: Libro de Ri[sic] Imperaturi, Principi, Signori, gentilhomini, & de tucti Armigeri continente Disfide, Concordie, Pace, Casi accadenti, & Iudicii.* Naples, 1518.

Sansovino, Francesco. *Origine de cavalieri.* Venice, 1566.

"Scritture di duelli e pace dal 1543 al 1613." ASF, Miscellanea Medicea, filza 129.

Susio, G. B. *Della ingiustizia del duello et di coloro che lo permettono.* Venice, 1555.

Tasso, Bernardo. *I tre libri de gli amori.* Venice, 1555.

Thonnina, Francesco. *Discorso in materia di duello, Nel quale si ragiona, qual sia l'honor Cavallaresco, & qual il duello hoggidi usato; et della Cavallaria, & conche ragione, si debbano decidere le querele fra cavalieri; et qual Reo; & del l'Ingiuria et mentita.* Mantua, 1557.

Vulpellius, Octavianus. *Tractatus de pace.* Urbino, 1573.

Zamorensis, Rodericus [Rodrigo Sánchez]. *Speculum humane vite.* Louvain, ca. 1480. [British Library IB 49226 (3).]

Zilettus, Franciscus, ed. *Tractatus universi juris duce & auspice Gregorii XIII Pontefice Maximo in unum congestorum.* 11 vols. Venice, 1584. Includes treatises on nobility and dueling by Boni de Curtili, Paris de Puteo, Giovanni Legnano, Iacopo da Castello, and Alciato.

Treatises on Women, Love, and Love Letters

Atanagi, Dionigi. *De le lettere di tredici huomini illustri.* Venice, 1554.

Bruni, Domenico da Pistoia. *Difese delle donne.* Florence, 1552.

Gli ornamenti delle donne. Venice, 1569.

Guarini, Battista. *Il segretario dialogo nel quale non sol si tratta dell'ufficio del segretario et del modo del compor lettere.* Venice, 1600.

Guazzo, Stefano. *Lettere volgari di diversi gentilhuomini del Monferrato.* Brescia, 1566.

Lettere amorose di Madonna Celia gentildonna romana scritte al suo amante. Venice, 1562.

Muzio, Girolamo. *Lettere.* Ed. Luciana Borsetto. Ferrara, 1985.

Pallavicino, Ferrante. *Panegirici, epitalami, discorsi accademici, novelle, et lettere amorosi.* Venice, 1652.

Parabosco, Girolamo. *Quattro libri delle lettere amorose di nuovo ordinatamente per Thomaso Porcacchi* (1566). Venice, 1607.

Pasqualigo, Alvise. *Lettere amorose libri III ne' quali sotto maravigliosi concetti si contengono tutti gli accidenti d'Amore.* [2nd ed.?]. Venice, 1581.

Porcacchi, Tomaso. *Lettere di xiii huomini illustri.* [Enlarged edition of Atanagi.] Venice, 1576.

Ruiz, Juan (the archpriest of Hita). *The Book of True Love* (1343). Ed. and trans. Saralyn R. Daly and Anthony N. Zahareas. State College, Pa., 1978.

Sansovino, Francesco. *Il segretario.* Venice, 1584.

Savorgnan, Maria, and Pietro Bembo. *Carteggio d'amore (1500–1501).* Ed. Carlo Dionisotti. Florence, 1950.

Tasso, Torquato. *Dialoghi.* Ed. Ezio Raimondi. 2 vols. Florence, 1958.

Selected Studies

Andreini Galli, N. "Un grande patrimonio terrestre: la villa detta della Magia." *Il tremisse pistoiese* 14, no. 38 (1989).

Angelozzi, Giancarlo. "Cultura dell'onore, codici di comportamento nobiliari e stato nella Bologna Pontificia: un ipotesi di lavoro." *Annali dell'Istituto Storico Italo-Germanico in Trento* 7 (1982): 305–24.

———. "La trattistica su nobiltà ed onore a Bologna." *Atti Memorie della Deputazione di Storia Patria per le Province di Romagna,* n.s. 25–26 (1974–75).

Arlette, Jouanna. "Recherches sur la notion d'honneur au XVIème siècle." *Revue d'histoire moderne et contemporaine.* T.15 (1968): 597–623.

Artigiani e salariati secoli 12–15. Pistoia, 1984.

Baldacci, Luigi. *Il petrarchismo italiano nel cinquecento.* Milan, 1957.

Baldick, Robert. *The Duel: A History of Duelling.* London, 1965.

Bartlett, Robert. *Trial by Fire and Water: The Medieval Judicial Ordeal.* Oxford, 1986.

Beani, G. *Cenni storici riguardanti S. Iacopo Apostolo il maggiore, patrono di Pistoia.* Pistoia, 1886.

———. *Di alcune chiese, oratori e compagnie soppresse in Pistoia nel 1783.* Pistoia, 1908.

———. *La chiesa pistoiese dalla sua origine ai tempi nostri.* 2nd ed. Pistoia, 1912.

Bell, Rudolph M. *How To Do It: Guides to Good Living for Renaissance Italians.* Chicago, 1999.

Benadusi, Giovanna. *A Provincial Elite in Early Modern Tuscany: Family and Power in the Creation of the State.* Baltimore, 1996.

Benson, Pamela. *Invention of the Renaissance Woman.* University Park, Pa., 1992.

Bergiaschi, Luigi. *Storia degli istituti di benificenza d'istruzione ed educazione in Pistoia e suo circondario.* 2 vols. Florence, 1883–84.

Berner, Samuel. "Florentine Society in the Late-Sixteenth- and Early-Seventeenth Centuries." *Studies in the Renaissance* 18 (1971): 203–46.

————. "The Florentine Patriciate in the Transition from Republic to Principate, 1530–1609." *Studies in Medieval and Renaissance History* 9 (1972): 3–15.

Betti, Claudio. *De l'honore.* Bologna, 1567.

Bianchi, Dante. "Trattati d'epistolografia nei secoli xvi e xvii: per la storia del Seicentismo." *Giornale storico della letteratura italiana* 89 (1927): 111–26.

Billacois, François. *Le duel dans la société francaise des XVIe e XVIIe siècles: essai de psycho-sociologie historique.* Paris, 1986.

Bliese, John R. E. "When Knightly Courage May Fail: Battle Orations in Medieval Europe." *Historian* 53 (1991): 489–504.

Bonatti, Franco. *La Lunigiana nel secolo XV attraverso i protocolli del notaio Baldassare Nobili.* 2 vols. Pisa, 1977, 1981.

Borghini, Vincenzio. *Storia della nobiltà fiorentina discorsi inediti o rari.* Ed. J. R. Woodhouse. Pisa, 1974.

Bossy, John, ed. *Disputes and Settlements: Law and Human Relations in the West.* Cambridge, 1983.

Boulton, Jonathan D'Arcy Dacre. *The Knights of the Crown: The Monarchical Orders of Knighthood in Later Medieval Europe, 1325–1520.* Woodbridge, Suffolk, 1987.

Branchi, Eugenio. *Storia della Lunigiana feudale.* 3 vols. Pistoia, 1897; repr. Bologna, 1971.

Brown, William. "Trial by Combat." *Yorkshire Archeological Journal* 23 (1915): 300–307.

Bryson, Frederick R. *The Point of Honor in Sixteenth-Century Italy: An Aspect of the Life of the Gentleman.* New York, 1935.

————. *The Sixteenth-Century Italian Duel: A Study in Renaissance Social History.* Chicago, 1938.

Buraggi, Gian Carlo. *Le prime leggi sabaude contro il duello.* Asti, 1913.

Burke, Peter. *The Historical Anthropology of Early Modern Italy: Essays on Perception and Communication.* Cambridge, 1987.

Cantini, Monica Stanghellini. "Giustizia criminale a Pistoia agli inizi del secolo xvii." *Bullettino storico pistoiese* 15 (1980): 53–104.

Capecchi, Ilvo, and Lucia Gai. *Il Monte della Pietà a Pistoia e le sue origini.* Florence, 1975.

Cardini, Franco. *Alle radici della cavalleria medievale.* Florence, 1981.

————. Marco Tangheroni. *Guerra e guerrieri nella Toscana del Rinascimento.* Florence, 1990.

Castro, Amerigo. *Le drame de l'honneur dans la vie et dans la littérature espagnoles du XVIe siecle.* Paris, 1965.

Cini, Domenico. *Osservazioni storiche sopra l'antico stato della montagna pistoiese con un discorso sopra l'origine di Pistoia.* Florence, 1737; repr. 1976.

Cipolla, Carlo M. *Il fiorino e il quattrino.* Bologna, 1982.

————. *La moneta nel Cinquecento.* Bologna, 1987.

Civiltà ed economia agricola in Toscana nei secoli 13–15. Pistoia, 1981.

Cohen, Elizabeth S. "Between Oral and Written Culture: The Social Meaning of an Illustrated Love Letter." In *Culture and Identity in Early Modern Europe (1500–1800): Essays in Honor of Natalie Zemon Davis,* ed. B. B. Diefendorf and C. Hesse, 181–201. Ann Arbor, 1993.

Cohen, T. V., and E. S. Cohen. *Words and Deeds in Renaissance Rome: Trials before the Papal Magistrates.* Toronto, 1993.

Colloquio internazionale su "potere e elites" nella Spagna e nell'Italia spagnola dei secoli 15–17, 1977–1978. Rome, 1979.

Connell, William J. "Clientelismo e lo Stato territoriale fiorentino: Il potere fiorentino a Pistoia nel XV secolo." *Società e storia* 14 (1991): 523–43.

————. "Il commissario e lo Stato territoriale fiorentino." *Ricerche storiche* 18 (1988): 591–617.

————. "Republican Territorial Government: Florence and Pistoia, Fifteenth and Early Sixteenth Centuries." Ph.D. diss., University of California, Berkeley, 1989.

————. "Un cronista pistoiese sconosciuto: Bastiano Buoni e la sua cronaca *De'casi di Pistoia.*" *Bullettino storico pistoiese* 95 (1993): 23–39.

Corradi, Alfonso. *Annali delle epidemie occorse in Italia dalle prime memorie fino al 1850.* 4 vols. Bologna, 1865–70.

Cortese, Ennio. *La norma giuridica.* 2 vols. Milan, 1962–64.

Crane, Thomas Frederick. *Italian Social Customs of the Sixteenth Century and Their Influence on the Literatures of Europe.* New Haven, 1926.

Cuomo, Raffaelle. *Ordini cavallereschi antichi e moderni.* 2 vols. Naples, 1894; repr. 1968.

D'Alessandri, Torquato. *Il cavalier compito.* Viterbo, 1609.

Davidsohn, Robert. "I campioni nudi ed unti." *Bullettino della Società Dantesca Italiana* 7 (1899): 39–43.

Davies, W., and P. Fouracre, eds. *The Settlement of Disputes in Early Medieval Europe.* Cambridge, 1986.

Davis, Natalie Zemon. *The Return of Martin Guerre.* Cambridge, Mass., 1983.

Day, James F. "Trafficking in Honor: Social Climbing and the Purchase of Gentility in the English Renaissance." *Renaissance Papers.* Papers of the Southeastern Renaissance Conference, 1987. Ed. D. B. J. Randall and J. A. Porter, 61–70. Durham, 1987.

Dean, T., and K. J. P. Lowe, eds. *Crime, Society, and the Law in Renaissance Italy.* Cambridge, 1994.

Dedola, Marco. "'Tener Pistoia con le parti': governo fiorentino e fazioni pistoiesi all'inizio del '500." *Ricerche storiche* 22, no. 2 (1992): 239–59.

———. "Governare sul territorio: Podestà, capitani e commissari a Pistoia prima e dopo l'assoggettamento a Firenze (14–16 secolo)." *Istituzioni e società in Toscana nell'età moderna,* 215–30. Rome, 1994.

Del Vecchio, A, and E. Casanova. *Le rappresagli nei comuni medievali e specialmente in Firenze.* Bologna, 1894.

de Waal, Frans. *Peacemaking among Primates.* Cambridge, Mass., 1989.

Diaz, Furio. *Il Granducato di Toscana—I Medici.* Turin, 1987.

Donati, Claudio. *L'idea di nobiltà in Italia secoli 14–18.* Bari, 1988.

Dorini, Umberto. "I duelli a morte nel sec. 14–15." *Rivista storica degli archivi toscani* 1 (1929): 209–11.

Enriques, Anna Maria. "La vendetta nella vita e nella legislazione fiorentina." *Archivio storico italiano,* ser. 7, 1 (1933): 85–146, 181–223.

Erspamer, Francesco. *La biblioteca di Don Ferrante: duello e onore nella cultura del Cinquecento.* Rome, 1982.

Fasano Guarini, Elena. "Arezzo, Pistoia, Pisa nelle note del Commissario Giovan Battista Tedaldi (1566–74)." In *Studi di storia pisana e toscana in onore del Prof. Cinzio Violante: Biblioteca del Bollettino storico pisano,* 161–76. Pisa, 1991.

———. "Gli stati dell'Italia centro-settentrionale tra Quattro e Cinquecento: continuità e trasformazioni." *Società e storia* 21 (1983): 617–39.

———. "Potere centrale e comunità soggette nel Granducato di Cosimo I." *Rivista storica italiana* (1977): 490–538.

———. *Lo stato mediceo di Cosimo I.* Florence, 1973.

Ferrante, Joan M. *Self-improvement of Man and Society in Courtly Codes.* New Orleans, 1984.

Ferrario, G. *Storia e analisi degli antichi romanzi di cavalleria e dei poemi romanzeschi d'Italia.* Milan, 1928.

Ferretti, Jolanda. "L'organizzazione militare in Toscana durante il governo di Alessandro e Cosimo I de'Medici." *Rivista storica degli archivi toscani,* pt. 1 (1929): 248–75; pt. 2 (1930): 58–80.

Fioravanti, Jacopo Maria. *Memorie storiche della città di Pistoia.* Lucca, 1758; repr. 1968.

Fontana, Fulvio. *I pregi della Toscana nell'imprese più segnalate de'Cavalieri di Santo Stefano.* Florence, 1701.

Foucault, Michel. *Discipline and Punish: The Birth of the Prison.* Trans. Alan Sheridan. 2nd ed. New York, 1995.

Gai, Lucia. "Interventi rinascimentali nello spedale del Ceppo di Pistoia." *Bullettino storico pistoiese* 79 (1977): 71–128.

———. *Le feste patronali di S.Jacopo e il Palio a Pistoia. Incontri Pistoiesi di storia arte cultura* 39. Pistoia, 1987.

———. *Pistoia nel secolo 15. Incontri Pistoiesi di storia arte cultura* 14. Pistoia, 1982.

———. *Pistoia nel secolo 16. Incontri Pistoiesi di storia arte cultura* 15. Pistoia, 1982.

Gai, Lucia, ed. *San Francesco: La chiesa e il convento in Pistoia.* Pistoia, 1993.

Galluzzi, Riguccio. *Istoria del Granducato di Toscana sotto il governo della casa Medici.* 5 vols. Florence, 1781; repr. Milan, 1974.

Ganucci Cancellieri, Girolamo. *Pistoia nel xiii secolo saggio storico sulla stirpe dei Cancellieri di Pistoia.* Florence, 1975.

Gardiner, Cynthia P. *The Sophoclean Chorus: A Study of Character and Function.* Iowa City, 1987.

Gatrell, V. A. C., B. Lenman, and G. Parker, eds. *Crime and the Law: The Social History of Crime in Western Europe since 1500.* London, 1980.

Geary, Patrick J. "Vivre en conflit dans une France sans État: typologie des mécanismes de règlement des conflits (1050–1200)." *Annales E.S.C.* 41 (1986): 1107–33.

Gelli, Jacopo. *Il duello nella storia della giurisprudenza e nella pratica italiana.* Florence, 1886.

Giaxich, Paolo. *Vita di Girolamo Muzio Giustinopolitano.* Trieste, 1847.

Gilbert, Creighton. "When Did a Man in the Renaissance Grow Old?" *Studies in the Renaissance* 14 (1967): 7–32.

Girard, Rene. *Violence and the Sacred.* Trans. P. Gregory. Baltimore, 1977.

Graff, Harvey J. *Literacy and Social Development in the West: A Reader.* Cambridge, 1981.

Greenberg, Kenneth S. "The Nose, the Lie, and the Duel in the Antebellum South." *American Historical Review* 95 (1990): 57–74.

Greenblatt, Stephen J. *Renaissance Self-fashioning: From More to Shakespeare.* Chicago, 1980.

Grossi, Paolo, ed. *Storia sociale e dimensione giuridica: strumenti d'indagine e ipotesi di lavoro: Per la storia del pensiero giuridico moderno.* Milan, 1986.

Guarnieri, G. *L'ordine di Santo Stefano nella sua organizzazione interna.* Vol. 4. Pisa, 1966.

Hale, John R. "The Military Education of the Officer Class in Early Modern Europe." In *Cultural Aspects of the Italian Renaissance: Essays in Honour of Paul Oskar Kristeller,* ed. Cecil H. Clough, 440–61. Manchester, 1976.

———. "Sixteenth Century Explanations of War and Violence." *Past and Present* 51 (1971): 3–26.

Halkin, Léon-E. "Pour une histoire de l'honneur." *Annales* 4 (1949): 433–44.

Herald, Jacqueline. *Renaissance Dress in Italy, 1400–1500.* London, 1981.

Herlihy, David. "Le relazioni economiche di Firenze con le città soggette nel sec. XV." In *Egemonia fiorentina ed autonomie locali nella Toscana nord-occidentale del Primo Rinascimento: vita, arte, cultura,* 79–109. Pistoia, 1978.

————. *Medieval and Renaissance Pistoia: The Social History of an Italian Town, 1200–1430.* New Haven, 1967.

————. "Population, Plague, and Social Change in Rural Pistoia, 1201–1430." *Economic History Review* 18 (1965): 225–44.

Herlihy, David, and Christiane Klapisch. *Les Toscanes et leurs familles; une étude du catasto florentin de 1427.* Paris, 1978.

Hess, Andrew C. "The Battle of Lepanto and Its Place in Mediterranean History." *Past and Present* 57 (1972): 53–73.

Holme, J. W. "Italian Courtesy Books of the 16th Century." *Modern Language Review* 5 (1910): 145–66.

Höltgen, Karl Josef. "Sir Robert Dallington, 1561–1637: Author, Traveler, and Pioneer of Taste." *Huntington Library Quarterly* 47 (1984): 147–77.

Huizinga, J. *The Waning of the Middle Ages.* New York, 1949.

Huppert, George. *The Bourgeois Gentleman.* Chicago, 1977.

I ceti dirigenti nella Toscana tardo comunale. Committee for the Study of the History of the Governing Classes in Tuscany (third conference, Florence, 5–7 December, 1980). Florence, 1983.

Il patrimonio artistico di Pistoia e del suo territorio Catalogo storico descrittivo. Pistoia, 1967–68.

Italia, 1350–1450: tra crisi, trasformazione, sviluppo. Papers of the conference at Pistoia, 10–13 May, 1991. Pistoia, 1993.

Jacoby, Susan. *Wild Justice: The Evolution of Revenge.* New York, 1983.

Jones, Philip. *The Italian City-State from Commune to Signoria.* Oxford, 1997.

Keen, Maurice. *Chivalry.* New Haven, 1984.

Kelso, Ruth. *The Doctrine of the English Gentleman in the Sixteenth Century.* London, 1929.

King, Margaret. *The Death of the Child Valerio Marcello.* Chicago, 1994.

Kirshner, Julius. "Wives' Claims against Insolvent Husbands in Late Medieval Italy." In *Women of the Medieval World: Essays in Honor of John M. Mundy,* ed. J. Kirshner and S. F. Wemple. Oxford, 1985, 256–303.

Klapisch-Zuber, Christiane. *Women, Family, and Ritual in Renaissance Italy.* Trans. Lydia G. Cochrane. Chicago, 1985.

Kuehn, Thomas. "Arbitration and Law in Renaissance Florence." *Renaissance and Reformation* 11 (1987): 289–319.

————. "Reading Microhistory: The Example of Giovanni and Lusanna." *Journal of Modern History* 61 (1989): 514–34.

Labov, William. *Language in the Inner City: Studies in the Black English Vernacular.* Philadelphia, 1972.

Laqueur, Thomas. *Making Sex: Body and Gender from the Greeks to Freud.* Cambridge, Mass., 1990.

Lea, Henry C. *Superstition and Force: Essay on the Wages of Law, the Wages of Battle, the Ordeal, etc.* Philadelphia, 1866.

Le Blant, Edmond. "Note sur quelques anciens talismans de bataille." *Memoires de l'Académie des Inscriptions et Belles-Lettres* 34, pt. 2 (1893): 113–23.

Lenzi, M. L. "Fanti e cavalieri nelle prime guerre d'Italia, 1494–1527." *Ricerche storiche* 7 (1977): 7–92; 8 (1978): 359–415.

Litchfield, R. Burr. "Office-holding in Florence after the Republic." In *Renaissance Studies in Honor of Hans Baron,* ed. A. Molho and J. Tedeschi. De Kalb, Illinois, 1971, 533–55.

Martines, Lauro, ed. *Violence and Civil Disorder in Italian Cities, 1200–1500.* Berkeley, 1972.

Massai, Ferdinando. "Duelli mancati a Firenze nel secolo 17." *Atti della "Società Colombaria"* (Florence, 1931): 3–16.

Meader, William G. *Courtship in Shakespeare, its Relation to Traditions of Courtly Love.* New York, 1971.

Montagna, Davide Maria. *Feste liturgiche ed altre "allegrezze" all'Annunziata di Pistoia fra il '500 e il '700. Incontri pistoiesi di storia arte cultura* 42. Pistoia, 1987.

Moore, S. F., and B. G. Myerhoff, eds. *Secular Ritual.* Van Gorcum, Netherlands, 1977.

Mor, C. G. "La cavalleria." In *Nuove questioni di storia medievale.* Milan, 1964.

Morel, Henri. "La fin du duel judiciaire en France et la naissance du point d'honneur." *Revue Historique de Droit Français et Etranger,* ser. 4, 42 (1964): 574–639.

Muir, E., and G. Ruggiero, eds. *History from Crime: Selections from Quaderni storici.* Baltimore, 1994.

Muratori, Lodovico Antonio. *Introduzione alle paci private.* Modena, 1708.

Neuschel, Kristen B. *Word of Honor: Interpreting Noble Culture in Sixteenth-Century France.* Ithaca, 1989.

Nobiltà e ceti dirigenti in Toscana nei secoli xi–xiii strutture e concetti. Committee for the Study of the Governing Classes in Tuscany (proceedings of the fourth conference, Florence, 12 December, 1981). Florence, 1982.

Paliotti, V. *Storia della canzone napoletane.* Milan, 1958.

Patetta, Federico. *Le ordalie: studio di storia del diritto e scienza del diritto comparato.* Turin, 1890.

Peltinelli, Rosanna Alhaique. *L'immaginario cavalleresco nel Rinascimento ferrarese.* Rome, 1983.

Pennington, Kenneth. *The Prince and the Law, 1200–1600: Sovereignty and Rights in the Western Legal Tradition.* Berkeley, 1993.

Pinto, G., ed. *Storia di Pistoia,* III. Florence, 1999.

Pistoia: una città nello stato mediceo. Catalog of the Exhibition, Pistoia Fortezza, Santa Barbara, 28 June–30 September, 1980). Pistoia, 1980.

Prosperi, Adriano. "Il 'miles christianus' nella cultura italiana tra '400 e '500." *Critica storica/Bollettino A. S. E.* 26, no. 4 (1989): 685–704.

Quondam, Amedeo, ed. *Le "carte messaggiere": Retorica e modelli di comunicazione epistolare: per un indice dei libri di lettere del cinquecento.* Rome, 1981.

Raggio, Osvaldo. *Faide e parentele: Lo stato genovese visto dall Fontanabuona*. Turin, 1990.

Rauty, Natale. *L'antico palazzo dei vescovi a Pistoia*. Florence, 1981.

———. "L'incastellamento nel territorio pistoiese tra il X e l'XI secolo." *Bullettino storico pistoiese* 92 (1990): 31–57.

———. "Schede storiche delle parrochie della Diocesi di Pistoia." *Annuario della Diocesi di Pistoia*, 37–143. Pistoia, 1986.

———. *Storia di Pistoia*, vol. 1, *Dall'Alto Medioevo all'età precomunale*. Florence, 1988.

Roberts, Simon. *Order and Dispute: An Introduction to Legal Anthropology*. New York, 1979.

Rocke, Michael. *Forbidden Friendships: Homosexuality and Male Culture in Renaissance Florence*. New York, 1996.

Salvi, Michelangelo. *Historie di Pistoia e fazioni d'Italia*. 3 vols. Rome, 1656–1662; repr. Bologna, 1978.

Santoni, L. *Le feste principali della città e Arcidiocesi fiorentina*. Florence, 1853.

Schmidt, S. W., J. C. Scott, C. Landé, and L. Guasti. *Friends, Followers, and Factions: A Reader in Political Clientelism*. Berkeley, 1977.

Setton, Kenneth M. *The Papacy and the Levant, 1204–1571*, vol. 4, *The Sixteenth Century from Julius III to Pius V*. Philadelphia, 1984.

Shankland, Hugh. *The Prettiest Love Letters in the World*. London, 1987.

Sole, Antonino. *Il gentiluomo cortigiano nel segno di Petrarca: modelli sociali e modelli etico-retorici in quattro autori del Cinquecento: Castiglione, Berni, Bembo, Della Casa*. Palermo, 1992.

Sonnino, Sydney. "La mezzeria in Toscana." In Leopoldo Franchetti, ed., *Condizioni economiche ed amministrative delle province napolitane*, 177–223. Florence, 1875.

Spacks, Patricia Ann Meyer. *Gossip*. New York, 1985.

Spini, Giorgio, ed. *Architettura e politica da Cosimo I a Ferdinando I*. Florence, 1976.

———. "Architettura e politica nel principato mediceo del Cinquecento." *Rivista storica italiana* 73 (1971): 792–845.

Stern, Laura I. *The Criminal Law System of Medieval and Renaissance Florence*. Baltimore, 1994.

Stewart, Keith. "Towards Defining an Aesthetic for the Familiar Letter in Eighteenth-Century England." *Prose Studies* 5 (1982): 179–92.

Storr, Anthony. *Human Aggression*. New York, 1968.

Tempestini, Luciano. *La religiosità popolare pistoiese nelle sue espressioni festive*. Incontri pistoiesi di storia arte cultura 40. Pistoia, 1987.

Trexler, Richard. *Public Life in Renaissance Florence*. New York, 1980.

Vocino, Michele. *Storia del costume: Venti secoli di vita italiana*. 2d ed. Rome, 1961.

Weissman, Ronald F. E. *Ritual Brotherhood in Renaissance Florence*. New York, 1982.

Patronymics are preceded by *di, del,* or *d'* (son, or daughter, of) or by *fu* if the father is deceased. Page numbers in *italics* denote illustrations.

Library of Congress Cataloging-in-Publication Data

Weinstein, Donald, 1926–

    The captain's concubine : love, honor, and violence in
Renaissance Tuscany / Donald Weinstein.

      p.   cm.

    Includes bibliographical references (p.   ) and index.

     ISBN 0-8018-6475-5 (alk. paper)

     1. Pistoia (Italy)—History. 2. Cellesi family. 3. Bracciolini
family. 4. Honor—Italy—Pistoia—History. 5. Dueling—Italy—
Pistoia—History. I. Title.

DG975.P65 W45 2000

945'.5207'0922—dc21   00-008337